BLUEBEARD

The trial of Gilles de Rais.

LEONARD WOLF

BLUEBEARD

The Life and Crimes of Gilles de Rais

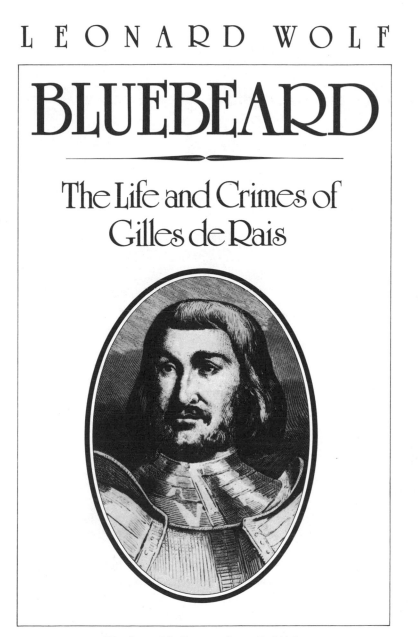

Clarkson N. Potter, Inc./Publishers
DISTRIBUTED BY CROWN PUBLISHERS, INC.
NEW YORK

Inquiries should be addressed to Clarkson N. Potter, Inc., One Park Avenue, New York, New York 10016

Printed in the United States of America

Published simultaneously in Canada by General Publishing Company Limited

Library of Congress Cataloging in Publication Data

Wolf, Leonard.
  Bluebeard, the life and crimes of Gilles de Rais.

  Bibliography: p.
  Includes index.
  1. Rais, Gilles de Laval, seigneur de, 1404-1440.
2. Jeanne d'Arc, Saint, 1412-1431—Friends and
associates—Biography.   3. Crime and criminals France—
Biography.   I. Title.
  DC102.8.R2W7 1980   364.1′5′0924 [B]   79-28345
  ISBN: 0-517-540614

10 9 8 7 6 5 4 3 2 1

First Edition

Photo Credits

Map of France during the reign of Charles VII (p. viii) from *Charles VII* by
   M.G.A. Vale (Berkeley: University of California Press, 1974). Used with
   permission.
Map of Gilles de Rais country (p. 10) from *The Soul of Marshal Gilles de Raiz* by
   D. B. Wyndham Lewis (London: Eyre & Spottiswoode, 1952). Used with
   permission.
The trial of Gilles de Rais (frontispiece), the execution of Gilles de Rais (p. 214),
   and the trial transcript (p. 189), courtesy Bibliothèque Nationale de Paris.
Photograph of Jeanne d'Arc's birthplace (p. 73), courtesy French Government
   Tourist Office.
Photographs on pages 25, 82, 122, 139, and 170 taken by Leonard Wolf.

THIS BOOK IS DEDICATED
TO THE VICTIMS

ACKNOWLEDGMENTS

Many people in various parts of the world have been generous
with their time or their suggestions while I was making this book.
First, I want to express my thanks to the librarians and staffs of
the Bibliothèque Nationale in Paris and the University of Califor-
nia Library in Berkeley. I also want to express my gratitude to
M. G. Borleteau of Machecoul; Dr. Alexandra Botwin; Robert
Berg, Acquisitions Librarian, San Francisco State University;
Chantal Damey of the Bibliothèque Municipale in Nantes; Dr.
Bernard Diamond of the University of California School of Crim-
inology; Madame Ghislaine Fortin of the Bibliothèque
Municipale in Nantes; Professor Daniel Knapp of San Francisco
State University; Dr. Wolfgang Lederer; Professor André Martin
of San Francisco State University; Nancy Noda, Inter-library
Loan Librarian at San Francisco State University; Brother S.
Robert of St. John's College, Annapolis; Professors Sally Scully
and Richard Trapp of San Francisco State University; and to
Virginia Verrill. As always, I have many reasons to thank Dr.
Deborah Goleman Wolf, whose anthropological insights have
sharpened my own.

To Pamela Roberts for her help as a researcher, translator, and
critic, I owe a special thanks.

CONTENTS

THE VALLEY OF THE LOIRE

0 ——— 20 Miles

0 ——— 20 Km

Orléans

R. Loire

Vendôme ▲

Angers •

Tours ▲

Amboise ▲

Mehun-
sur-Yèvre ▲

Montsoreau •

Chinon ▲ Montbazon ▲

Loches ▲

Bourges •

▲ Residences of Charles VII between 1418 and 1461

Calais

Bruges •

Ghent •

FLANDERS

ARTOIS

Lille •

Liège •

Arras •

Cherbourg •

Dieppe •

PICARDY

Beauvais •

Laon •

Rouen •

Rheims •

Metz •

Caen •

NORMAN D Y

1449–50

Senlis •

Coutances •

Avranches •

Evreux •

CHAMPAGNE

Nancy •

Paris

1436

L O R R A I N E

Fougères •

ALENÇON

•Chartres

Seine

Troyes •

BAR

MAINE

PERCHE

Orléans •

Angers •

Blois •

Loire

Dijon •

Tours •

ANJOU

Nantes •

TOURAINE

B E R R Y

•Bourges

NEVERS

DUCHY OF
BURGUNDY

COMTÉ OF
BURGUNDY

BRITTANY

POITOU

Poitiers •

BOURBONNAIS

Mâcon •

LA MARCHE

SAINTONGE

Angoulême •

•Limoges

Lyon •

LIMOUSIN

Vienne •

Bordeaux •

AUVERGNE

Rhône

DAUPHINÉ

1456

GUYENNE

1451/3

Garonne

Albi •

Avignon •

ALBRET

Tartas •

Nîmes •

ARMAGNAC

Toulouse •

LANGUEDOC

PROVENCE

Aix en
Provence

Nice •

NAVARRE

BÉARN

BIGORRE

COMMINGES

FOIX

Montpellier •

Béziers •

Narbonne •

0 ——— 100 ——— 200 Miles

0 ——— 100 ——— 200 Kilometres

▬ ▬ ▬ Kingdom of France (including
principalities dependent upon it)

1451/3 Date of annexation to the Crown,
or recovery

M. Verity

France during the reign of Charles VII.

Do not construe these words as images.
They are attempting to construct an abominable wisdom.

—Antonin Artaud

The greatest difficulty, you see, is to explain how this man, who was a brave captain and a good Christian, all of a sudden became a sacrilegious sadist and a coward.

Metamorphosed overnight, as it were.

Worse . . .

—J. K. Huysmans, Là-Bas

INTRODUCTION

This book is about Gilles de Rais, who, more than anyone in history, deserves to be called "the world's wickedest man." Until very recently, his biographers have felt it necessary to put up warning signals about Gilles's wickedness.

> The monstrous details of his crimes may be found in the archives of the château [at Nantes]; but one has believed it one's duty to spare the public horrors of that kind.[1]

Or

> His crimes are of such a nature that modern editors of his trial dossier leave blanks even in the original Latin.[2]

Or

> I must warn my sadistic readers that they will be disappointed because I haven't the least intention of enumerating in detail those atrocities which Gilles, in tears, confessed publicly. . . .[3]

And yet the terror no one wants to talk about, or talks about in hushed tones or euphemistically, is part of the mystery of Gilles de Rais, whose cruelty and whose mysticism are of the sort that make us think of "the religious greatness of the damned; genius as disease, disease as genius . . . where saint and criminal become one."[4] The problem is that Gilles was not merely brutal, not merely religious, not merely a man of sensibility, but a paradoxical mixture of the three, who at some point seemed to become aware of himself as one of those people with "a gifted normal intellect who [moves upward to icy, abnormal spheres of comprehension and moral isolation]; to a frightful, criminal degree of knowingness."[5] Before that, however, he played to perfection all that we imagine is required of the great knight in the age of chivalry: He was tall and handsome; he was skilled at arms, devoted, loyal, passionate, and

devout; he was, too, one of the richest men of his day, the owner of
territories larger than counties. He was a man of quality: a Latinist, a connoisseur of the arts. He was a man moved to tears by
music—especially religious music as he heard it sung in the clear
voices of children. He was everything Ophelia deemed Hamlet to
be: "the courtier's, soldier's, scholar's, eye, tongue, sword. The glass
of fashion and the mould of form, the observ'd of all observers."

To his contemporaries, he was the Lord Baron Gilles de Rais,
count of Brienne, lord of Laval, of Pouzauges, Tiffauges, Champtocé, Machecoul, and other places; he was also marshal of France
and lieutenant general of Brittany. To compound the paradox of
his life, he was also the companion-in-arms of Jeanne d'Arc. To
these titles, his age learned to add that he was "the beast of extermination" and "the devourer of Machecoul"—the poor fool who
tried to catch God and Satan in the same net.

For all of that, if his name means anything at all to our own age,
it is because it has been dimly connected with the story of Bluebeard, that nobleman whose habit it was to punish the curiosity of
a succession of wives with death. Gilles de Rais, at least in the
popular imagination, is the historical Bluebeard.

That there is a vast difference between Perrault's jewellike tale
and the story of Gilles's life, the pages to come should make clear.
In Perrault's fiction, Bluebeard is the enameled image of the
merely wicked. There is good and there is evil, and Bluebeard has
chosen the second. Gilles's story, on the other hand, leads us to the
more problematical and biblical Man of Iniquity, whose soul
seems vaguely familiar even as we contrive to let it elude us. History in the story of Gilles seems to be "attempting to construct an
abominable wisdom." [6]

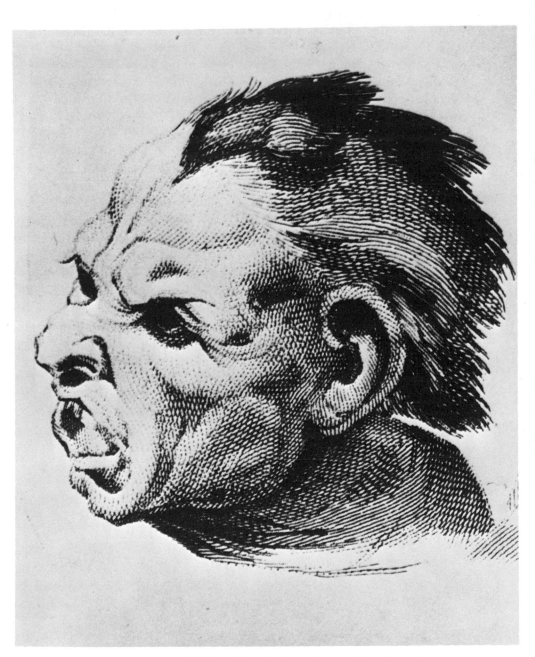

Rage (one of "Two Heads from Dante" by Fuseli.

PROLOGUE

oe understood the Rage, as did Dostoevsky, and Isidore
Ducasse, and Baudelaire. The Rage is a seizure that can
overtake even children who grow giddy with the pleasure
that assails them as they tear apart the wings of the butterfly
which, by destroying, they possess. It seized the children in T. F.
Powys's story "The Hunted Beast," who gouged out the eyes of a
rabbit they had taken on the English downs; and it gripped Mr.
Gidden, the kindly, peace-loving vicar who came upon them and
who, seeing what they had done, grew dizzy with voluptuous despair. He chased the children but

> the boys escaped his hands and ran off. But the girl wasn't so fortu-
> nate; she did not run so quickly as the boys; perhaps she wanted to
> know what the clergyman would do to her.
>
> Mr. Gidden threw himself upon her. He tore at her clothes. She
> struggled and fell into the ditch. He struck her, lay upon her in his
> fury, and held to her throat. His stick was broken; he took up a great
> bone that lay near and struck her with that. There was blood upon the
> bone, and Nellie lay very still.
>
> During the struggle Mr. Gidden had wished to do the very worst a
> man could do. He had wished to violate her—to give her cruelty for
> cruelty, pain for pain. . . . He was satisfied, he had avenged the rabbit.
> Though the world delivered no justice, he had delivered it. He had
> toppled over the world.[1]

Mr. Gidden, for thirty years the vicar of East Dodder, was a man
of sedentary habits, a devoted Christian, a good husband and father. Powys says that "the family were united lovingly and their
thoughts were for one another." And then, in one instant, Mr.
Gidden became a hunted beast who had—*because he wished it*—done
"the very worst a man could do." By a single gesture he "had
toppled over the world." What T. F. Powys knows is that the
impulse to such self-destruction is all but independent of character
(or is so secretly linked to it as to escape the most scrutinizing eye).

1

More than that, Powys knows that the lust to topple the world with wickedness is lascivious beyond all other temptations.

The Rage, though it may come as a seizure, is not madness. There is no letting go of the sense of right or wrong. It is only that when the Rage happens one is filled with a terrible lucidity in which one sees all the known seams of the creation ripping apart, and is flooded with joy at the sight. It is as if one were standing like God in the midst of chaos, in the gorgeous moment *before* the creation, watching the interplay of possibility. At the center of that excitement, there is only one age: youth. Only one mood: power. Only one person: self.

Poe has given us a near portrait of the Rage in his story "The Black Cat." There, Poe's narrator describes the Rage as a reflex against moral law. He calls it

> the spirit of PERVERSENESS. Of this spirit, philosophy [science] takes no account, yet I am not more sure that my soul lives than I am that perverseness is one of the primitive impulses of the human heart, one of the indivisible primary faculties, or sentiments, which give direction to the character of Man. Who has not a hundred times, found himself committing a vile or a stupid action, for no other reason than because he knows he should *not?* Have we not a perpetual inclination, in the teeth of our best judgment, to violate that which is *Law,* merely because we understand it to be such: This spirit of perverseness, I say, came to my final overthrow. It was this unfathomable longing of the soul *to vex itself*—to offer violence to its own nature—to do wrong for the wrong's sake only—that urged me on.[2]

It is the Rage that prompts Dostoevsky's character Stavrogin (in *Stavrogin's Confession*) to rape, and by his silence, to destroy Matryusha, his twelve-year-old victim. Stavrogin says of himself that "every unusually disgraceful, utterly degrading, dastardly, and above all, ridiculous situation, in which I ever happened to be in my life always roused in me, side by side with extreme anger, an incredible delight. . . . If I stole, I would feel, while committing the theft, a rapture from the consciousness of the depth of my vileness. It was not the vileness that I loved (here my mind was perfectly sound), but I enjoyed the rapture from the tormenting consciousness of the baseness."[3] And Ivan, in *The Brothers Karamazov,* says, "In every man, of course, . . . lies hidden the demon of lustful heat at the screams of the tortured victim, the demon of lawlessness let off the chain."[4]

CHAPTER ONE

ONCE UPON A TIME

The supereminence of man is like Satan's,
a supereminence of pain.

—Percy B. Shelley, in *Notes on Queen Mab*

illes de Rais and his sovereign, Charles VII, were born within a year of each other. Charles was born on February 22, 1403, the son of Isabella of Bavaria and the mad Charles VI, king of France. Gilles de Rais was born at the end of 1404 in the Black Tower of the family castle at Champtocé. For Isabella, childbearing was nearly a habit—the infant Charles was her eleventh; for Catherine de Rais, Gilles was her firstborn. Each woman had been attended by a midwife who, when the child emerged, washed it and tied its umbilicus. The midwife rubbed honey and salt over the infant to "dry and comfort its members." [1]

Though it was common practice to consult astrologers after the birth of a child, we have no astrological prediction made for either Charles or Gilles, though the latter would one day say that he was born under a malevolent star. The star in fact was Scorpio, "the sign of water, of night, of intelligence, of anguish, of suicide." [2]

The infant Charles and his highborn vassal, Gilles, each received baptism. It was a festive occasion, with many guests and elaborate displays of hospitality. At Champtocé, a lady named Marce-Garsenheu rang the baptism bell. Each of the infants had several godparents. For the rich the number was a matter of prestige; for the poor the many godparents served, in an age where birth registers were either not kept, or kept badly, as a way of making certain that there were witnesses to the child's existence and baptism. (Jeanne d'Arc, for instance, had seven or more godparents, including the wife of the mayor of Domrémy. [3])

These worldly considerations to one side, the baptism was a solemn enough matter. Cradled in the arms of his godfather, each infant took his part in a tiny play:

PRIEST: Do you renounce Satan?
GODFATHER (speaking for the infant): I do renounce him.
PRIEST: And all his works?
GODFATHER: I do.
PRIEST: And all his pomps?
GODFATHER: I do renounce them.
PRIEST: Go in peace. I baptize you in the name of the Father, the
    Son, and the Holy Spirit.

It was too soon for Gilles to know just how glorious the pomps of Satan are, but for the medieval world they represented a daily temptation, since for mortals Satan represented "a semblance of the Being of God." According to the popular imagination, he was the perpetual spy of God, licensed to be an *agent provocateur,* testing the strength of one's faith and morals. In daily life there was a constant possibility that one's behavior was instigated by Satan. The danger was graver still since Satan, as a consequence of Christian baptism, had no access to the Christian, unless there was collusion with the devil. There had to be consent—one had to be an accomplice to one's own damnation. The surest remedy against the devil was an act of will: "Get thee behind me, Satan."

The penalties for collusion with the devil—leaving to one side such bodily torments as the Inquisition might see fit to use in its effort to save the soul from damnation—were terrible.

Paul and Michael prayed to our Lord Jesus Christ of his great grace to show the pains of hell to his disciple Paul, that he might declare them in opening (preaching) to Christian people. Wherefore, our Lord granted him power by the leading of his angel Michael for to see the pains of souls punished in that fearful place.

And the angel Michael brought Paul before the gates of hell for to see the pains of hell, and there Paul saw before the ages burning trees, and in those trees sinful souls tormented and hanged, all burning, some by the hair, some by the neck, some by the tongue, some by the arms. And furthermore, Paul saw a furnace all burning in which the souls were punished with seven manner of pains: the first, snow; the second, frost; the third, fire; the fourth, adders; the fifth, lightning; the sixth, stench; the seventh, sorrow without end. And in that furnace be souls

punished the which did no penance by their life-day and every-each
after his deeds that he had in this world wrought, wherein is sorrowing,
weeping, waymenting (lamenting), burning, seeking of death. This
place is to be dreaded, in the which is sorrow of adders and sorrow
without gladness, in the which is plenty of pains with burning wheels,
and in every wheel a thousand crooks (hooks), smitten a thousand
times with devils, and in every crook hanging a thousand souls.[4]

Gilles, wrapped in the innocence of infancy, might squall at the
touch of the water from the baptismal font, as indifferent to Satan
as he was to the live hare that the abbot of Saint-Georges-sur-Loire
brought him as a gift.

If one could choose when to be born, the fifteenth century would
be a poor choice. In 1404, France and England were almost three
quarters through the Hundred Years War.

That endless quarrel over real estate began in 1337, when the
French king, Philip VI, sent his troops into the duchy of Aquitaine
and the county of Ponthieu—territories that were then ruled by the
English king, Edward III. The troops were on a punitive expedition because Edward III had harbored Robert of Artois, a "capital
enemy of the king of France." Edward III, as a liege vassal of the
French king, incurred by his act of hospitality "the penalty of
commise, that is, the confiscation of his fiefs." [5]

The Hundred Years War consisted of occasional formal battles
followed by periods of truce; of endless guerrilla operations and
perpetual bad feeling. The devastation to France, which was the
scene of nearly all of the fighting, was continuous and overwhelming. When we recall the further devastation visited upon England
and France by the plague of 1347, we may get some sense of the
literalness with which a fourteenth-century Christian heard that
"in the midst of life we are in death." The plague, devastating as it
was, lasted only two years. By 1403, 1404, when Charles and Gilles
were born, the French and the English had been at each other's
throats, in what was essentially a family quarrel, for more than
sixty years. For the peasantry, life was peaceful between raids. But
during them, there were "devastated farmlands, dead and rotting
cattle, ruined orchards, broken bridges, deserted villages, grass
grown roads, and a familiar atmosphere of desolation and
death." [6] When the English and French were not plundering the
fields, land pirates, free knights, and assorted other gangsters swept

down on the villages, either for pillage or for kidnapping, since even respectable soldiers derived part of their income from ransom pay.

The situation of the embattled powers could not be adequately conveyed by the image of a unified national France being invaded by marauding English troops. Though France had an anointed king to whom the individual magnates owed military allegiance, these peers were all but independent rulers in their own territories. They coined money, collected taxes, prescribed behavior, or ennobled each other. What they owed to the king was military allegiance, not subservience. Even their allegiance they could interpret loosely enough so that while they could choose to send troops to help the king against the English, they were just as capable of choosing to hold strategically still or even to make direct alliances with the English.

If the peers had nearly regal powers in their own domains, there was no impulse among them to overthrow the monarchy. For one thing, they were members of an extended family, continually marrying and remarrying their young to bolster alliances and agreements. Still there was plenty of reason to defer to the throne. Money and power were to be found there. The royal power turned on the careful distribution of gifts, grants, lands, jewels, pensions. A peer's income (unless he could manage some other alliance) was inversely proportional to how closely he stood to the throne.

At the beginning of the fifteenth century, the Valois throne, though not vacant, was, in terms of power, absent and France was governed by a coalition of peers that included Jean, duke of Berry, Philippe le Hardi of Burgundy, and Louis of Orléans. These last two had a fated detestation for each other. For years they got into each other's way in every conceivable fashion. If Orléans favored taking Aquitaine from Henry IV by conquest, Burgundy urged a personal challenge to Henry to fight it out on the frontier of Guienne: each prince to be accompanied by eight hundred knights. If Burgundy was hostile to Pope Benedict XIII, then Orléans urged reconciliation.

The two men nursed their hatred until April 1404 when Philippe le Hardi died, leaving the quarrel to his son, Jean sans Peur, who greedily took it up.

The younger Burgundy, "harsh, cynical, crafty, imperious, gloomy, and a kill-joy" [7] saw no reason to devote years to endless snapping at heels. Taking advantage of the duke of Orléans' habitual visits in Paris to Isabella of Bavaria, "that plump harridan of many amours," [8] Jean had Orléans assassinated by no fewer than seventeen *bravos* who nearly cut him apart one dark November night in 1407 before 47, rue Vieille-du-Temple. That quarrel, at least, was over.

For a while, there was talk of vengeance, but it remained talk until 1409 when Jean sans Peur, who had fled Paris after the assassination, was invited back and, after a ceremony of forgiveness at Chartres, resumed his seat on the royal council. More than that, seized with the litigious spirit of the age, which, in the midst of anarchy or crime, insisted on invoking the authority of law, he hired Jean Petit, a famous scholar at the University of Paris, to prepare a *Justification* that demonstrated how the assassination of Orléans had really been tyrannicide and therefore permissible. Having hired assassins, Jean sans Peur proved that he could also hire scholarship—in impeccable Latin. "In vain did Valentine Visconti, Orléans' widow, hire her own lawyer to refute the propositions of Burgundy's man point by point. . . . Jean sans Peur had appealed to public opinion and, on the whole, it supported him." [9] Jean, confessing his crime, made no such highfalutin claims for it. He did it, he said, "through the intervention of the devil." [10]

The quarrel was far from finished. Charles, the new duke of Orléans, son of the murdered man, had married a daughter of the count of Armagnac. With the count's powerful help, the young Charles struck out against Burgundy and the civil war between Armagnacs and Burgundians was launched. It would be a war that, terror for terror, would match anything the English-French battlefields could show.

In Paris, the chronicler known as the Bourgeois de Paris described daily life there as a constant fluctuation of bloodshed and high prices, as this montage of passages from his *Journal* shows:

> Corn was now so dear that a *setier* [two gallons] of good corn costs two francs or more . . . a sixteen ounce loaf, made with the chaff, eight *blancs* [a coin worth between five and ten English pence]. . . . For more than a month a *setier* of good flour cost fifty-four or sixty francs . . . the Armagnacs did as much damage as Saracens would have done; they

hanged people up by the thumbs or by the feet; they killed or took for ransom; they raped women, and started fires. Whoever it was that did these things, everyone said 'it is the Armagnacs. . . .' The rulers of Paris suddenly announced that no one of any rank whatsoever should accept *gros* [a large coin, in this instance being devalued] nor have them accepted. . . . They gave only eight shillings *parisis* for a mark's weight of *gros* . . . this was a dreadful thing for everyone in Paris. . . . On the fifth day of May, the Bastard Vauru was dragged all over the town of Meaux and then beheaded. . . . One damnably cruel thing this de Vauru did proves clearly that he was a crueler man than ever Nero or anyone else was. He captured a young man once who was going about his work. . . . Then he had him tortured. The young man sent a message to his wife, whom he had married that year and who was soon to bear their child, telling her the huge sum he was supposed to pay to save his life and limbs. . . . His wife went there, hoping that she would soften the tyrant's heart. . . . De Vauru told her that if he had not got the ransom by a certain day he would hang her husband on the elm tree. . . . But she could not get it till about a week after the appointed day. [When the wife, exhausted, and near her time, came, finally with the money, and paid the ransom, she was told her husband was dead] . . . she was in an agony of grief. . . . That cruel and evil monster, the Bastard of Vauru, hearing her say things that annoyed him, had her beaten with sticks and then dragged off at a great rate to his elm. . . . All her clothes were cut off . . . as far as her navel. . . . Above her hung four score or a hundred men, some up, some down, and the feet of those hanging lower down brushed against her head when the wind stirred.

The Bourgeois has more details, "[until] In all this pain and crying, the pains of childbirth took her . . . she shrieked so loud that the wolves which used to go there for the corpses heard her." And were fierce midwives to her.

"This happened in Lent." [11]

Years later in Paris. When Jeanne d'Arc was asked, at her trial, "Did the people of Domrémy take the Burgundian side or that of their opponents?" she replied: "I knew only one Burgundian there and I could have wished his head cut off—however," she added quickly, "only if it pleased God." After which she recalled fights between the men of Domrémy (Armagnac) and the nearby village of Maxey (Burgundian) "whence they came back sometimes much wounded and bleeding." [12]

CHAPTER TWO

CHILDHOOD AND EARLY MANHOOD

The lake gleamed in the sun, glistening like
diamonds and stinking to high heaven.

—Sholom Aleichem

Gilles de Rais's country—those territories in which Gilles
had land or bastions—extended from Champtocé on the
east, north of the Loire, to the mouth of the river on the
west; north as far as Saint-Aubin and south to La
Mothe-Achard. Most of Gilles's life was spent, however, in a region
that forms a crude half-circle with Nantes as its center, south of the
Loire, with Pouzauges and La Mothe-Achard as points on the arc.

For the most part, it is level, very fertile farming land. Springtime is a tender time, moist, sparkling; in autumn, the wheatfields
and orchards are breathtakingly beautiful; summers are hot and
moist. There is nothing in the landscape to which one can point as
shaping the monster Gilles, unless one speaks of the harsh, damp
winters during which fogs drift in from the salt marshes near the
coast. There are no crags or raging rivers, no stark glaciers such as
Gothic novelists require for their works. But there are Gilles's castles on or near the Loire, now suitably cold and ruined.

Gilles, as we have seen was born in the family castle at Champtocé, about thirty-five miles from Nantes, the capital city of Brittany. The date was 1404, nine months after the February 5
marriage of his parents, Guy de Laval and Marie de Craon. The
godparent who held Gilles in the crook of his arm and renounced
the pomps of Satan for him was Jean de Craon, Gilles's grandfather, for whom the birth of his grandson marked the end of a
series of schemes having to do with property and power.

9

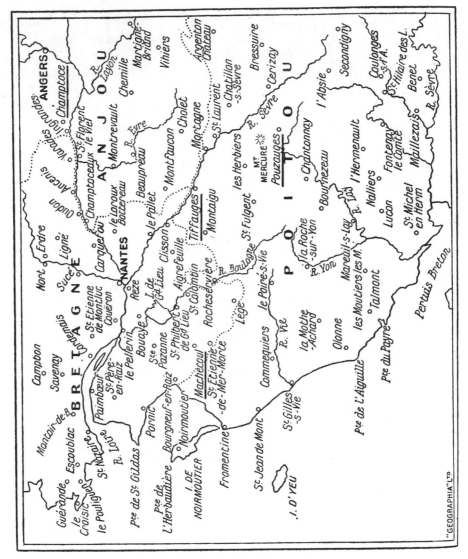

Gilles de Rais country.

The once-upon-a-time of Gilles's story begins in 1400 when Jeanne la Sage, the last representative of the de Rais family, whose marriage to Jean de Parthenay had been annulled on the grounds of consanguinity, fearing that her great fortune would revert to the state if she died without an heir, adopted her kinsman, Guy de Laval, requiring of him only that he renounce the Laval name and that he take a vow to wear the Rais coat of arms on his shield. To ask a feudal nobleman to give up his family crest was just short of an insult, but the inheritance was large and Guy de Laval accepted his destiny. On January 1, 1402, he became Guy de Rais.

If Guy accepted his destiny, Jeanne la Sage suddenly backed away from hers. She changed her mind and disinherited Guy, leaving her estates to Catherine de Machecoul, the mother of Jean de Craon.[1]

But Guy de Laval, having swallowed one insult, decided not to swallow another. He sued, and for more than a year, the matter lay with the Parlement of Paris (National Court). It was then that de Craon, whose passion was the acquisition of land and who was a genius at making deals, devised a compromise that was accepted by all sides: Guy de Laval, restored to favor, would marry Jean de Craon's daughter, Marie. It was a brilliant solution that bound the Laval, Chabot, and de Craon fortunes together and created an inheritance, through Marie de Craon, which one day would descend on Gilles de Rais and make him one of France's richest men.[2]

The infant's immediate needs were looked after by a wet nurse, Guillemette la Drapière. Guillemette was not called in because Marie de Rais could not breast-feed her son—the wet nurse was an indulgence of the rich, a sign of prestige. But it was taken very seriously since it was believed that a child imbibed character along with the milk that it took from the breast of the wet nurse. Choosing a wet nurse was no casual matter. In the royal family, for example, to be sure that imperial infants would not be corrupted, wet nurses were sometimes chosen from women of noble families.[3]

In the beginning, Gilles, like any medieval child, was tightly swaddled. Tightly enough "to give him the aspect of a mummy." [4] Later, when he began to walk, he was dressed in clothes not specially different from those worn by adults, since children were conceived to be simply adults in miniature.

Just the same, in the real world, differences were noted. The regime recommended for the first five years of a child of noble or royal blood was as follows: He was to sleep in an airy, but not windy room, looking out on the east, to take advantage of the morning sun. He ought to be bathed, but not too often, for fear of softening his skin. Consommés of veal, beef, partridge were recommended, while fish, because fish was inclined to make the child "phlegmatic," was held in low esteem. A noble child drank boiled, sugared water "to which one added one-sixth part French wine." [5]

The child Gilles, like other children of his time, spent the first seven years of his life chiefly in the company of women. For the most part, they would be nursemaids and servants of the household. Occasionally, his parents might come to the nursery to visit him, in which case a great deal of suppressed excitement pervaded the meeting, since it was the *manner* of even the most loving parents to appear formal in their children's presence.

After the seventh year, the child was presumed to have entered into the state of reason and his formal education began. For Gilles, that meant a series of tutors, from whom it would appear he acquired "a taste for letters and the arts. . . . All the historians who have had occasion to mention him in passing . . . represent him, not only as a generous man, but also as one of the best educated of his times . . . one of the finest intelligences of his age." [6] There is a famous sentence of Michelet's that is constantly cited: "He was, it was said, a lord with a fine understanding, well-mannered, and one who had a fine appreciation for those who spoke elegant Latin." "If only," sighs the Abbé Bossard, "if only he had been able to moderate his desires, he might have become a hero." [7] There is a way in which Gilles did become a hero, but of quite another sort than those who inhabit the *Roman de la Rose* or the *Tesseide*. Gilles became one of those heroes of iniquity—the great rebels, the great monsters, and sometimes the great fools.

In the real world, they include Antiochus IV, Nero, Heliogabalus, Lucrezia Borgia; in literature, where their lives are more blazing still, they are the various Fausts, Chaucer's Pardoner, Byron's Cain, Milton's Satan, Shakespeare's Iago, Lady Macbeth, or Richard III, H. G. Wells's Dr. Moreau, or Dostoevsky's Svidrigailov. They are the wicked naysayers, the great self-indulgents who, in life as in literature, make us think of grandeur while their works are death. That they are immensely wicked hardly needs saying, but anyone reading—or writing—about them is sometimes enveloped in a fever of recognition so fierce as to seem, for a moment, like admiration.

From Bossard onward, the story of the well-taught Gilles, "who spoke Latin fluently, had a passion for the sciences, music and the plastic arts, who illuminated manuscripts with his own hands, and prepared enamels with which to enrich the bindings of his books . . ." [8] has been repeated as a matter of wonder. "[What] a truly remarkable thing! a patron of the arts, he did not content himself with supporting them: he cultivated them himself." [9] As if the study of the humanities humanized anyone. As if, in Oscar Wilde's phrase, one could tell anything about a murderer from his prose.

In 1415, Gilles's father, Guy de Laval-Rais, pursued a wild boar into a wood where the creature turned on him and inflicted wounds that proved to be mortal. Michel Bataille, in his biography of Gilles, has imagined an affecting scene in which Gilles learns of his father's death. Gilles is at his studies, while his tutor, Michel de Fontenay, bored, is examining his own fingernails. Gilles is reciting his Latin declensions. "Suddenly, both of them raise their heads as they hear a stamping which they recognize as marching men entering the courtyard. Then silence, though the clinking of metal on harness and the breathing of horses can still be heard. It is not a normal silence . . . Gilles makes no move, not because he is indifferent but because he is in anguish and trying to pull himself together . . . [because] he knew.

"Gilles had lost his father." [10]

And, if that catastrophe was not enough, it was followed not long afterward by the death of Gilles's mother, Marie de Craon—though there is some dispute about whether she did in fact die, or whether she married Charles d'Estouteville, lord of Villebon, not long after her husband's death.[11] The essential point is that Gilles lost both of his parents in a single year.

It is an easy temptation to imagine a psycho-history for Gilles that would see him, in this respect also, in the mold of Hamlet. The trouble is, we do not know what Gilles's relationship to either of his parents was. Was it his father he adored, and over whose loss he brooded? Or his mother? Or did he brood at all? Nothing of that sort is known.

There was, however, a documented event that leads to interesting speculations. When Guy de Laval's will was read, it was discovered that it specifically barred Jean de Craon, Gilles's grandfather, from supervising the education of Gilles and his brother René. That task, instead, was turned over to Jean Tournemine de la Junaudaye who, however, did not get the chance to perform the duty imposed on him because Jean de Craon, a man of great vitality, capable of taking great umbrage, promptly had his son-in-law's proviso set apart by the courts and took the boys in hand. But it is the proviso itself that teases the imagination. Does it suggest that there was still a smoldering resentment on Guy de Laval's part for the way in which he had been manipulated into his marriage settlement; or was there some other quarrel between the two men that, by flaring up from time to time, might have been the source of family battles between Guy and his father-in-law; or were there battles between Guy de Laval and Marie de Craon, Gilles's parents, battles still more disconcerting for the boys to watch? The simplest answer might be that Guy de Laval, knowing too much of Jean de Craon's character, preferred not to let his sons be too closely affected by it.

In any case, it was Jean de Craon who reared his grandsons, creating thereby a paradox. The same writers who find themselves impressed with Gilles's courage, his chivalric prowess, his Latin, and his aesthetic sensibility are also those who blame de Craon for neglecting the education of their paragon. De Craon, it is said, gave Gilles a "tutelage . . . so lax as to be almost negligible." [12] Vizitelly says that de Craon "abandoned [Gilles] to laxness and the disorders of childhood." [13] "Gilles and René [his brother] could not have found a worse mentor . . . ," says Villeneuve.[14] "Everything we know suggests that he [de Craon] was little better than a bandit." [15] And Georges Bataille says, "[de Craon] taught Gilles to believe himself above the law." [16]

This dispraise is an uncritical echo of Abbé Bossard: "All the documents agree [that] de Craon was soft, indulgent, too indulgent, alas . . . [and] governed his grandchildren according to their capricious natures. He bent to all their wishes." [17]

It is easy enough to see how Bossard came to his conclusion.

There was Guy de Laval's will, excluding de Craon. Then there were the paragraphs in *Le Mémoire des Héritiers* (1460), a document prepared by Gilles's heirs twenty years after his execution, which describe de Craon as "his maternal grandfather, who was old and ancient and of great age," and imply that he was too old to manage his grandson properly. Bossard also believed too literally Gilles's assertion at the time of his trial that he had led an unsupervised childhood in the course of which he had the freedom to "do as he pleased, and had taken pleasure in all illicit acts." [18]

De Craon is central to the story of Gilles's development, but not, I think, as the oversimplified doting old man for whom Gilles could do no wrong. For one thing, he was hardly more than sixty years old when he took Gilles and René into his care. Moreover, there was nothing feeble about him. If he was sly, he was also vigorous; if he was canny, he could also be fierce.

That to one side, what has been overlooked about de Craon and Gilles is that the year 1415 was catastrophic not only to Gilles and René who lost their parents, but to de Craon, and to France. This was the year of Agincourt, when French fortunes of war plummeted to a new depth. That happened when, on October 25, Saint Crispin and Saint Crispinian's day, a small army of English troops led by Henry V, who had not intended a major battle, was overtaken by a French army twice its number and forced, as the sun was setting, to fight. The English stood, a mass of dismounted men, their front a solid mass of Welsh archers with their famed longbows. Behind the archers, infantry; behind them, dismounted cavalry. "The French repeated the mistakes of Crécy and Poitiers in mounting a cavalry charge across unfavourable terrain. The English victory was overwhelming." [19]

There was carnage among the French nobility:

First, the Duke of Brabant and the Count of Nevers, brothers of the
    Duke of Burgundy,
the Duke of Alençon,
the Duke of Bar,
Charles d'Albret, Constable of France,
the Count of Marle,
the Count of Roucy,
the Count of Salm,
the Count of Vaudémont,
the Count of Dammartin, . . .[20]

And so on and so on. Not included in the Bourgeois's list is the name of Amaury de Craon, son of Jean de Craon, uncle to Gilles de Rais.

The death of Amaury touches our story closely. If we recall that Guy de Laval, Gilles's father, died sometime after October 28, 1415 (the date of his will); and that de Craon's son was killed at Agincourt; and that the likelihood is great that Jean de Craon's daughter, Marie, died in the same year, we get a view of Jean considerably different from the one that has come down to us. Because it was de Craon's life fixation to amass land for the sake of an imagined dynasty of which he would be the founder, the death of his only son must have been a crushing affair; then the death of his son-in-law; then the death of his daughter; all within the same year. It was a heavy load of grief to bear and it puts a very different color on de Craon's eagerness to take over the education of his grandsons. The children and the grandfather, in that year, must have felt surrounded by death; and it is not hard to see why they might cling together.

Such a view of de Craon and his grandsons in 1415 makes of de Craon something better than merely an old river pirate who insisted on being the guardian of his grandchildren out of cantankerous pride. And it gives us a more dynamic reason for what, certainly, became what we nowadays call an "overdetermined" relationship between grandfather and grandson, that is that these two, grandfather and grandson, loved each other however mysteriously. One was a scion; the other a father of sorts. One thing is certain—when, at his trial, Gilles was asked when he began to commit his crimes, the reply was "in the year when the Lord of La Suze [his grandfather] died." [21]

One almost has to believe that Gilles had an unlucky star: to become an adolescent and an orphan at the same time. An adolescent, and an orphan, and a fledgling knight. To be in a whirl of sense and loneliness and terror; of military disciplines, and misinforming dreams; of sensualities, present, deferred, or horrifying.

He was the boy-man training for war, learning to put on thirty-three pounds of chain mail, to peer out at what might be enemies through a slit in an eleven-pound basinet; learning to sit astride a *destrier,* while he was locked inside arm-plates, shoulder-plates, leg-plates; and his hands inside their metal gauntlets handled reins as

Portrait of a fifteenth-century knight.

well as eleven pounds or more of weaponry: a "lance of ten to twelve feet in length, made of wood, but terminating in a metal spearhead or *glaive*. He also carried a sword, a dagger (often a *misericord* [sic], used for slipping between the plates of armor or through the *vizor*) and frequently a truncheon or an axe." [22]

The first task was to learn to stand, then to breathe, then to see, then to survive inside the expensive, usually Italian-made, oven of one's armor. Later came the picturesque riding, the hacking and the smashing of metal on metal, the excitement of giving or evading death.

Chaucer, in "The Knight's Tale," has given us both a realistic and a romanticized portrait of what knighthood could mean. By the end of the fourteenth century, when Chaucer was writing, though knighthood had become a debased profession (Froissart was already complaining that "the burning of abbeys and raping of nuns [were] decidedly unworthy of good knights"),[23] Chaucer could still describe with pleasure a medieval tourney: in the course of which Palamon and Arcite, young cousins who both love the fair Emilye, fight for her hand. Each of the cousins, accompanied by one hundred chosen knights, is ranged at one opposite end of a field:

> Then the gates were shut, and it was loudly cried:
> Now do your duty, proud young knights.
>
> The heralds stopped their riding up and down.
> Now rang the trumpets loud and clear
> There is no more to say, but east and west,
> The spears are firmly set in their sockets;
> In go the spurs into their [horses'] sides
> And there it's seen who can ride and who can joust;
> There shiver the shafts upon thick shields;
> Now one feels the thrust against his breast bone,
> Up spring the spears, twenty feet in height,
> Out drawn the swords that are like silver bright
> They hack at helmets, hew and shred them,
> Out gushes blood with dreadful bursts of red;
> With mighty maces they shatter bones
> Now one pushes his way through the thickest of the throng,
> There, strong steeds stumble, and down goes all,
> Rolling under foot as does a ball.[24]

And here is Jean de Bueil rhapsodizing about war:

> It is a joyous thing, is war. . . . You love your comrade so in war. When you see that your quarrel is just and your blood is fighting well, tears rise to your eye. A great sweet feeling of loyalty and of pity fills your heart on seeing your friend so valiantly exposing his body to execute and accomplish the command of our Creator. And then you prepare to go and die or live with him, and for love not to abandon him. And out of that there arises such a delectation, that he who has not tasted it is not fit to say what a delight it is. Do you think that a man who does that fears death? Not at all; for he feels so strengthened, he is so elated, that he does not know where he is. Truly he is afraid of nothing.[25]

All this enthusiasm for stylized bone-crushing, despite the assertion by a modern historian that "the massive armor of the period made it essentially improbable that either participant [of a joust] would be hurt." [26] The same historian, Painter, also gives us examples of the idiotic penalties that might be required of a knight defeated in a tourney, "For instance, if a knight were knocked down in the combat with the axes, he was obliged to wear a gold bracelet for a year unless before that he could find the lady who held the key."

Warfare itself, however, could be bloody enough, and it is only fair to Chaucer to quote a few of his more realistic lines from "The Knight's Tale" about the nature of war. Describing a mural painted on the wall of the Temple of Mars, the god of war, he writes:

> There, I saw . . .
> Cruel anger, red as any coal,
> The pickpurse, and pallid Fear,
> The smiler with his knife under his cloak,
> The burning barn, and the black smoke,
> The treasonable murder in the bed,
>
> . . . .
> The slayer of himself I saw there,
> His hair bathed in his own heart's blood.
> The nail, driven at night through the skull,
> Cold death, with gaping mouth
>
> . . . .
> And I saw madness, laughing in a fit
>
> . . . .

Chaucer's list goes on, inexorably noting the other aspects of war: burning ships; corpses of men lying in bushes with their throats cut; destroyed towns. "The sow eating the child in the cradle; the scalded cook, despite his long ladle." [27]

For the young Gilles, wearing his shiny, heavy new armor, imported from the great armor factories in Genoa, and riding his expensive, lightly armored *destrier,* the panoply of war was, at the beginning of his career, sufficiently exciting. He was a tall, blond, blue-eyed, broad-shouldered youth who had been trained to violence as the only honorable career open to a member of his class. High deeds at arms were the most obvious demonstrations of his manhood—that curious goal that haunts men from the first moment they hear of it; that haunted, one is sure, the blind King John of Bohemia, when he insisted on being carried into battle at Crécy where, after a few wild swings of his sword, he joined the other dead on the field.[28]

Gilles learned his chivalric skills within the three years that passed from the time of his parents' deaths to the time that he first rode out as a *yonge squier.* He learned them well, but only by endless hours spent under the tutelage of a fencing master, or in the saddle riding to hounds, or by lowering his lance over and over again against a target in the tilting yard.

The pretense for Gilles and all his ilk—the *chevaliers,* the knights-at-arms—was that they were in training for membership in a holy order. "First and foremost, knighthood was ordained to maintain and defend the holy church and the faith. . . ." [29] After that, there was a litany of other excellences. The knight was required to

defend his "natural lord."

have the virtues of "justice, force, prudence, and temperance, charity and verity, loyalty and humility, faith, esperance, subtlety, agility, and with all other virtues touching wisdom."

maintain and defend widows, maidens, fatherless, motherless bairns, and poor miserable persons . . . and to help the weak against the [strong] and the poor against the rich. . . .

be "meek and full of clemency, and not pridey na presumptuous no orguillous . . . For orguille [*sic*—pride] is contrary to justice and enemy to concord." [30]

All of this, to the sound of hacking swords, the truncheon wielded with such force that it would smash through a helmeted skull; of training for battlefields from which knights, if they were lucky enough to capture a rich foe, could emerge rich men; or, that failing, might enrich themselves by the pillage of towns and villages and, though it was technically forbidden, the ransacking of churches and church land.

It would be some years, however, before Gilles would go to war. For the moment, we have him before us as an adolescent living through what are probably the worst years in any man's development. Adolescence is a self-curing disease if one lives past it, but before the arrival of the cure, the self is assailed from every quarter. Every breeze, every sunset, every word spoken or heard is both an accusation and a promise. All questions of will, of judgment defer to the tricks played on one by his glands. At the same time, there is the consciousness of new power; visions of new ways to achieve success—or failure. There are floods of energy; whole galleries of dreams in which the outlines of God are confused with orgies. All the world seems to be coupling, and every coupling is forbidden.

> Everywhere obscene forms rise from the ground and spring, disordered, into a firmament which satanizes. The clouds swell into breasts, divide into buttocks, bulge as if with fecundity, scattering a train of spawn through space. They accord with the sombre bulging of the foliage in which now there are only images of giant or dwarf hips, feminine triangles, great V's, mouths of Sodom, glowing cicatrices, humid vents.[31]

The most normal youth hears the word *manhood* and cringes. It is, therefore, a pity that the early years of Gilles's adolescence are not accounted for, though there is a hint that—not surprisingly—Gilles "sacrificed to the pleasures of Onan." More intriguing is the hint that Gilles discovered his own homosexuality in those years: His nurse, Guillemette, or his grandfather, is said to have surprised Gilles one day "all too eloquently unbuttoned in the presence of a page." [32]

Whatever Gilles's unspecified adolescent misbehavior was, it had little to do with de Craon's eagerness to get the boy married. De Craon, as we have seen, was an indefatigable schemer, especially about property. And Gilles was, in terms of the holdings that would come to him after de Craon's death, a very eligible twelve-

and-a-half-year-old when he was contracted to Jeanne Paynel, the four-year-old orphan daughter of Foulques Paynel, lord of Hambuie and of Bricquebec. She was too young to know that she was a considerable heiress, and that her guardians, the Roche-Guyons, had been paid by de Craon to arrange the marriage, and that it was her inheritance, and not her person, that had charmed de Craon. To avoid the match and the inevitable scandal, the Parlement of Paris turned the child over to other guardians.[33] Gilles, of course, had nothing to say in the matter.

Foiled once, de Craon tried again. This time, the matrimonial target was Béatrice de Rohan, daughter of Alain de Porhoet. Again, this time without hint of scandal, de Craon was foiled when the girl died.[34]

While de Craon was canvassing the field for a third candidate to be Gilles's bride, there was a final flare-up of the "Little Hundred Years War," that quarrel in Brittany between the Montfort and Penthièvre families. The two great houses had been rival claimants for the throne of the duchy ever since 1341 when Duke Jean III died, leaving the question of succession "a nice problem suited to fire lawyers with enthusiasm." [35] In the decades that followed, more than lawyers would be involved. There were plots, petty wars, and, on the part of the Montforts, appeals for English help.

The Montfort-Penthièvre hostilities were renewed in 1420 as a consequence of one of those simpleminded plots that seem endemic to the fifteenth century. This one was instigated by Marguerite de Clisson (a Penthièvre) and carried out by her son, Olivier de Blois, against the reigning Montfort duke of Brittany, Jean V. Since the fortunes of the duke were to be closely linked to Gilles's, on this occasion and in years to come, one must pause to pay some attention to what transpired.

The duke was as politically undependable as a man with great power could be, continually vacillating in his loyalties between the French throne and the English invaders. He arrived, for instance, at the Battle of Agincourt when the fighting was over, "though he might have changed its outcome had he hastened ever so little." [36] The young duke was perhaps something of a realist; his family motto was, "The jingle of money in the country house is not disagreeable," and he did not like to send good money after bad. But

his vacillation had not ingratiated him to Charles VII, who re-
sented the absence of Breton men and money when it was needed,
and there is some reason to suppose that Charles encouraged the
plot against the duke.

That plot, on the face of it, was simple enough. The duke was a
good-looking young man, who, though married, had an amorous
eye for women. Marguerite de Clisson invited him to a banquet
where, he was led to suppose, there would be several "young, beautiful and lively damsels." Unable to resist, the duke of Brittany
rode cheerfully off looking forward to having "a right pastime." [37]

He got more than he bargained for. Accompanied by his entourage, Jean headed for Champtoceaux and the festivities. Near a
little river, La Divatte, there was a narrow bridge some of whose
planks, at the instructions of Olivier de Blois, had been removed.
Olivier came forward to greet the duke, then, pointing to the gaps
in the bridge, suggested to the duke that he dismount, since crossing on horseback might prove inconvenient.

It was a gentle courtesy from one knight to another. The duke
dismounted and, accompanied by Olivier and Olivier's brother,
Robert, walked onto the bridge. There, Olivier, "still jesting, flung
[still more boards] into the water. Thus the duke could not retreat,
nor could his guards join him." [38] With the water of La Divatte
below him, and forty armed Penthièvre men on the other shore,
Jean proved not to be another Horatius at the bridge. He went
forward peacefully enough. "Had he thought more of his devoted
wife and less of the belles damoyselles," says a chronicler, "he
might have escaped this unpleasant adventure." But, sighs the
same chronicler, ". . . it would be difficult to name any prince of
that age who really had any inclination to conjugal fidelity." [39]

Jean V's wife, whatever she knew of her husband's philandering
ambitions, on the day he was trapped made dramatic gestures in
her husband's favor. While one woman, Marguerite de Clisson,
saw to it that the young duke of Brittany was kept in chains and
continually threatened with death, the duke's wife, Jeanne of
France—Charles VII's sister—appeared dramatically before the estates general of Brittany, accompanied by her two children, and
begged for help. Surprisingly enough, in a time of broken oaths
and scorned truces, she got it. The estates general and all of Brit-

tany "rose like one man to punish the Penthièvres, and, by the destruction of their house, to put an end to their felonies." [40]

Again, there was war. This time, breaking a long tradition of loyalty to the Penthièvre household, Jean de Craon offered his sword and his allegiance to the duke of Brittany. This switch in loyalty has been cited as one more sign that de Craon, ever shifting with the prevailing winds, had chosen to come down on the winning side.

De Craon offered more than his own sword. On February 23, 1420, the sixteen-year-old Gilles de Rais and his grandfather took an oath "on the cross . . . to employ our bodies and our goods, and to live or die in this quarrel." For its part, the estates general empowered Alain de Rohan to levy troops. Meanwhile, de Craon and a cousin, Guy de Laval, were sent to England to treat with Henry V for the release of Arthur de Richemont, the young military genius, the duke of Brittany's brother, who had been disfigured and taken captive at the Battle of Agincourt. The reasonable assumption was that with de Richemont leading Jean V's troops against the Penthièvres, the duke would be swiftly rescued.

For their part, the Penthièvres were already on the march. Infuriated by Jean de Craon's switch in allegiance, they unleashed their troops through sections of the barony of Rais, and de Craon's territories south of the Loire. They "turned their anger against the unfortunate inhabitants of the countryside . . . all was turned to fire and blood; the ravages, in a word, were such as those one can imagine in a civil war, in an epoch in which personal animosity found such easy expression in public hatred." [41]

In the Penthièvre war, as with so many other skirmishes, battles, and feuds of the fifteenth century, there was so little of what anyone could call reason, and so much of something else—an upthrust of rage whose origins were only dimly related to policy. The frenzies were so personal, the mistreatment of individuals so urgent that one gets a glimpse of other energies at work, besides the official reasons given for the quarrel. There is the presence of dream longings, of sexual confusion, outbursts of the mystery of chaos and blood which may be at the heart of all warfare, but which, in the

The ruins of Gilles's château at Champtoceaux.

fifteenth century, seem weirdly unmasked. Why was it necessary to starve the duke; to drag him about from castle to castle; or to make him "promise his weight in gold to the church of the Carmelites, and his weight in silver to Saint Yves of Trégier, and even to go on pilgrimage to the Holy Sepulchre?" [42] The starvation, the chains, the forced promises, the holy penances, all lumped together, make no political sense.

The Penthièvre war was quickly over. For a time, their soldiery continued to ravage de Craon's lands, partly to pay him off for having shifted his allegiance to the duke, but they were no match for the forces, led by Alain de Rohan, that were put into the field against them. Champtoceaux, the stronghold in which Marguerite de Clisson and her sons had taken refuge, was besieged and taken. "On July 15, 1420, her son Jean, Sire de l'Aigle, came forth from Champtoceaux in all humility, and handed the duke of Brittany over to his subjects." [43] The freed duke caused the fortress to be razed; the Penthièvres were declared guilty of felony, of treason, and of *lèse majesté* and condemned to decapitation. They managed, however, to flee the country.

De Craon and his grandson Gilles, whose properties had been damaged in the brief war, were compensated by a grateful duke, though it is noteworthy that the duke's subjects modified the compensation downward—the gift of land was replaced by a gift of money. As for the Penthièvres, they were "deprived into perpetuity of all honor, of name, and [the coat] of arms of Brittany." [44]

That Gilles participated in the war is clear. Just what he did, or how much, is not known.

The year was 1420, and Gilles, at sixteen, had been to his first war.

With quiet restored to Brittany, it was time for de Craon to think again of marriage for his grandson. There was a certain grand estate that included Tiffauges, Pouzauges, Savenay, Confolens, Chabanai, and other territories that, it just so happened, were adjacent to the properties that one day the young Gilles would inherit. This neighboring estate would descend to a sixteen-year-old woman named Catherine de Thouars, daughter of Milet de Thouars and Béatrice de Montjean. For that old stitcher of fortunes, Jean de Craon, it seemed natural to bring together Catherine's territories and those Gilles would inherit. Marriage was to be the mechanism.

There are two versions of how that marriage was made. One has it that de Craon proposed Gilles for a husband and since Gilles was in every way suitable, the proposal was accepted.[45] The other, more complicated story smacks of the real de Craon.

In that version, when de Craon made his proposal, Catherine's family did indeed think Gilles was a fine *parti*, but there was just the slightest impediment: Catherine de Thouars was Gilles's cousin to some distant degree and Gilles could not, therefore, marry her without violating the Church's laws of consanguinity. Without time-consuming and expensive petitions back and forth between the families and the papal court, nothing could be done.

If, that is, one was a law-abiding Christian. Jean de Craon, however, whose instincts were those of a river pirate, saw no reason to waste the lives of the young people while their elders played paper games. With the zest of a man much younger than his more than sixty years, he took Gilles and a number of other armed men with him and marched off to the bride's castle where, since Catherine's father, Milet de Thouars, was off in Normandy, the coast was clear enough to make what was essentially a marauding expedition a success.

Tennille Dix, in her *The Black Baron,* has given us her romantic and wholly imagined scene as if a stolid Walter Scott were describing it. Catherine, she tells us, was out on her white horse, taking her morning ride accompanied by a few of her women, a forester, and his two sons, when

> she was considerably surprised to find her way barred by a handsome and most determined young man about her own age, blocking her path upon his tall black horse. She recognized him at once as the hero of the late war [the Penthièvre affair], Gilles, Baron de Rais, who had so lately ridden beside the Duke on the occasion of the triumphal return to Nantes. He bowed most respectfully and motioned her to approach him.
>
> Her attendants drew rein and waited anxiously close together in the center of the road, while Catherine walked her horse slowly toward the motionless horseman and said:
>
> "My Lord de Rais, have you wish to speak to me?"

De Rais bowed. He turned his horse so that he was beside her and
his hand grasped her bridle. "Mademoiselle Catherine," he said with
great formality, "I regret my rudeness in so interrupting your pleasure,
but I have decided to make you my bride. . . ."

Catherine was startled and quite suddenly frightened.

"Would you carry me off, sir?" She pulled at the reins with frantic
terror. "Leave go, sir! I demand that you loose my horse. What right
have you to hold me here? Let me go!"

De Rais allowed a slow smile. "My dear child," he said, "don't be
fractious. We are about to commence our wedding journey. Come," he
said sternly.[46]

There is something just a touch askew in the notion of the sixteen-
year-old Gilles calling the sixteen-year-old Catherine "My child."
But if we imagine ourselves watching a Technicolor movie in
which the characters are posturing delightfully, the scene will do.
In the real world, what took place was kidnap and rape, since there
was a coldly planned consummation on the day that Catherine
was carried off . . . the twenty-second of November.

D. B. Wyndham Lewis who is indulgent to all things medieval,
since Christian allegory was everywhere in that age, is indulgent to
this bit of violence too. He writes:

> [The English] Simon Lord Lovat snapped up his heiress no more
> efficiently in 1692; and it seems only fair to recall that precisely the
> same kind of abduction . . . was common in Wales and on the Welsh
> Marches down to the second half of the Seventeenth Century." [47]

Lewis adds, "The attitude of Gilles's bride to this adventure is not
recorded."

Whatever mixture of the romantic and the clammy the story
has, one needs to remember that the acquisition of property, not
abduction or rape, was the motive for the excursion. The idea was
very simple: Now that the young woman was spoiled past mar-
ketability, it was to everyone's best interest to get the young people
married just as quickly as possible. That happened on November
30, when a suborned priest married the couple, despite church
law.[48] Again, "the attitude of the bride is not recorded."

Now began the charade of paper work that de Craon had
counted on. The bishop of Angers immediately declared the marriage annulled, though Catherine went right on being the Lady de
Rais. A slow correspondence was developed between the offenders,

Gilles and de Craon, on the one hand, and the bishop, on the other; then between the bishop and Rome. Eighteen months later, long after Catherine had been delivered of, and had lost, her baby, the bishop of Angers was instructed by the papal nuncio to separate the technically incestuous couple; to impose a penance on them; then to give them a dispensation that would let them marry again, this time under the proper sponsorship of the Church. On June 22, 1422, that second wedding took place.

Now, let us retrace our steps a little. In 1420, some time after Gilles's improper marriage, Jean de Craon's wife, Béatrix de Rochefort, died and de Craon, who did not know that he was "old, ancient, and very old," was suddenly free to make one more venture into estate building. Land was his monomania. Before he left this world, he wanted to have more estates than even the fabulous marquis de Carabas of the Puss-in-Boots story. Since marriage was a favorite means of acquiring property, de Craon looked about for a bride for himself, and settled on Anne de Sillé, grandmother of Catherine, Gilles's young bride.

We have then 1420 as a year for marriages in the de Craon-de Rais households. Two years later, these marriages produced in Jean de Craon one more expression of "the Rage," that sudden outburst of self-will coupled with violence that we have already observed in the treatment of the duke of Brittany in our brief account of the Penthièvre war. In respect to that rage, Gilles and his grandfather were alike. Again, property was the precipitating factor. This time the victim was Gilles's mother-in-law.

Although in 1420 Gilles and Catherine de Thouars had been, if without Church sanction, married, some of the land that belonged to Catherine's dowry was still in the possession of her mother, Béatrice de Montjean, especially the castles of Tiffauges and Pouzauges, which could not be transferred to Gilles until after the flow of documents legalizing the marriage had taken its course. De Craon fumed at the delay. Then he acted.

Béatrice, newly widowed, had found for her protection a husband in the knight Jacques Meschin. Meschin, young, handsome, and not very rich, saw financial advantages in the marriage to the widow, while Béatrice, rich, alone, and unprotected, must have had genial interests of her own. From de Craon's point of view, the marriage presented a financial threat to Gilles's welfare. "There was always the possibility of an heir," writes Jean Benedetti, "and that would complicate the problem of inheritance which, as always, he [Jean de Craon] had so carefully thought out." [49] No sooner were the two married than de Craon acted. While Meschin was on a visit to La Roche-sur-Yonne ("to show the good people his handsome clothes"),[50] de Craon suborned de la Noë, the captain of the garrison at Tiffauges, promising among other things to give de la Noë's son Meschin's young sister for a bride. With de la Noë's help, Béatrice, Gilles's mother-in-law, was kidnapped and, in her turn, brought back to Champtocé and thrown into an oubliette.

M. Bataille writes that de Craon advised the jailer to keep Béatrice hungry for several days.[51] "When he [de Craon] judged that she [Béatrice] had had time to reflect—she was half dead with thirst—de Craon paid her a visit and explained to her the reason for the misunderstanding." He wanted Béatrice to renounce her rights to the château. "Unfortunately, the old woman could not [do it] because she wished to keep her young husband and feared that, without the castle [of Tiffauges], he would leave her." [52]

De Craon, then, had Béatrice sewn into a leather sack and taken to the banks of the Loire where he threatened to drown her, unless she immediately signed a transfer of property agreement. Lest she not take the threat seriously, "Béatrice was dipped into the water for a bit, then withdrawn coughing, because one dared not leave her to the river's current: Was she not Gilles's mother-in-law?" [53]

Meschin, Béatrice's young bridegroom, meanwhile sent to de Craon to arrange for a discussion. The messengers (one of whom was Meschin's brother) were thrown into prison cells of their own, and de Craon decided with or without documents to take possession of Tiffauges, which, promptly, he did.[54]

Meschin made some further appeals first to reason, then to the Dauphin. Charles, then at his shadow capital at Poitiers, had the matter investigated. *His* investigators were flogged and sent back to their master. Charles then imposed a fine on de Craon who forgot all about it.

Presumably, de Craon sent the hapless Béatrice back to her husband. The fate of the too biddable de la Noë, captain of Tiffauges, and of his lovestruck son, is not known.

Thus, de Craon: avaricious, scheming, sly, brutal. Land was his *idée fixe,* cupidity his religion, violence his reflex. Regarding those attributes he was, except that he was less brutal than other of his contemporaries, a man of his time. But his avarice was linked to the creation of an estate that was passed down from father to son, and might be said to have a certain selflessness about it; it might even be called avarice in the service of love. His grandson, Gilles, was to inherit all.

THE KNIGHT'S TALE

The Duke de Fronsac is generally credited
with the invention of a kind of chair for
rendering women powerless against rape.

—Guy Endore

In 1420, the year in which Gilles and his grandfather each took
wives for themselves, two men, Philippe le Bon, the duke of
Burgundy, and Henry V of England, with the connivance of
Isabella of Bavaria, wife of the mad King Charles VI, divided
the Gaul they controlled into two parts: Lancastrian France and
Anglo-Norman France. The document negotiated between Philippe and Henry V was called the Treaty of Troyes and, says
Edouard Perroy: "North of the Loire no voice was raised against
[it]. When he negotiated it, Philip of Burgundy probably antici-
pated that Henry would be overburdened by his two kingdoms,
and would leave him the *de facto* administration of France while
helping him to conquer the rebel provinces." [1] As a consequence of
the treaty, Isabella's son, Charles VII, the Dauphin, who had been
declared a bastard by his own mother, was banished from France
for "horrible and enormous crimes and offences." [2] Charles, however, clung to territories south of the Loire that were still loyal
to him. From his capital at Bourges, the young prince ruled a
shadowy kingdom, called derisively by his enemies, the kingdom of
Bourges. From this kingdom, which comprised the Loire valley,
Languedoc, and the Dauphiné, Charles hoped to build sufficient
strength to take power as the rightful heir to the French throne.

Then, on August 31, 1422, less than two years after Henry V of

Philippe Le Bon.

England was made heir to the French throne, that hero of Saints
Crispin-Crispinian's day died, leaving behind his eight-month-old
son. Two months later, at the end of October, Henry's father-in-
law, Charles VI of France, who had been in and out of madness
some forty-three times, gave over that losing game and died, unat-
tended by any members of his family. At his funeral it was said
"by his enemies and scoundrels that it was the funeral of the national monarchy." [3] The French kingdom now descended to the
boy King Henry VI of England.

With the deaths of the figureheads, and the French crown not
yet firmly in anyone's possession, the hopes of the nineteen-year-
old French Dauphin, Charles VII, rose. Charles was a sallow-
skinned, slope-shouldered, spindly-legged, fearful young man; a
prince whose portrait would be used in the twentieth century in
advertisements for antacid pills. He had good reason to be hopeful.
For one thing, the duke of Bedford, who ruled France as regent in
the infant Henry VI's name, did not get on well with his Burgundian allies; for another, English financial support of their troops in
France was beginning to lag. Urged on by his ambitious mother-
in-law, Yolande d'Aragon, the young Charles stirred himself to a
series of military and political tentatives.

It is in connection with one such political move that Gilles de
Rais's life first intersects with that of his sovereign, Charles VII. In
1425, Charles and the duke of Brittany were brought together at
Saumur in a meeting contrived by Jean de Craon and Yolande
d'Aragon. The aim of the meeting was to produce a reconciliation
between the duke and the young king who needed all the friends
he could muster. Charles had had some severe setbacks at the battles of Cravant (July 31, 1423) and at Verneuil (August 17, 1424).
At Verneuil, Charles's losses had been especially heavy. There the
French forces, numbering twenty thousand men, met the English
enemy, to the number of fourteen thousand. In the battle that
followed, the French were soundly beaten and, as at Agincourt,
they left an extraordinary number of their leaders either dead or
taken on the field. Verneuil was a supreme blow to French morale;
and one can understand how Charles, in the straits he was in,
might yield to his mother-in-law's prodding to achieve by policy
what his military efforts had failed to accomplish. The task at
Saumur was to wean the duke of Brittany from his English alliance.

In exchange for Jean V's pledge of loyalty, Charles promised to purge from his court any surviving members of the Penthièvre faction. As part of the realignment of forces, Charles was persuaded to accept the proffered loyalty of Arthur de Richemont, Jean V's redoubtable brother. De Richemont, who had formerly served the Burgundian cause (indeed, he was, along with the English duke of Bedford, one of the duke of Burgundy's sons-in-law), was now named constable of France, that is, commander in chief of Charles's armies. The peace between Charles and the duke of Brittany, and the adherence of de Richemont to Charles's cause, inaugurated a new phase in the French struggle against the Anglo-Burgundians. "It was," says the Abbé Bossard, "the dawn of liberation for France." [4]

The meeting is important because it was at Saumur that Gilles was introduced at court and learned courtly manners. He learned too, at least to some degree, to know his sovereign.

Charles at this time was twenty-one years old and Gilles was twenty. Charles had been long overburdened by troubles of a particularly cruel sort. In an age when the image of manhood was that of a strong, broad-shouldered knight, for whom physical violence was something of a sacred duty, Charles, as we have seen, was a model of weakness and apparently incapable of making decisions. That his ineptitude was merely a mask for fairly subtle skill in manipulating the people around him has only in recent years become clear. Still, if to be unprepossessing was one of his tricks, it was a trick he played convincingly. His fears, however, were not intended to deceive. He was timid, studious, nervous, and suffered from a notable phobia—a fear of floors and bridges. We have seen already in the story of the Penthièvre episode that bridges, for potentates, could be dangerous places and Charles was himself involved in a similar "bridge-assassination," that of Jean sans Peur at Montereau in September 1419. In that betrayal, there is evidence that Charles, if not an accomplice to the murder, at least consented silently to it.[5] His fear of floors was based on a narrow escape he had when a floor collapsed while he was holding court at La Rochelle.[6]

To all of his disabilities, one must add the fact that his own mother publicly declared him a bastard (the father of the child was unstated), and the pain of that bit of cruelty cannot be overestimated. That he not only survived, psychologically and politically, but became famous before his reign was over as Charles *le roi très victorieux,* and the creator of France as a modern national monarchy, is a demonstration of just how much psychological strength (not health—that is an entirely different matter) he would learn to muster.

With de Richemont commanding, French military action took on fresh vigor, though it is notable that the first major action he undertook, the attack against the English stronghold, Saint-James-de-Beuvron, ended in disaster. As had happened so frequently before, a French force heavily outnumbering its English enemy managed to get itself cut to bits as a consequence of confusion, complicated, it may be, with a certain amount of French treachery. "Jean de Malestroit, Chancellor of the Duchy of Brittany," writes Benedetti, "had always been opposed to the alliance with France. . . . Equally opposed to de Richemont was Pierre de Giac, the king's favourite. . . . Jean de Malestroit withheld the necessary funds with which de Richemont hoped to pay his troops, while de Giac re-routed essential food supplies. Unpaid and unfed, the French army was demoralised before the battle even began." [7] When it was over, the French forces were completely routed.

If the Sire de Giac really was guilty of the treachery ascribed to him, then he paid for it dearly. Some time later, the amorous de Giac, anxious to enjoy more freely the caresses of the young Catherine de l'Isle-Bouchard, poisoned his wife. Then, while she was in the throes of her death agony, he mounted her on a horse and led her at a gallop through the forest until she slid dead to the ground; after which the noble chevalier returned to the royal palace where Catherine, already pregnant by him, waited. One night, after these two were married, the unforgiving de Richemont accompanied by Georges de la Trémoille, Gilles de Rais's kinsman, about whom we will hear more later, and several men-at-arms smashed into de Giac's bedroom. Catherine, now de Giac's wife, hastened to protect the silver service while de Giac was hauled away to his death. Before he died, he begged his assassins to cut off his right hand, claiming that with it he had signed a pact with the devil. His hope was that Satan would be content with the guilty hand and that he would leave the rest of de Giac to take his chances of getting into heaven. His request was granted, and the hand was lopped off. Five months later, his widow, Catherine, married Georges de la Trémoille and, one supposes, brought de Giac's child with her.[8]

One guesses that for the twenty-one-year-old Gilles, those years in combat (1427–1429) were among the happiest of his life. He was young and strong; he was good-looking and rich. On the field of battle, at Le Mans and Saint-Lô, he was permitted to indulge his taste for violence—even for carnage, without being regarded as especially bloodthirsty. While it is true that he hanged Burgundians at Rainfort and Malicorne, there is no sign that any of his fellow-captains protested the executions. The Abbé Bossard writes approvingly that "it was in his eyes a necessary lesson to traitors." [9] It was harsh behavior, but not significantly different from what his master, the Dauphin, had done in 1418 when he executed the two or three hundred Burgundian defenders of Azay-le-Rideau [10] and beheaded their captain.

Even if it is true that Gilles as a young warrior was not particularly more bloody-minded than his companions-in-arms, it would be a mistake to suppose that Gilles was not affected by the cruelties that frequently were part of his life. Georges Bataille suggests that "in the training of Gilles de Rais, the only elements that can be traced are, on the one hand, the violence of war, eliciting as in the times of the German tribes, extraordinary courage and the ferocity of wild beasts." [11]

Michel Bataille, in his *Gilles de Rais,* has developed this view in a powerful chapter entitled "Le Métier des Armes." He writes:

> There were days of drunkenness after the pillage of an enemy convoy; nights of hunger in which one could not sleep. When one found friends who had been taken prisoner and tortured [and], in revenge, [one] tortured enemy prisoners, to make an example . . . without hate, with indifference. *Par métier.* One brutalized the peasants one met. To avoid being betrayed by them, one needed to treat them worse than the enemy. One hanged many; the population did not get indignant. On the days of a hanging, the condemned formed a line waiting their turn without anger, without tears, without cries. They helped to put the cord into place. They cooperated in [the] abominable rites that belong to war. . . .
>
> . . . the meanness and the menace of death were tonics, on the contrary, conferring upon life its immediate savor.[12]

M. Bataille, for his part, has identified a particular event that, he believes, crystallized the monster Gilles de Rais out of the inchoate human mass. He fixes the occasion as taking place during the battle for the Château of Lude, when Gilles, climbing the assault ladder, found himself on the ramparts, the first of his troops, where he encountered the English captain Blackburn. Bataille, in a close description that would do justice to Hollywood, studies the moment carefully: Blackburn, his back against the stone rampart, looked into Gilles's eyes and "Gilles was not afraid *because he knew that he would not die this day.*" Blackburn, understanding this, understood too that he, Blackburn, would. "At the moment of crisis, the two exchanged farewell looks. . . . In Gilles's eyes, Blackburn read immediate death. . . . The edge of the sword in Gilles's hand tore a way for itself between the plates of mail and buried itself in the flesh, cutting the knot of life. . . . *Pour notre malheur,* Gilles de Rais had found his métier." [13]

I think it did not happen quite as dramatically as this. In any case, Gilles's métier, when finally he did discover it, required helpless victims, not armed combat-ready opponents. And there is the difference between even the most savage warrior and the creature Gilles long afterward became.

Gilles lived, then, the virile life of a combat soldier. His commander-in-chief was the famous scar-faced de Richemont, a Breton like himself. A man with a taste and a talent for battle, who had fought at Agincourt. Gilles's companions-in-arms were the Sire de Broussac, Ambroise de Loré, Beaumanoir, and La Hire, the peppery warrior who had blasphemy ever poised on his tongue and who is remembered for the frank prayer he addressed to God: "O Lord, I pray you to do today for La Hire what, if you were a warrior and La Hire was God, you would want La Hire to do for you." They were tough, strong, fierce, and determined young men riding into danger together, celebrating their successes, consoling each other for failures.

JEANNE D'ARC

It is proved by experience that if a harlot tries to plant an olive it does not become fruitful, whereas if it is planted by a chaste woman it is fruitful.

—Malleus Maleficarum

While Gilles was exulting in his youth and his feats of arms alongside La Hire and Beaumanoir, another young person, some two hundred miles to the east, was making her moves to enter history. Her name was Jeanne and she was the daughter of a prosperous farmer, Jacques d'Arc, and of his wife, Isabelle Rommée, who lived in the village of Domrémy in the duchy of Bar. Jeanne was the fourth of the d'Arcs' five children.

For most of her childhood, Jeanne was not much different from the other children of her village. She had been baptized in the local church where, since her father was a substantial citizen, some half-dozen respectable villagers stood godparents to her. From her birth, her life, like theirs, was lived according to the canonical hours, in which prayer, not clocks, divided the day. There was *matins* (or *laudes)* at sunrise; *prime,* one sixth of the time between sunrise and noon; *tierce,* one half of that interval; *sexte,* midday; *none,* a sixth of the time between noon and sunset; *vespers,* halfway between noon and sunset; and *compline,* the time for sunset prayers. It was a rhythmic, rather than a regular division, so that in the winter when the days were short, a canonical hour could be as brief as twenty minutes.

As Jeanne grew up, she learned the tenets of her religion from her mother and from the village priest to whom she made an annual confession, though sometimes, when a mendicant friar passed through Domrémy, she confessed to him as well. Beyond her re-

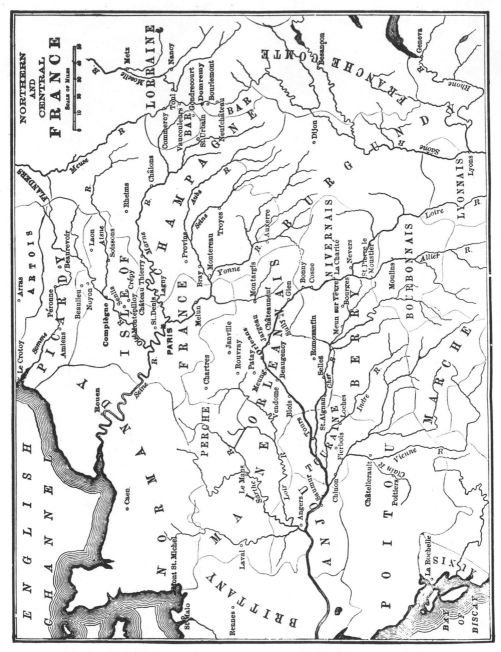

Northern and central France (fifteenth century).

ligious instruction, she received no other education. She would say
later that she "could not tell A from B"—a disability that was
hardly surprising in a village girl who lived in an age when most
knights and lords were hardly more literate.[1]

By all accounts, Jeanne was a good child. Unbelievably "good,
simple, pious, fearing God and his saints, she went often and of her
own will to church and to sacred places, caring for the sick and
giving alms to the poor." [2] She also did the usual sorts of chores
that were expected of girls in hardworking peasant families: She
helped her mother with the housekeeping and she took her turn
with the other children looking after the village cattle. She was
taught to spin and sew, and it would be said of her later that "in
sewing and spinning, she feared no woman in Rouen." [3]

She was then an ordinary enough child, though perhaps just a
bit too pious—given to sneaking away from her duties to spend
moments of rapt contemplation in the chapel at Bermont. Then, in
1424, in her thirteenth year, her life changed. She was standing in
her father's garden when she heard a voice: "And the first time she
was much afraid. And this voice came towards noon, in summer. . . . She heard the voice on her right, in the direction of the
church; and she seldom heard it without a light. This light came
from the same side as the voice, and generally there was a great
light." [4]

She learned that the "ineffably grave and sweet voice" belonged
to Saint Michael, the archangel, the provost of Paradise and pro-
tector of France,[5] and it brought her a message that she was to
hear reiterated later by the voices of Saint Catherine and Saint
Margaret as well: "Before all things [Saint Michael] told me to be
a good child and that God would help me. And, among other
things, he told me to come to the help of the King of France. . . .
And the Angel told me the pity that was in the Kingdom of
France." [6]

There is a more fanciful version of the annunciation to Jeanne in
a letter by Perceval de Boulainvilliers, one of Jeanne's contemporaries. In that account, Jeanne was involved in some child's game
when she heard a voice coming from a cloud that said: "Jeanne,
you are destined to lead a different kind of life and to accomplish
miraculous things, for you are she who has been chosen by the king
of Heaven to restore the Kingdom of France, and to aid and pro-

tect King Charles, who has been driven from his domains. You shall put on masculine clothes; you shall wear arms and become head of the army; all things shall be guided by your counsel." [7]

Such visions came to Jeanne once or twice a week for nearly five years. Always, they urged her to go to France where she would raise the siege of the city of Orléans.[8] They told her, too, to go to the nearby town of Vaucouleurs where Robert de Baudricourt, the Dauphin's military commander, would provide her with the means for her journey. When Jeanne begged off, saying she was "a poor maid, knowing nothing of riding or fighting," [9] the voices reiterated their injunction.

The five-year interval between the first appearance of her voices and the time in 1429 when she finally obeyed them and made her move must have been hard for the child to bear. She was not naturally secretive or disobedient, but she did not tell her parents about her voices. She did not mention them to her confessor either. Then, in May 1428, she begged her parents to let her go on a visit to her cousin Jeanne Laxalt (Lassoit) who lived with her husband, Durand, in the village of Bury-le-Petit, some ten miles from Domrémy. She made her request at the instigation of her voices, which may a little have assuaged her guilt for hiding from her parents the real motivation for her journey—to get Laxalt to take her to Vaucouleurs where she hoped to meet Robert de Baudricourt. When Jeanne was later taxed for hiding her purpose from her parents, she replied sensibly enough that . . . "above all I greatly feared my father, that he might prevent me from making my journey. . . . In all other things I did obey my father and my mother, save in this leaving them, but afterwards I wrote to them about it and they gave me their forgiveness." [10]

Her father might well have forbidden the journey had he known she intended to visit one of the Dauphin's soldiers, because Jacques d'Arc, some two years before this time, had been troubled by certain recurring dreams about Jeanne. In those dreams of his, he saw his well-behaved daughter suddenly abandoning her home to run off with a troop of passing soldiers. While Jacques d'Arc was a villager and a provincial, he knew or had heard enough about soldiers, and the sorts of women who followed them from camp to

Jeanne d'Arc listening to her voices.

camp, to be horrified by his dreams. He confided to his sons, "If I thought what I dreamed was going to happen, I should want you to drown her, and if you would not, I would do it myself." [11] The story of those dreams was well known to Jeanne, who had been told of them by her mother, and it helps to explain why the otherwise dutiful Jeanne deceived her parents with a white lie. Though she was perfectly willing to die grandly to save France, she did not wish to risk being drowned like a cat in a well even before her mission began.

Sometime near the end of her visit to Bury-le-Petit, Jeanne confided the real motive for her visit to Durand Laxalt, her cousin's forty-year-old husband, whom she called "uncle."

She did not, however, get to see de Baudricourt on this first visit to her cousin's house. That did not happen until January 1429, when Jeanne left Domrémy (forever, as it would turn out) to be with the Laxalts again; this time, ostensibly to help her cousin Jeanne get ready for the coming of her first baby. Durand Laxalt lodged his wife's young cousin in the home of the respectable Catherine le Royer. Evidently, Laxalt handled both the coming of his firstborn child and Jeanne d'Arc's insistent pleas to take her to de Baudricourt with equal calm. Why he finally took Jeanne to see de Baudricourt is not certain. Perhaps he was stirred by Jeanne's eloquence, or perhaps, being a simple farmer, he was predisposed to believe in miracles. One may even speculate that Laxalt, unwilling to quarrel with his wife's young cousin, simply decided to give the crazy young woman all the rope she wanted to see if she would hang herself with it. Whatever his motive, he took her to Vaucouleurs to see Robert Liebaut, Seigneur de Baudricourt, captain of the garrison there. De Baudricourt was not as yielding as Jeanne's "uncle" Laxalt had been. When he heard what Jeanne had to say, he told Laxalt "several times that [he] should return her to her father's house after having cuffed [her] soundly." [12] De Baudricourt rebuffed Jeanne twice, though he was prudent enough between times to send a letter to the Dauphin describing Jeanne and the nature of her mission.[13] When, on February 12, Jeanne complained to de Baudricourt about his long inaction, she cried out, "Don't you know that this very day the Dauphin's soldiers have suffered a terrible defeat near Orléans?" [14] When de Baudricourt heard the remark, it must only have perplexed him, but when, a few days later, the news reached Vaucouleurs that

Charles's forces had been badly beaten at Rouvray, in the so-called Battle of the Herrings,[15] his skepticism was shaken.

By then, Jeanne had impressed, or ingratiated herself with, two of de Baudricourt's men, Bertrand de Poulegny and Jean de Metz. When they pleaded her cause, de Baudricourt allowed himself to be persuaded, and provided Jeanne with an escort, a horse, and a sword. Then he sent her off to the Dauphin's court at Chinon.[16] Since the English and the Burgundians controlled the roads by day, the little group (Jeanne, Jean de Metz, de Poulegny, and Colet de Vienne) traveled by night. "Every night she lay down with Jean de Metz and me [Poulegny] keeping upon her her surcoat and hose, tied and tight. I was young then and yet I had neither desire nor carnal movement to touch woman, and I should not have dared to ask such a thing of Joan, because of the abundance of goodness which I saw in her." [17]

When Jeanne left Vaucouleurs, she was dressed in men's clothes which de Baudricourt "reluctantly, and with great repugnance, finally consenting to her demand" [18] had had made for her. Jeanne's choice of dress was to have fatal consequences for her because it struck her contemporaries—and especially, of course, her enemies—with something of the force of a blatantly acknowledged sexual perversion, implying as it did her denial of her place in nature. The simple explanation for her choice of clothes—that they were more suitable for a woman who would be riding and fighting in the company of men and that male attire made her sexually less visible and less accessible to the men among whom she lived—did not count for much when weighed against the offense she gave by acting "contrary to the honesty of womankind, in a way forbidden by divine law, abominable to God and man, and prohibited under penalty of anathema." [19] The only defense Jeanne herself ever made for her choice of clothing was that she was acting on the advice of her voices.[20]

Jeanne and her escort arrived in Chinon on or about the twenty-third of February 1429. Once again, care was taken to find her respectable lodging; then she was taken to the castle to meet King Charles. That meeting has been described many times, but it bears retelling because there is reason to believe that Gilles de Rais was one of the courtiers present on that momentous occasion.

Jeanne was not unexpected at Chinon. The rumors of her mission had preceded her from Vaucouleurs, and there was such lively curiosity about her in Charles's court that there were several hundred knights and ladies present in the audience chamber when Jeanne was led into it. It is well known how she was made to go through some kind of testing charade in the course of which she identified Charles who had deliberately hidden himself in the crowd. "Coming in from the darkness of the night, the Maid, in her page's dress of black and grey, was not dazzled by the torches burning; was not confused by such a throng of men in velvet and cloth of gold, in crimson and in azure, as she had never seen." [21] Instead, she found the prince at once. Approaching him "with great humility and simplicity . . . [she said] 'Most noble Dauphin, I come from God to help you and your realm.' " [22] The Dauphin, then, drew her apart and there followed a tête-à-tête between them "that seemed, when it was over, to make the Dauphin extremely happy. Speaking with the certainty of a visionary, Jeanne assured the unselfconfident Charles that he was truly his father's son, and therefore the legitimate heir to the throne of France. Though her words soothed his greatest anxiety, Jeanne's bare assertions might not have moved Charles to belief if she had not also demonstrated her authority by revealing to him her knowledge of a secret prayer he made sometime in 1428 when he had implored "God that, if he were indeed the true heir, of the blood of the noble house of France, and the kingdom rightfully his own, God would please to guard and defend him." [23]

What the hot-blooded young Gilles de Rais thought of the meeting between the bandy-legged Dauphin and the dark-haired, stocky young woman from Lorraine is not known. What he thought of Jeanne herself has roused much romantic speculation. There is a tradition that several of Gilles's biographers have not hesitated to exploit—that Gilles was immediately smitten by Jeanne so that he fell irrevocably in love with her. The Abbé Bossard, Albert Jean, Raffaele Ciampini, and Tennille Dix each in his or her own way deals with this theme. Bossard sees Jeanne as having an immediate spiritual ascendance over Gilles, while Tennille Dix has Gilles at Chinon, "staring [at Jeanne] rudely. For a moment she stared back, then turned her eyes from him. . . . But in that moment, an intimacy had been established. De Rais experienced a sudden and warm enthusiasm, and adopted this sturdy wench as his friend." [24]

In Raffaele Ciampini's fiction, Gilles is seen as madly in love with Jeanne. "Gilles loved Jeanne, and he knew that it was wrong. Jeanne was not a woman to love; she was not even a woman. Jeanne was one of God's mysteries." [25] Gilles is described as ashamed to love Jeanne, but he writhed in the toils just the same, struggling with himself against seeing her, because he felt that in loving the Maid he was committing a sin. "He was afraid of himself, knowing the power of his instincts . . . that sooner or later he would embrace her." Gilles and Jeanne finally have a confrontation at Reims in the course of which Gilles tells Jeanne that he is leaving her.

> Jeanne says petulantly, "It's as I told you on the field at Patay. Gilles wants all the glory for himself and is afraid he will be robbed of it by a woman."
>
> "No, Jeanne," Gilles says. Then, after an instant of silence, "I'm going because I love you."
>
> The maid turns serious and lowers her eyes. . . . "I know, Gilles. You told me at Orléans. And you kissed me; and you sought your own death on the battlefield at Patay. But no one has the right to love me; and I love no one."
>
> She had raised her head and now her voice was hard and imperious. . . . "I love no one. Still . . . no kiss that my mother ever gave me was as sweet as the one you gave me at the gates of Orléans." [26]

In Albert Jean's *Le Secret de Barbe-bleue,* Gilles is depicted once more as in love with Jeanne, only this time that love is an expression of spiritual as well as of erotic longing. Gilles, in Albert Jean's reading, suffered from erotic frustration because of his wife Catherine's frigidity. Catherine loathed Gilles's touch. As a consequence, Jeanne d'Arc became for Gilles a symbol of both spiritual and physical longing: She was not only a woman alongside whom he fought, but also the desirable woman whose purity kept her forever out of his reach. Gilles was smitten with her in both manifestations, and when she was lost to him, he lost the single thread that still attached him to humanity.

The idea that Gilles and Jeanne were romantic lovers is, let me confess, a tremendously attractive but most unlikely notion. In 1429, Gilles was twenty-five years old. He was a battle-hardened veteran who had, surely, by then discovered something of his inner nature. One thing he must have known: that he was not interested in the physical love of women. And Jeanne, as we have seen, is said to have given off no sexual aura whatsoever.[27]

On the other hand, there may have been some kind of bond between these two strange people. Perhaps they did love each other, if by that we mean that they recognized that they shared the cataclysmic destiny of people who do not fit the usual human mold. They were both, in an evolutionary sense, "sports"—throwbacks to primordial times when physical and spiritual ecstasies were more closely linked to each other than Christianity permitted these two Christians to believe. In Gilles's life, as we will see later, that bizarre link is easy to show; but the rhetoric of nationalism and sainthood in which Jeanne's story is usually couched has tended to obscure the fact that Jeanne, too, in her brief career was continually swinging between bloodshed and prayer; between mystical ardor and battlefield noise. If she was the Maid, she had also her war-horse and her armor; her sword and her little combat hatchet slapping at her side. Her war cry and her pennon are not mere copybook emblems waiting to be colored beautifully. Once Jeanne was invested with power and went into action, real men were mangled and died.

Nothing that has just been said is meant to make a moral equation between Jeanne's life and Gilles's. Gilles deserves to be called the Beast of Extermination, and Jeanne was, no doubt, a certain kind of spiritual innocent. What I am suggesting is that these two, the Monster and the Maid, may have had inklings of the ways in which their destinies were alike and that that recognition may have revealed to them an affinity that has in it some of the elements of love.

Affinity and the comradeship that comes from shared battlefield experiences; and the perhaps greater intimacy of night around the woodsmoke of military campfires, with the fatigue of the day's battle over, reminiscing over dangers passed, and those yet to come. The bonds of comrades-in-arms are strong because pain and death are in their weaving. In those half-quiet times, I think, these two young people must have stepped aside from the allegories they were living, and aware that they might be dead before the next day ended, surely yielded to their ordinary need for affection.

Gilles, in any event, was deeply moved by Jeanne. Just how deeply we will see later. For the time being, we may accept Charles

Lemire's view that in the brief battle-scarred epoch during which Gilles and the Maid were together almost daily, "the demon was subjugated by the angel." [28]

That angel, meanwhile, though she had impressed the Dauphin, did not at once get her heart's desire, which was to be given troops with which to raise the siege of Orléans. Instead, Jeanne was subjected to nearly two months of delay at Chinon, and then at Poitiers, while she was tested by various churchmen who "reported to [King Charles] that they had found nothing but what was good in her." [29] Despite this, she was subjected to an examination that had nothing to do with the theological cast of her mind. In order to be sure that Satan was not inspiring the young woman, Jeanne's claim to virginity had to be checked, on the theory that the notoriously lecherous Satan never left any of his minions intact.[30] The learned doctors of the church at Poitiers had found no evil in Jeanne. Now, a committee of ladies, headed by Yolande d'Aragon, Charles's mother-in-law, "visited and secretly regarded and examined in the secret parts of her body. But after they had seen and looked at all there was to look at in this case, . . . she and her ladies found with certainty that [Jeanne] was a true and entire maid in whom appeared no corruption." [31]

Reassured once more, Charles finally decided to give Jeanne what she wanted—the opportunity to go to the relief of Orléans. Though she was not put in charge of anything,[32] she had armor made for her as well as a costly banner of white silk on which was painted a picture of a kneeling Christ "holding the world in his hand, and on each side an angel kneeling, one of whom presents him with a fleur-de-lis." [33] She had, in addition, a small staff of men: two pages, two heralds and two ordinary servants, as well as a priest, Jean Pasquerel, who was assigned to be her personal confessor. There is some evidence to suggest that Gilles de Rais was assigned to her staff at this time.[34] Certainly, he was in the group of notable men at arms that included La Hire, Gaucourt, Saint-Sévère, and Xantrailles that rode with her toward the besieged city.[35] Of them all, La Hire was perhaps the most uncomfortable, since he had to deal with Jeanne's spirited hostility to swearing. In her presence, the usually foulmouthed warrior was reduced to such maddening euphemisms as *par mon Martin* (by my Martin).

Jeanne's journey to Orléans was, on the face of it, all panoply and high-hearted optimism, but there was an unseen cloud of court politics that hovered over the glitter. King Charles VII, who was still young, still uncertain of himself, governed as much by whim as by policy. His judgments were frequently modified by the attitudes and interests of whatever favorite was in the ascendant. At the time when Jeanne and her captains were riding to the relief of Orléans, Charles's reigning favorite was Gilles's distant cousin, the fat, forty-seven-year-old Georges de la Trémoille.

La Trémoille was a slippery character, as wily and full of ruses as Gilles's grandfather, Jean de Craon, to whom the fat man was related. La Trémoille had been installed in his position of power at the instigation of the Count de Richemont who, no doubt, assumed that La Trémoille would then prove a loyal and biddable ally. The tough, scar-faced de Richemont could not have been more mistaken—though he might have taken warning from the sly comment the young King Charles is said to have made about La Trémoille on that occasion: "Dear cousin, you give him to me, but you'll repent of it, because I know him better than you do." [36] And de Richemont dearly did repent of it because La Trémoille "sly, audacious and corrupt . . . could be a precious helper, but also a redoubtable enemy." [37] For the next six years, La Trémoille would do what he could to impede or to mar de Richemont's career.

For La Trémoille, the arrival of Jeanne d'Arc at Charles's court was a signal to be alert. Who knew just what effect the presence of the strangely luminous young woman in the unstable Charles's vicinity would have on him? Or on de Richemont's party at court? Or on his own? Like any sensible Machiavellian, La Trémoille took precautions to keep himself informed of Jeanne's doings at the same time as he set himself to dimming the luster of that rising young star.

It is in connection with La Trémoille that we come upon evidence that Gilles de Rais may have played a murky role in his relationship to Jeanne d'Arc. Vallet de Viriville, who is responsible for the charge against Gilles, puts it brusquely: "[Gilles's] principal task [in relationship] to *La Pucelle* was to be La Trémoïlle's man. He accompanied the heroine until September 18, 1429. Obedient to superior orders, he abandoned her in the course of the reverse before Paris and the retreat of the king toward the Loire." [38] According to de Viriville, Gilles not only played the spy for La Trémoille, but he participated in the court plot to "lose" Jeanne to her enemies.

De Viriville bases his accusation on the existence of a letter of agreement between Gilles and La Trémoille in which "Gilles, Lord of Rais and Pouzauges, engages on his honour to observe inviolable fidelity towards George, Lord of La Trémoïlle, Sully and Craon, for the King's service . . . he swears to serve him until death against all lords and others of whatever estate they may be, always with regard to the good grace and love of the king." [39] It is easy enough to dismiss de Viriville's charge against Gilles, as the Abbé Bossard and Vizitelly do, by arguing that such letters of engagement were a commonplace of Gilles's age; that they were not much more than rhetorical flourishes exchanged between people accustomed to breaking their word. As Vizitelly puts it: ". . . leaving the Maid altogether on one side, the document is amply accounted for by the distrustful and jealous disposition of La Trémoïlle. It was in all likelihood a precaution taken by him to deter the young and flighty Gilles from entering into any conspiracies with other nobles." [40]

Beyond that, it is tempting to argue that Gilles, whatever else he was to become, did not have in him the makings of a petty sneak.[41] One prefers to think of Gilles as the stuff of which tragic heroes or grand villains are made. And yet, there is a way in which the shabby role of Gilles, the spy, may also fit our grand and tragic sense of Gilles as well.

The task here is to intuit, as much as to know, what sorts of things were happening to Gilles in this so-called honorable period of his life, which may in some way help us understand how he could be transformed into the monster he became. We know that he was ferocious in battle; that he was a skilled and capable commander; that he was married to a woman with whom he had as little to do as possible; that, though he was twenty-five years old, he was still under the sway of his domineering grandfather, Jean de Craon. We know, too, that he was a passionately devoted Christian who nurtured the ambitions of a mystic. He was also a glutton and a lecher. The gluttony we might dismiss as an occupational hazard, since feasting grandly was one of the ways in which the medieval rich could demonstrate their wealth. Gilles's lechery, on the other hand, was not the usual wenching of a man-at-arms.

Gilles was a homosexual in an age when homosexuality was considered a "crime against nature"—a crime only slightly less loathsome than downright bestiality. Anyone charged with sodomy (the crime was often linked to heresy) could be punished by death.[42]

For a sensitive young man to be buffeted by the paradoxes of his nature was bad enough. How much more anguishing, then, must it have been for Gilles to know that his relationship with Jeanne—on the face of it so pure, so frank and affectionate—was, on his part, tainted by the sleazy role of a paid spy. One can hardly imagine a situation better calculated to shatter Gilles's self-esteem or one more likely to load his conscience with guilt. Had he spied on Jeanne, and had she survived King Charles's wars and gone back to live out her life at Domrémy, Gilles might have had some squeamish memories to deal with. But she was captured before the walls of Compiègne; she was tried and burned for a witch at Rouen. Now *there* is cause for self-loathing if one has been a friend and a petty spy. Whether his guilt was severe enough to prompt his crimes is open for discussion.[43]

Meanwhile let us turn again to the epoch of glory that began for Jeanne after her departure from Poitiers with a French force bound for Orléans. The troops were commanded by such warriors as d'Alençon, Dunois, and Gilles, but Jeanne was treated like a commander. It was April, the time of sweet showers and quickening fields, birds in the trees and fragrant blossoms in the orchards along the line of march. It was a cavalcade that moved the hearts of villagers as Jeanne's silk-fringed standard fluttered by. The standard showed, "supported by two angels, a portrait of Our Lord and the words Jhesus Maria . . . painted upon it." [44] The sword that had been found for her, considerably rusty, but exactly where her voices told her it would be behind the altar in the church of Saint Catherine at Fierbois, slapped against her side.[45]

In her exalted progress from Chinon to Poitiers, from Poitiers to Orléans, Jeanne grew giddy with self-realization and self-display, as her high-pitched letter to the duke of Bedford reveals. She demanded of the English duke that he and his lieutenants should turn over to her the keys "of all the good towns which you have taken and violated in France." [46] Referring to herself in the third person as "the Maid here sent by God the King of Heaven," she commanded them to "go away into your country, by God. . . . I am chief-of-war and in whatever place I attain your people in France, I will make them quit it willy nilly and if they will not obey, I will have them all slain: I am here sent by God, the King of Heaven, body for body, to drive you out of France. . . . If you will not believe the news conveyed by God and the Maid, in what place soever we find you, we shall strike into it and there make such a great *hahay* that none so great has been in France for a thousand years, if you yield not to right." [47]

The "great *hahay*" was made before Orléans, which had, for more than half a year, been under siege by a combined English and Burgundian force. The last French effort to relieve Orléans had been the ill-fated Battle of the Herrings about which Jeanne had, as we have seen, received supernatural advice at Vaucouleurs. That engagement, shameful to the French, had taken place on February 28. Now, in late April, the city, commanded by the Bastard of Orléans, was in desperate straits, though its despair was mixed with wild flashes of hope as the rumors of the coming of the Maid sped through the town.

On Friday, April 29, along with "victuals, powder, cannon and other equipments of war," the Maid appeared "to comfort the town," [48] riding on a white horse, accompanied, on her left, by Dunois, the Bastard of Orléans, and followed by knights-at-arms. Gilles de Rais was not part of that evening entry into Orléans. He and Ambroise de Loré were on their way back to Blois to arrange provisions and reinforcements for the Dauphin's undersupplied troops. [49]

The next several days, Jeanne spent being a public person, showing herself to the ecstatic citizens, and being something of a pest to Dunois and his captains. Vita Sackville-West says that Jeanne probably "had formed no practical idea of Orléans . . . and had thought of it in her simple faith as a second Jericho whose walls would fall before the trumpet-blast of the Lord." [50] But that did not prevent her from having decided ideas on what to do about the English. Dunois, the professional soldier, considered that his forces were inadequate for an immediate attack. Jeanne insisted on action. There followed an interval in which nothing happened while Dunois rode off to Blois to see about getting additional recruits; Jeanne and La Hire stayed in Orléans where "the crowd of people insatiable for her presence" followed her about. Jeanne got what comfort she could from their adulation, and from occasional sallies out of the city to harangue the English garrisons inside their forts. The English shouted back, calling her "Whore!" [51]

Then, on May 4, with Dunois back, the occasion for action Jeanne had been waiting for literally caught her napping in an upstairs room of her inn. She was roused from her sleep by her voices that told her, "In God's name . . . go out against the English." [52] But the voices did not specify just where to go. The frantic Jeanne berated her page, Louis de Contes, "Ah, bleeding boy, you told me not that the blood of France was spilling!" With de Contes's help, she was armed and mounted, then taking her pennon in her hand, she rode off to the Burgundy Gate where she met a party of French soldiers who had been wounded in a skirmish at Saint-Loup. Jeanne put herself at once at the head of a small force and rode pell mell to Saint-Loup. Benedetti writes: "This was not a wise move. Talbot [the English captain] immediately sent out troops from the other forts to attack the French in the rear. Joan was thus caught between two fires. Lookouts on the city ramparts saw what was happening and raised the alarm by ringing the church bells. Gilles immediately called his troops together and with La Hire at his side rode out to the rescue. . . . The combined French forces then attacked the fortification." [53]

And took it! Jeanne d'Arc and Gilles de Rais, her "valorous and faithful" companion-in-arms, were victorious.[54] While Gilles panted from his exertions, Jeanne, who had earlier wept for the wounded French, shed tears for the many Englishmen who were killed in the action, lamenting that "they had been killed without confession." [55]

Hotheaded—even wrongheaded—as Jeanne's part in the skirmish against Saint-Loup was, her victory there signaled a change in the French fortunes of war at Orléans. Jeanne herself predicted that within five days, the siege of the city would be raised. Two days later, she was with Gilles in the thick of the assault against the fortress of Les Augustins [56], where she went against the specific orders of the Sire de Gaucourt who had been instructed to keep the city's gates closed.

The Augustins was taken on Friday, May 6, despite arrow and longbow fire. When the captains urged a rest period, Jeanne cried, "You have been at your counsel and I at mine; and I know that my Lord's counsel will be accomplished and will prevail and that

that (other) counsel will perish." It was no way to speak to seasoned warriors, but by then Jeanne had become, even in her own
eyes, a symbol. She represented action—more than that, she was
victory. To her auditors, her will had a momentum that could not
be gainsaid, especially since she added the affective news that:
"Tomorrow I shall have much to do, and more than I ever had,
and tomorrow the blood will flow out of my body above my
breast." [57]

On Saturday, May 7, from sunrise until sunset, Jeanne and
Gilles fought on the ramparts before Les Tourelles, an English
bastion commanded by Glasdale, without being able to take the
place. Sometime in midmorning, Jeanne was struck by an English
arrow in the shoulder. It must have been a petrifying moment for
her, since she had sensed herself, until then, as an exultant idea
behind whom victorious events would cohere. Suddenly, she was
immobilized, bleeding and in pain, on a heaving battlefield where
at any moment she might die. If ever there was a time for a delu-
sional young woman to come to her senses, this should have been
it. Instead, Jeanne enclosed herself in her idea and reanimated it.
Though she allowed her comrades to dress her wound with olive oil
and lard, she insisted on returning, with Gilles at her side, into the
thick of the action.[58]

It was a long, weary day. As evening approached, Dunois, the
Bastard of Orléans, feeling that the French forces were at a stale-
mate, prepared to sound the retreat when Jeanne implored him to
delay a little while—just long enough for her to withdraw for a few
moments of silent prayer. Dunois gave her the time she needed.
Reanimated by her voices, she returned to the field of battle to
precipitate "one of the grandest feats of arms that there had been
for a long time before." [59]

It was a feat of arms that began with a misunderstanding.
Jeanne's beloved standard had somehow been passed to a soldier
named Le Basque, who carried it into the *fossé,* or ditch, below the
Tourelles. According to Jean d'Aulons, "When the Maid saw her
standard in the hands of Le Basque and thought that she had lost
it . . . she went and seized the end of the standard in such manner
that he could not carry it away, crying 'My standard, my standard!' and waved the standard in such fashion that I imagined
that so doing, the others would think that she was making them a
sign. . . . Then Le Basque tugged so at the standard that he tore it

from the Maid's hands and so doing came to me and raised the standard. This occasioned all who were of the Maid's army to come together and to rally again." [60]

It was Jeanne's genius to shape confusion into miracle. The contretemps over the standard was interpreted by her troops as a signal for a renewed effort and they rushed to join her as she led them in a charge, crying to Glasdale, the English commander, " 'Classidas, Classidas, yield thee, yield thee to the King of Heaven; thou hast called me "whore," me; I take great pity on thy soul and on thy people's.' Then Classidas, armed (as he was) from head to foot, fell into the river of Loire and was drowned." [61] Once again, Jeanne wept for the souls of her enemies, but the Tourelles were taken and the six hundred English defenders were killed or captured.

The following day, Sunday, the English, who still camped before Orléans, were mustered and marched away to Meung-sur-Loire and the nearly seven-month siege of Orléans was over. Jeanne d'Arc's mission was finally, and fully, validated. She had said that she would raise the siege and, however bumblingly it had been accomplished, it was over. King Charles, in whose ears there still echoed the rest of her promise—to see him crowned at Reims—sent out a circular letter of exultation in which the Maid received honorable mention.[62]

Orléans was relieved on the eighth of May. From then until the seventeenth of July when the king was crowned at Reims, Jeanne d'Arc and Gilles entered a restless period of military activity. Gilles, now officially assigned to protect Jeanne, rode beside her as she led the increasing numbers of men who flocked to her banner. Wherever she rode, she was accompanied by a troop of mendicant friars singing pious songs. Wherever she camped, soldiers had to watch their language and hide their doxies if they would avoid her pious tongue-lashings. Jeanne might have done better to be kind to the whores, but remembering, perhaps, her father's dream that she herself might one day be a camp follower, she lashed out at the women on every occasion. One day, she swung the flat of her good luck sword—the one that had been found for her miraculously behind the altar of the church of Saint Catherine at Fierbois—against a whore's backside. In the collision between sanctified metal and corrupted flesh, the flesh proved sturdier and the holy sword broke beyond mending. Jeanne took the loss of the sword as an evil omen, as indeed it proved to be.

Jeanne was exigent in another, more important, matter. No sooner was Orléans liberated than she went off to Tours where she set about persuading Charles to betake himself to Reims where he should be properly anointed as the king of France. The matter was pressing because the English had their own candidate, the young Henry VI, whose claim to the French throne was not frivolous. In the popular imagination, the king who was anointed at Reims (as all the kings of France since Charlemagne had been) would be the true ruler of the kingdom. Charles's natural indolence, as well as the advice of his councillors, contrived to delay the journey to Reims, though Jeanne's voices were saying, "Daughter of God, go, go, go. I will help you, go." [63] Instead, in a compromise military decision, the French turned their attention to the liberation of various cities along the Loire.

Gilles was with Jeanne at Jargeau, as we know from a receipt that shows that he was paid the sum of one thousand *livres* to "recompense him for the great expenditure he had incurred by assembling, according to agreement, a certain large body of men-at-arms, and bowmen, whom he had kept at his own expense and employed for the service of the king and in the company of the Maid, in order to reduce to obedience the town of Gergeau [*sic*] which was held by the English." [64]

Jeanne and Gilles were together also at Beaugency [65] and again at Patay. It was before Patay on June 18, 1429, that Jeanne urged the French troops to look to their spurs. The strange advice produced wonder. The French asked whether she meant that they would lose the fight; Jeanne replied, "It will be the English who will turn their backs. . . . You will need spurs to pursue them." [66] It was a grandiose promise, but by then the French were confident that whatever Jeanne promised would come true. The trouble was that though the English were somewhere before them on the plain of La Beauce, they were so well hidden by trees that no one knew where to find them. It was then that a party of French scouts inadvertently started a stag that "bounded off immediately into the English lines, a sight which the English evidently could not resist, especially in this game of hide and seek, over the wide area of La Beauce. . . . It was scarcely to be expected that Englishmen seeing a stag should not set up a shout of delight. They set it up." [67] Now the French knew where the enemy was and the battle was joined. By two o'clock in the afternoon, the French had carried the day. "The pursuit was murderous. Two thousand [English] corpses were strewn on the plain. The Maid wept when she saw the carnage, and she wept more grievously still when she had to witness the brutal behaviour of her soldiers and the ruthless treatment of the prisoners who could not offer ransom." [68]

After Patay, even the hesitating King Charles was moved to action. On June 29, he began the slow progress that would take him from Saint-Benoît-sur-Loire to Reims, pausing from time to time to take the submission of the towns on his route. It was something of a conquering procession. "[W]hen they set out, they were only 12,100; but on the way their numbers grew; more kept coming, and others still." [69] Finally, on July 16, Charles and his armies reached Reims, which only hours before his arrival was still hesitating whether to receive him or not.

For Jeanne, Charles's entry into Reims on that day was the beginning of another of those giddy-making moments on which her soul fed. She had had the annunciation of her voices when she was thirteen; then only four months before (on March 6) there had been her meeting with Charles at Chinon; two months after that, as she had promised, she had raised the siege of Orléans; and now here she was, six weeks later, at the penultimate moment of her mission when her country-girl dreams and her nation's destiny were about to become one. The sanctification ceremony to come would mark the spiritual culmination of her mission. From the time that she first heard her voices, every breath she drew had been devoted to hallowing Charles's kingship. Only when the tiny drop of oil, teased out of its Holy Ampul with a golden needle, touched Charles's head could he be "truly, truly" the sovereign of France.

All questions of miracle to one side, one cannot help being amazed at what had, in less than two months, become of Jeanne. To think that an English military leader would treat with a woman of seventeen for a ten-day truce, as d'Evreux had at Beaugency! One guesses that of all the thousands of people dazzled that day at Reims by Jeanne's accomplishments, the one most over-

French coronation costume of the emperor.

BISSON ET COTTARD

whelmed and exhilarated was Jeanne herself. As a plot for fiction, the story of what she had done was improbable to the point of absurdity. A writer trying to pass it off on readers would have been laughed to scorn. And yet here she was, an illiterate country woman, looking chunky in her masculine armor, and wearing, it may be, the green cloak that had been her reward for raising the siege of Orléans, her pennon fluttering in the breeze, riding shoulder to shoulder with such famous captains as Xaintrailles, La Hire, Ambroise de Loré, Gilles de Rais, and the Bastard of Orléans.[70] And all of them on their way to witness a historic event for which she herself was primarily responsible: the anointing of a king.

It was a giddy and a busy time. Reims was not quite ready for the event, so there was much that had to be done. The vestments and jewels appropriate for the coronation were at Saint-Denis. Moreover, there was no proper crown, but one suitable enough was found in the cathedral treasury. In the midst of the general tumult, it was discovered that the Holy Ampul containing the precious oil of consecration could not be brought to Reims in just any old fashion. There was a particular "form and manner" that had to be followed. For that, Gilles de Rais, newly created marshal of France, was pressed into service. He, along with a second marshal, Jean de Brosse, Sire de Boussac and Saint-Sévère; as well as the Sire de Culan, admiral of France; and the Sire de Graville, commander of the king's crossbowmen, rode off, accompanying the abbot of Saint-Rémy to his abbey some miles away where the cleric, splendidly garbed, took the "little phial measuring only an inch and a half long, the neck being closed by a stopper of red silk; the holy contents had admittedly dried and shrivelled since a pigeon whiter than snow had arrived with the phial in its beak to the assistance of Saint-Rémi at the baptism of Clovis." [71] The vial was encased in a golden dove that swayed from a chain hung round the abbot's neck as he and his escort retraced their solemn, if hurried, way back to Reims, where the abbot and his bodyguard rode right into the cathedral to the very nave. The ampul was there received by Regnault de Chartres, archbishop of Reims, and the coronation continued. [72]

As part of the ceremony, Charles received knighthood at the hands of the Duke d'Alençon, and, if we are to believe the *Mémoires Concernant la Pucelle d'Orléans,* Gilles was made a count by Charles in recognition of his many services to him and to Jeanne. Jeanne, for her part, stood near the king throughout the nearly five-hour ceremony. When it was over, she knelt before the monarch and, says an old chronicle, "whoever had seen the Maid clasping the king about by the knees, kissing his foot weeping hot tears would have had great pity [as she said] 'Gentle King, now is God's pleasure accomplished Who wished that you should come to Reims to receive your holy anointing, showing that you are the true king and the one to whom the realm belongs.' " [73]

Jeanne had given the king his realm; now he gave her sixty *livres*—a gift to her father. He also made one of her brothers provost of Vaucouleurs.[74] Jeanne, one should say, was not totally oblivious to such worldly emoluments. Even in the heady days of the coronation in Reims, she took advantage of her prestige to ask for—and was granted—a tax remission into perpetuity for the villages of Domrémy and Greux. [75]

After Reims, if Jeanne had had good judgment, she would have gone back to Domrémy where she would have been a nine-day wonder; then the cycle of the seasons, the village's funerals and festivals would have resumed their rhythm and she would have lived out unremarkable days. Sackville-West suggests that after Reims "the first great gale of her inspiration left her, and . . . she was no longer capable in quite her old way of making men listen to her voice." [76] The compassionate Michelet thinks that by this time something essential in Jeanne had been touched by corruption: "What a misery for such a soul to be enmeshed in the realities of this world. Every day she must have lost something of her integrity." [77] I think myself that Reims had given Jeanne such a fatal taste of exultation that she could not bring herself to come down from the heights to which spiritual genius, physical courage, momentum, and luck had raised her.

She did not go home. Instead, she stayed to become the tragic epilogue to the success story that ended at Reims. From here on, the tone of her life loses some of the patina of innocence that had given it so much charm. In Jeanne, the world had condescended to be moved by innocence, and briefly innocence had proved stronger, truer, and braver than the accommodations that usually pass for wisdom among us. But the season for purity is as brief as was the appearance of the white butterflies that reportedly surrounded Jeanne at the Battle of Patay. After a flare of loveliness, reality takes over and the ceremony of innocence, not for the last time, is drowned.

Success had made Jeanne precious to the French. After Reims, success sustained her for a while longer. City after city yielded obedience to Charles's armies so that he grew sanguine and delayed the march on Paris that, had he made it following on the victory of his armies at Orléans, might have brought that city tumbling into his lap like ripe fruit. When at last he moved, the Paris campaign fluctuated between stalemates and victories. At Senlis (August 14–16, 1429), the English Bedford's troops skirmished with the French, though battle was never joined. It was in the course of one of these skirmishes that La Trémoille, Gilles's fat, conniving cousin, was thrown from his falling horse and "had he not been quickly rescued, he would have been killed or taken." [78] Fierce as the skirmishes were, the following morning the English turned their backs on the French and made their way back to Paris.

Jeanne and Gilles de Rais participated in the misfortunate attack on Paris by Charles's forces on September 8. Jeanne, her banner held high, led an attack against the Saint-Honoré Gate and managed to get past the outer barrier. Under heavy enemy fire, she and Gilles crossed the first *fossé*, or ditch, but they were stopped by the second one, which was filled with water. There, where "it was a marvel to hear the sounds and the voices of the cannons and culverins . . . ," [79] Jeanne was struck by an arrow.

The good Bourgeois de Paris describes what happened before the gate of Saint-Denis: "They [Charles's troops] assembled, a good twelve thousand or more of them, and came up, their Maid with them, at about the time of high mass. . . . Their Maid was there with her standard on the bank above the moat, and she said to the Parisians, 'Surrender to us quickly in Jesus' name! If you don't surrender before nightfall, we shall come in by force whether you like it or not and you will all be killed.' 'Shall we, you bloody tart?' said a crossbowman, and shot at her. The bolt went right through her leg; she ran for safety." [80] Presumably into the arms of Gilles de Rais who helped her out of range of further arrows. Fifteen hundred other French soldiers were also wounded on that day. Jeanne's hurt was not serious, and she was ready for yet another attack the following day, but King Charles ordered a with-drawal from Saint-Denis. Gilles, Jeanne, and d'Alençon, with great bitterness, obeyed their sovereign. There is some evidence that the discomfiture of King Charles's forces before Paris was actually contrived by the king himself and various of his counselors who wished by this means to injure Jeanne's reputation.[81]

After the retreat from Saint-Denis, Gilles de Rais was granted the right "to add the arms of France as a border to the shield of Rais. 'The said escutcheon,' says the document, 'shall bear an orle of our arms—that is, a field azure charged with flowers-de-luce or, in such form and manner as is here portrayed, figured, and emblazoned.' " [82]

Ironically enough, after so many shared hours, the rest of Jeanne's career is played out without further mention of her comrade-in-arms, Gilles de Rais. As we follow Jeanne to her death, we are haunted by the absence of his name. The Abbé Bossard asks, "Did [Gilles] stay on at the French court; or, like the Duc d'Alençon, irritated by the truce that had been signed, return to his estates to rest from his fatigues like many other captains? Was he made a governor of some important place. . . ?" [83] There is no answer. The teasing silence remains.

Jeanne, meanwhile, continued to campaign. She was active at Saint-Pierre-les-Moûtiers, and at the long but unsuccessful siege of La Charité. Then, as she stood on the ramparts of Melun, her voices came to her bringing the news "that before the feast of Saint Jean should come round she would be taken." [84] Her voices advised her to take the event well; not to be terrified; to count on God's help.

That was at Easter 1430. On May 23, at five o'clock in the evening, in the vicinity of French-held Compiègne, Jeanne d'Arc led a spoilers' raid against an isolated English outpost at Baudot de Noyelles, near the village of Margny. It should have been a nearly routine sortie; and it should have been successful—the English defenders had put aside their arms for the day: "Her task easy, Jeanne, on her grey horse, with her scarlet gold-embroidered *hucque,* must have sallied forth with a heart as light as it was resolute. She scattered the men of the outpost through the village. . . . At this hour, Jean de Luxembourg, with the Sieur de Créqui and eight or ten other gentlemen, was riding from Clairoix on a visit to

Baudot." [85] It was the accidental presence of Jean de Luxembourg on the heights above Margny that spelled doom for Jeanne d'Arc. De Luxembourg, observing the raid, sent for reinforcements and himself rode to engage Jeanne and her men. After a melee in which Jeanne is said to have done heroic "deeds beyond the nature of woman . . . ," [86] she and her men were forced to retreat toward the safety of Compiègne, within whose walls, once she crossed the drawbridge over the moat, they would have been safe. Jeanne's ill fortune was that Guillaume de Flavy, the governor of the town, seeing the pell-mell advance of five thousand English men-at-arms, did not dare wait for Jeanne, her brothers, and the three or four others who were still with her, to reach the city's gates. He ordered the portcullis to be lowered, and Jeanne's retreat was cut off.[87] Surrounded by men who clamored for her surrender, Jeanne sought her own death first by putting up a resistance, but she was pulled ignominiously from her horse by an archer. [88]

The archer who claimed Jeanne as his prisoner was named Lyonnel. He was a liegeman of the Bastard of Wandonne who, in turn, owed his allegiance to the duke of Luxembourg. Jeanne, therefore, was passed from hand to hand until May 27 when she was sent to the château of Beaulieu from which, after an abortive escape attempt, she was sent to Beaurevoir, where she arrived on June 8. At Beaurevoir, according to Quicherat, a soldier named Aimond de Macy tried to caress Jeanne's breasts and was soundly boxed on the ear for the outrage. It may have been fear of further such molestation, along with her dread of being sold to the English, that prompted Jeanne to make her famous escape attempt from Beaurevoir several days later.

It should have been a leap to certain death—some fifty-four feet down from the tower in which she was imprisoned, but amazingly she landed at its foot unconscious, but otherwise unhurt. As an escape attempt, her leap was unsuccessful, but her survival was further evidence, if anyone still needed it, that nothing about Jeanne was ever anything but extraordinary.

Meanwhile, Charles VII, the man who had the best reason to know just how remarkable she was, did all but nothing about the capture of the woman who had sanctified his reign. Charles, who "was the greatest danger to any cause which he defended," and his court "took no interest in her fate; the Chancellor Regnault de Chartres wrote to the people of Reims that she had been taken because she insisted on following her own desires, and moreover that her place had already been taken by a shepherd of Gévaudan, who would do as well as she had done." [89] For Michel Bataille, Charles's silence during nearly a year that passed from the time of Jeanne's capture until her execution, is loud with cruel implications. "It was a silence that cried out to the English not only that they might dispose of Jeanne in any way they saw fit without bringing down [on themselves] any French reprisals, but more than that [it implied] *that it was necessary to burn her.*" [90] And Edouard Perroy writes that "legal means were not lacking for stopping her trial at Rouen or suspending the enforcement of its sentence. Regnault de Chartres could have claimed jurisdiction, since his suffragan Cauchon had irregularly started the procedure in a neighboring ecclesiastical province. An appeal to the Pope and the council could have been in order, and Cauchon, a respecter of formality, could not have challenged it. But nothing of the kind took place." [91]

The inertia of the French who did nothing to save her, and the energy of the English who were passionate to destroy her had pretty much the same root: Jeanne d'Arc had passed beyond personality and had become a symbol, both for the English and for the French. For the English, she represented the only explanation for their various defeats. She was the uncanny creature, "Whose pow'rful Charms made th'English quit the Field,/No mortal Force could else have made 'em yield." [92] For the French, by a curious extension of the same logic, Jeanne had become a sort of hallowed mascot whose presence in their midst had produced victories for the armies of France, a fact that itself was an implied slur on French military skill—as if they could not win wars without her banner fluttering before them. For both sides, she was an embodiment of energy rather than a self; a saint or Satan's minion. It is hardly surprising that in Charles's court, now that he was safely anointed, there should be little concern for a woman who had little small talk and no vices. The English, for their part, were enchanted to get their hands on her. They intended to prove that Satan's slave, whatever her battlefield talents, could also burn.

Eventually, Jeanne's greatest fear came to pass: She was sold to the English, but only, it would seem, with the connivance of heaven because Jean de Luxembourg, whose prisoner she was, had a very rich aunt who made a will leaving her considerable property to her nephew on condition that he *not* turn the Maid over to the English. De Luxembourg hesitated, then, on November 13, his aunt died. Her property passed irrevocably into his hands and he was free to add Jeanne's purchase price from the English to the fortune left him by his kindly aunt. The price for Jeanne, in gold, was twenty thousand livres.

It was late November 1430 when Jeanne was handed over to the English. They had her moved from Beaurevoir to Rouen where, when she arrived in December, she was immediately imprisoned, under irons and behind triple-locked doors, in the town's secular prison. Had she been sent, as she repeatedly begged, to the ecclesiastical prison, she would have been considerably better treated, since "the Bishop of Rouen had at his disposal a room for women and . . . she might have been placed under the care of women." [93] As it was, she was in such danger of sexual abuse that she clung to her male attire, a fact that later would weigh heavily in the scales against her.

Saints and martyrs severely try the real world's patience. The rest of us spend our lives learning to endure uncertainty, adjusting ourselves to the continuous blurring of definitions. Things are, and they also *are;* "is" and "may be" are forever in flux. It is a trying life but somehow we get on with it. We make reasonable approximations and avoid calling them compromises; we modify our expectations. Under the guise of humility, we learn to yield to the real. Not so the saint or martyr, whom it would be a great mistake to invite to dinner, or to any easy, friendly gathering, because such folk, having learned what they know directly from God, have no patience with any voices but their own. At the very least, they are sure to be boring; at worst, they will confound, exasperate, enrage.

Because, though they may speak to society, they do not know how to live in it; they are unwilling to pay the quasi-hypocritical small coin that getting on with it requires. And their refusal can be a sore pain to friends and family, but most of all to those authorities with whom sometimes they have to deal.

One thinks, for instance, of the tale told by Prudentius (A.D. 348–410) of Saint Eulalia, that improbable Spanish ten-year-old, who, to her own cost, tried the patience of a Roman praetor. Eulalia, like Jeanne, had angels on her side. What they counseled *her* to do was to leave home one night and make her way to "the judgement seat of the Praetor, [where] she reviled the [Roman] gods before his face."

What was the poor praetor to do? There he sits, a reasonable enough man, with a panting ten-year-old standing before him committing capital offenses with every breath she draws. The kindly praetor (perhaps he has daughters of his own) "begged her to be sensible; he is ready to pardon, if she will but touch with her fingertips a bit of sacred Pagan salt and incense." [94] But no, Eulalia has been chatting with angels and has heavenly permission to be bad-mannered. She spits in the praetor's face, knocks his idols down, and stamps on the sacred salt.

The matter, by then, is out of the praetor's hands. He wipes his face and nods to the executioner who, no doubt, wonders why the praetor has waited so long as he puts his long knives to their proper use. When they are done, the child's body is consigned to the flames where it gives off a miraculously sweet odor; and her soul, in the form of a white dove, ascends to heaven.

For the Christian, St. Eulalia is an emblem of martyrdom; for the praetor, she must have been one more proof that a dialogue that begins at the pitch of crisis is likely to erode less costly options.

The trouble with Jeanne, as Article XXV of the Articles of Accusation said, was that for a long time she had been "usurping the office of angels." [95] Altogether, as her accusers believed, Jeanne was too prideful. In the face of an assembly of Doctors of Theology who had been trained in the belief that knowing God's will was the lifetime study of His church, Jeanne asserted that her own knowledge was a sufficient authority for the truth of her voices. The line, not for the first time, was drawn between the illuminated mystic and the Church's authority. For five months, beginning with January 9, some sixty learned men were to struggle with the nineteen-year-old Jeanne to persuade her that in matters of faith she was not sufficient authority to decide what was the truth. And she, worn from months of prison life, sometimes racked with illness, always harassed for her persistence in wearing her masculine clothing, gave them the sort of answers that make us admire tragic heroines when they speak of them in fiction but which would break our hearts if our daughters, facing death, made such replies: "The way that I have always spoken and held to in this trial, that will I still maintain. And if I was brought to judgement and saw the fire lit and the faggots ready, and the executioner ready to stoke the fire and that I should be within the fire, yet should I not say otherwise and should maintain what I have said in the trial even unto death." [96]

No wonder the scribe recording this speech termed it "Jeanne's haughty answer." [97]

Pierre Cauchon, bishop of Beauvais, was the trial's presiding judge, because Jeanne had been captured in his diocese. For six days, she endured a public examination. Later there were fifteen private interviews with her in prison. The various interrogations produced *seventy* charges against her "based upon hearsay and tales of sorcery and witchcraft." [98] When these were being read to Jeanne, she interrupted at the end of each clause with a denial. The prologue to these Articles of Accusation is a sonorous piece of outraged prose as it describes

the woman commonly called Jeanne *the Maid* [sic] found, taken and detained in the limits of your territory, venerable father, and the boundaries of your diocese of Beauvais . . . to be dealt with by the law and corrected, as one vehemently suspected, denounced, and defamed by honest and sober people; to the end that she should be denounced and declared by you her said judges as a witch, enchantress, false prophet, a caller-up of evil spirits, as superstitious, implicated in and given to magic arts, thinking evil in our Catholic faith, schismatic in the article *Unam Sanctam,* etc., and in many other articles of our faith skeptic and devious, sacrilegious, idolatrous, apostate of the faith, accursed and working evil, blasphemous towards God and His saints, scandalous, seditious, perturbing and obstructing the peace, inciting to war, cruelly thirsting for human blood, encouraging it to be shed, having utterly and shamelessly abandoned the modesty befitting her sex, . . . and for that and other things abominable to God and man . . . and [for having] allowed herself to be adored and venerated, giving her hands to be kissed . . . that she should be punished and corrected canonically and lawfully.[99]

From January 9 to May 30, 1431, Jeanne's two judges, Pierre Cauchon, bishop of Beauvais, and Jean Lemaître, vicar of the Inquisition, aided by sixty assessors, picked at, turned, and twisted their victim round and round, drawing from her the story of her life in such detail that the trial transcript makes an astonishingly full, if tormented, biography of Jeanne. Most of the time, her replies were calm, lucid, commonsensical. To the trick question asked by clerics in the pay of the English, "Do you know whether Saints Catherine and Margaret hate the English?" Jeanne replied, "They love that which God loves and hate that which God hates." [100] To the question, intended to prove that she was prideful, "But why was [your] standard carried into the Church at Reims for the king's anointing, rather than those of the other captains?" she replied, with the pride of accomplishment, "It [the banner] had seen all the dangers; it was meet it should share the honors." [101] To the petrifying question, "[Jeanne], do you believe that you are in a state of grace?" she gave the glowing reply, "If I am not, may it please God to bring me into it; if I am, may he preserve me in it." [102]

The truth is, however, that, unless she was willing to make an act of abjuration in which she denied the truth of her voices and, indeed, the truth of her entire mission, nothing Jeanne could say would have done her the slightest good. Given the English sponsorship of the trial and the Church's hostility to personal authority for revelation, the wonder is not that she was finally declared to be guilty, but rather that the court should have worked so long and hard to weave a tissue of substance around the charges.

The English masters of this French ecclesiastical court, exasperated finally at how long it did take to declare Jeanne guilty, sent the Articles of Accusation (now reduced to twelve major heads) to the University of Paris for its judgment at its May 14 meeting. The Anglophile University did not deliberate long. It "concluded by finding [Jeanne] guilty of being a schismatic, an apostate, a liar, a soothsayer, suspect of heresy; of erring in the faith and being a blasphemer of God and the saints." [103] The university clerics added their wish that the matter of Jeanne be quickly brought to an end. The unequivocal message was "Burn the witch. Soon."

Just the same, Cauchon's court tried once more to get Jeanne to abjure her testimony. On the twenty-fourth of May, she was taken to the cemetery at Saint-Ouen where one more cruel charade was played out. Jeanne, now wan and exhausted, was shown a freshly constructed scaffold and was told that she would be burned there and then unless she abjured.

The scene at Saint-Ouen is in many ways macabre. It was a dress rehearsal for martyrdom complete with important prelates: the bishop of Winchester; "the Bishop of Beauvais and Noyon; Louis of Luxembourg, Bishop of Thérouanne; and William Alnwick, Keeper of the Privy Seal and Member of the Grand Council of the Crown. The principal assessors were also present, and a crowd had collected all round the platforms." [104] The great men knew it was a dress rehearsal. Jeanne and, probably, the crowd, did not.

Just as if it were the real thing, a sermon was preached to her by Guillaume Erard. When that was done, she was exhorted three times to abjure, and a document was thrust into her hands that, since she was illiterate, she could not read. When she begged to have the paper read by clerics who should advise her whether to sign it, Guillaume Erard replied, "Do it now, if not this day shalt thou end thy days by fire." [105]

Jeanne had been recently bled and was exhausted physically and emotionally. To the astonishment of many of her admirers, she put her mark to the little document on which she was now on record as expressing "penitence for mendaciously forging the revelations of her saints, for making supposititious divinations, for blaspheming God and the Saints, for indecently wearing man's dress contrary to the honour of her sex, for despising God and his sacraments, for adoring and invoking evil spirits, for being seditious." [106] It was a shabby bit of writing that effectively made a mockery of Jeanne and her entire miraculous history. We may be sure that she was in a daze when she signed it. When she took the pen in her hand, the mark she made on the paper was the only mark she ever made in despair.[107]

Her abjuration produced its reward. She was sentenced to life imprisonment "on the bread of sorrow and the water of affliction." But she was not to burn, a fact that rankled many, but especially the English who saw in Jeanne's presence on earth (even if clinging to life on bread and water) a rebuke to their honor. "A girl had filled them with fear," Michelet writes, "it was not certain that even now, chained though she was, they were not still afraid of her." [108]

They need not have been afraid. Once back in her prison, a series of degrading events there, as well as certain messages from her voices, conspired to ease the English of their fear. First, an unnamed but titled Englishman tried to rape Jeanne. Then her guards played a wicked game with her. Jeanne had been forbidden to wear masculine attire, but the guards refused to return to her the dress she had been given, and, instead, threw the bundle of her male garb into her cell. Rather than wear it, she crawled into bed and stayed there as long as, physically speaking, she could. When, finally, she had to get out of bed to perform a bodily function, she put the offending garments on. The matter was reported to Cauchon who immediately pronounced her a relapsed heretic. The theater of death was to be played once more, but this time it would not be a dress rehearsal.

On May 28, Jeanne, reconciled to death, turned herself from a survivor back into a symbol: She abjured her abjuration, saying

that her voices had told her that, when she was on the platform, she should answer the preacher boldly. And she said that the preacher was a false preacher, for he said that she had done many things which she had never done.

She said further that in saying that God had not sent her she had damned herself, for truly God had sent her. And since Thursday her voices had told her that she had done great wrong in confessing that what she had done was not well done.

She said also that everything she had said and revoked, she had done only through fear of fire. [109]

It was a reply that would lead her surely to the fire, but she had understood at last that for a Jeanne d'Arc, who was no longer a person but an idea, there was nowhere else to go.

On Wednesday morning of May 30, some ten thousand people gathered about four freshly built scaffolds in the Old Market of Rouen. On one, stood Jeanne's judges and other ecclesiastical notables; on a second platform, stood various civic dignitaries. On a third scaffold, the priest Nicholas Midi, one of her assessors, stood ready to preach to Jeanne. The fourth scaffold, built with a plaster base into which was set the stake, was reserved for the Maid of Orléans. At its base, was a placard that read, "Jeanne, self-styled the Maid, liar, mischiefmaker, abuser of the people, diviner, superstitious, blasphemer of God, presumptuous, false to the faith of Christ, boaster, idolater, cruel, dissolute, an invoker of devils, apostate, schismatic, heretic." [110] In addition to the placard, there was more language on display. In a deliberate parody of the crown of thorns that circled Christ's head, Jeanne wore a paper crown with the legend, "Heretic, Relapse, Apostate, Idolater." Jeanne, dressed in female garb, stood tied in place on her plaster platform. She was already exhausted because she had a terror of fire and had worn herself out in futile protest against it. "Alas! Do they treat me thus horribly and cruelly, so that my body, clean and whole, which was never corrupted, must be this day consumed and reduced to ashes! I had rather seven times be decapitated than to be thus burned. Alas!" [111]

Nicholas Midi, chafed by zeal, preached an endless sermon on a theme from the First Epistle to the Corinthians (12:26): "And whether one member [of the Church] suffer, all the members suffer with it; or one member be honoured, all the members rejoice with it." It was a weary hour for Jeanne and a weary one for the English soldiery, which was growing impatient keeping the huge crowd in order, but finally the preaching was done. Midi gave over, and Pierre Cauchon, in the grieving accents of a responsible cleric doing his tragic duty, announced to Jeanne that "hardened heretics must be separated from the midst of the just . . . [and] you, Jeanne, commonly called the Maid . . . are fallen again—O sorrow—into these errors and crimes as the dog returns to his vomit. . . . We [therefore] denounce you as a rotten member which, so that you shall not infect the other members of Christ, must be cast out of the unity of the Church . . . we cast you off, separate and abandon you, praying this same secular power on this side of death and the mutilation of your limbs, to moderate the judgement towards you, and if true signs of repentance appear in you to permit the sacrament of penance to be administered to you." [112]

It was now the executioner's turn on the dreadful stage. As a compassionate gesture, he had piled green wood around the plaster base of Jeanne's scaffold with the expectation of using it to create a dense smoke that would bring death quickly to Jeanne, but the plaster base turned out to be too high and the green wood could not be used. Consequently, Jeanne was spared none of her destined pain. [113]

Jeanne cried out for a cross and an English soldier fashioned a crucifix for her by binding together two bits of wood. She kissed the makeshift thing and tucked it into her garment, but makeshift at that moment was not enough for her. She begged for a real cross that would have Christ's image on it. The priest, Isambard de la Pierre, ran to a nearby church from which he brought back a processional cross, which he held before her eyes. As the flames leaped up, Jeanne cried out, "Jesus, Jesus, Jesus, Jesus, Jesus, Jesus." In the midst of her agony, Jeanne took an instant for a final courtesy to Père Isambard whom she warned away, crying, "Get down, take care of [look out for] the fire." [114]

Then, writes Mark Twain, "the pitchy smoke shot through with red flashes of flame rolled up in a thick volume and hid her from sight and from the heart of this darkness her voice rose eloquent in prayer. . . . At last, a mercifully swift tide of flame burst upward, and none saw that face any more nor that form, and the voice was still." [115] When, at last, Jeanne's head fell to one side, the column of smoke rising from her body was already thick and high, giving a smell that, say those who know, is like greasy soot.

But Authority was not yet done with Jeanne d'Arc. The executioner, following instructions, halted the blaze at one point so that he might step in to tear the clothes from Jeanne's body. This was done, says the Bourgeois de Paris, to let the people see "all the secrets that could or should belong to a woman, to take away any doubts from people's minds. When they had stared long enough at her dead body bound to the stake, the executioner got a big fire going again round her poor carcass, which was soon burned up." [116]

All of this was done on the morning of May 30, 1431. When the flames were finished, the ashes that had been Jeanne d'Arc were cast into the Seine. For Gilles de Rais, wherever he was at that moment, the drifting ash would prove a presage of even more dreadful things to come.

On October 29, 1449, nearly twenty years after Jeanne d'Arc's death, Somerset, the English military governor of Rouen, fled because of an insurrection in the town and Charles VII retook the place that, for thirty years, had been under English occupation. Then, "[Charles] did, shortly after his entry into Rouen, undertake to find out what had really happened in the matter of Joan. He sent out a letter to the canon of Noyon cathedral requesting him to

'inquire into and inform yourself diligently on that which is said about [the trial of Jeanne] and the information (gathered) by you in this matter, bring it close and sealed before us and people of our council.' " [117]

The key phrase was "We would know the truth of the said trial" and the letter was the instigating gesture for what would later become the Rehabilitation Proceedings. For nearly three years, various inquiries were made in the king's name and surviving witnesses were heard. Then on November 7, 1455, Isabelle Rommée, Jeanne's mother, carried a petition to the papal commission appointed by Calixtus III to rehabilitate Jeanne. The commission was meeting at the cathedral of Notre-Dame in Paris, and there the old woman, along with a number of people from Orléans, took her petition, which said:

> I had a daughter born in lawful wedlock, whom I had furnished worthily with the sacraments of baptism and confirmation and had reared in the fear of God and respect for the tradition of the Church, as far as her age and the simplicity of her condition allowed, in such sort that having grown up amid fields and pastures she was much in the church and received every month, after due confession, the sacrament of the Eucharist, despite her youth, and gave herself up to fasts and orisons with great devotion and fervour, for the wants at that time were so great which the people suffered and which she compassionated with all her heart; yet although she did never think, conceive or do anything whatever which set her out of the path of the faith, or spoke against it, certain enemies . . . had her arraigned in religious trial . . . and . . . despite her disclaimers and appeals, both tacit and expressed, and without any succour given to her innocence, in a trial perfidious, violent, iniquitous and without shadow of right . . . did they condemn her in a fashion damnable and criminal, and put her to death very cruelly by fire . . . for the damnation of their souls and in notorious, infamous and irreparable damage done to me, Isabelle, and mine.[118]

This "real trial," as Régine Pernoud calls it, moved from Paris to Rouen in December. In January 1456 the commission moved to Domrémy, in February to Orléans. Finally, on July 7, 1456, standing before the cathedral of Reims, the archbishop of Reims pronounced the not-unexpected verdict of the commission:

Jeanne d'Arc's birthplace.

We, in session of our court and having God only before our eyes, say, pronounce, decree and declare that the said trial and sentence (of condemnation) being tainted with fraud *(dolus malus)*, calumny, iniquity, contradiction and manifest errors of fact and of law, including the abjuration, execution and all their consequences, to have been and to be null, invalid, worthless, without effect and annihilated. . . . We break and annul them and declare that they must be destroyed (lit. *lacerated*). . . . In consideration of Joan's appeal to the Holy See . . . in consideration of the threats of torture. . . . We proclaim that Joan did not contract any taint of infamy and that she shall be and is washed clean of such and, if need be, we wash her clean of such absolutely.[119]

So she was innocent all along, and those scores of thoughtful clerics who had buzzed around Jeanne's body for the sake of her soul had been wrong. To make everything all right again, a copy of the "false Articles of Accusation" was condemned to be burned by the public executioner of Rouen. So, too, was a copy of the death sentence.

As for the judges who had produced the false and contumacious documents—nothing happened to them at all. "The rehabilitation process . . . condemned no one, because it could not afford to condemn anyone," writes M.G.A. Vale.[120] As for the flames that went up in the market square at Rouen, they had the crisp, clean smell of burning paper.

FAMILY WEATHER

On all sides the deep loathesome valley trembled so, that I thought the universe felt love, whereby as some believe the world has oft-times been converted into chaos.

—Dante, *The Inferno*

"And thus," says Mourain de Sourdeval, "ended the honorable period of [Gilles's] life; the rest was no more than a tissue of crimes or, better, a long access of madness." [1]

Madness.

It would be comforting to our image of humankind if we could really believe that Gilles, overwhelmed first by the horror of Jeanne's death and then by his grandfather's, withdrew morosely from warfare and the French court and retired to his estates where he went mad as a hatter. If we could point to him as insane, we could separate him from us. Make of him one of those "Others"; a creature one might fear and pity, but in whose life we would not expect to find any instructive allegory. Best of all, once we decide that *he* was mad, we can reassure ourselves that we are sane. Unfortunately for us, there was never any question in Gilles's lifetime but that he was sane, though it is true that his heirs, hoping to set aside the sequestration of his estates, put forward "the rather half-hearted plea of mental derangement twenty years after his death." [2] But the *Mémoire des Héritiers* is a self-serving document. No other contemporary report of Gilles's behavior so much as hints at his insanity. It is important to insist that Gilles was not mad; otherwise he becomes only another case history, on a grander scale no doubt, but of the same order as those sadly squalid creatures that haunt Krafft-Ebing's *Psychopathia Sexualis* and certain corridors in contemporary mental hospitals around the globe—

weary victims of disordered glands or incompetent minds—people whom our laws recognize as not responsible for their behavior. Gilles, on the other hand, as he would ringingly insist, knew from start to finish precisely what he was doing—and chose to do it. For his own pleasure; for his delight; for his sensual delectation.

But that description of Gilles risks turning him into one of those semi-comic figures out of a Renaissance revenge tragedy—Aaron the Moor, or Barnabas the Jew, for instance—rubbing his hands together and chuckling as he poisons wells or plots the destruction of innocent lives or female virtue. Gilles is far more protean than such inventions. To get at the mystery of evil that he represents, one must move round and round the kinds of unspectacular details that, taken together, give us a sense of the psychological texture of his life in the years before the murder of innocents became his pleasure.

We have already noted the intensely ambivalent relationship that existed between Gilles and his grandfather. That vigorous, stern, old man and his grandson loved each other, I think. And we have suggested, since they were equally willful and stubborn, they often hated each other as well. We have also seen that de Craon may have had an inkling of what Gilles's sexual life was really like; and we know that Gilles's grandfather left his sword, that medieval sign of manhood, not to Gilles, his heir, but to René de la Suze, Gilles's younger brother—about whom more soon.

There were other members of Gilles's household with whom Gilles's relationships were murky. With his wife, Catherine, for example.

Catherine, young as she was at the time of her abduction, could have had no illusions that she was being carried off by Gilles in a fit of passion. Medieval women understood what weddings were about. They were economic or political gestures, arranged by men. If a woman was lucky, she might discover that her husband was considerate and decent; if she was very lucky, starting from the neutral moment of the wedding day, she and her husband might build a relationship that could grow, amazingly, to resemble love. Catherine de Rais was not one of the lucky women of her age. The pell-mell ride on which she was taken on the day of her abduction ended in rape, and not in that sequence of scenes made dear to us by Errol Flynn movies in which the swashbuckling kidnapper learns to respect the woman he has abused. In those fantasies, the abductor moves from respect to tenderness, then to passion and finally, as angelic music fills the theater, true love suffuses the screen.

For Catherine—and for Gilles—the story was grimy indeed because Gilles, as a well-taught nobleman, understood the importance of begetting an heir and, therefore, periodically sought her bed, though he took no sexual pleasure from the bodies of women. It was not until 1430, after ten years of such dismal sexual encounters, that a girl was born to the couple. The baby was named Marie and with her coming, there was no further reason for Catherine and Gilles to go on with their haggard charade.[3] In 1434–1435, by which time Gilles was already far along in his double career of torturer-murderer and aspiring saint, Catherine retired to Pouzauges, where Gilles never went.

The Abbé Bossard speaks of Catherine as a shadowy woman, and in most of the other biographies of Gilles, she is treated as one of the supernumeraries of Gilles's drama. In the early years of her marriage, there was a color of necessity for her loneliness—Gilles's frequent absence at the wars. Later, after "perhaps some dreadful discovery on Katherine's part . . . they separated never to meet again."[4] She appears, like so many other medieval women of the nobility, to have been a dutiful *châtelaine*, moving from property to property, superintending repairs, looking over accounts.

Catherine was, no doubt, the pale figure described by Bossard. It is hard to know what other options besides silence and patience she had. But it would be a mistake not to wonder about the effect her silence must have had on Gilles's life. Her very muteness must have oppressed him with guilt, since there is no vengeance on a man more dreadful than the silent but visible suffering of the woman he torments. Over the years during which Gilles ignored or abused her, Catherine must have become the very icon of Gilles's cruelty, looking out upon him, wordlessly inciting him to self-contempt.

Catherine must have been, until they finally went their separate ways, very much present in Gilles's life. He and Catherine, given their social standing, frequently had to play the roles of the lord and his lady; they were required to appear at festivals and funerals, at baptisms or weddings, or at the various town processions in honor of saints or of municipal events that were characteristic of the medieval year. If nothing else, he had to attend mass with his lady at the churches in his domains: Machecoul, Champtocé, Tiffauges, Pouzauges. Medieval marriages were not designed to accommodate to love, so, in that sense, Gilles and Catherine were not much different from other fifteenth-century married folk, but one guesses that these two moved through the forms and responsibilities of their lives together with even greater coldness than was usual. Gilles's mind and body were already raging with fantasies that did not include Catherine; and she, more victim and prisoner than she was wife, had plenty of leisure in which to develop her detestation of him. The speed with which she remarried (a little more than a year after Gilles's death) is perhaps evidence of how little she grieved for her husband of nearly twenty years.

There is always Cain and Abel; Esau and Jacob; the older brother and the younger. For Gilles, the scion, there was René, the *puîné*, who was born on November 23, 1407. Considering that his character has come down to us in contrast to his monstrous older brother, he comes off rather badly. Gilles was bad, and grand; René, on the other hand, was the sort of man who, had he lived in our own day, would have created no greater moral ripple than that produced by a parking ticket. Still, René is worth pausing over since so many of the events that might have traumatized Gilles also happened to René. Indeed, since René was only eight years old when his parents died, one would expect him to have felt his loss even more than Gilles. Furthermore, René had the same education: religious training, Latin, and the tilting yard. Like Gilles, he too served honorably in the king's wars where, like Gilles, he was exposed to cruelties. With all that, René grew up to be respectable, petty, and insignificant.

Just the same, René's silent envy, like Catherine's equally silent rebuke, reached Gilles. Brothers begin very early the endless contention for their parents' love.

Siblings are preternaturally attentive: René envies his brother's strength and his place as heir; the boy Gilles is beleaguered by René's smallness, prettiness, newness. Each of them is perpetually alert against injustice. Each of them, as children do, believes that parental love is finite and that his brother is stealing from the diminishing supply. "It isn't fair!" is the most heartfelt of a sibling's cries, and in an ultimate sense, the charge is always true. There *are* shadings of parental touch and tone and response. And there is no way to persuade children that such shadings are not signs of preference. The wonder is not that siblings hate each other as they grow up but that they can learn to love each other at all. With Gilles and René, love never happened.

The best we can suppose is that their relationship, like that of Gilles with his wife, Catherine, was civil and that the amenities were performed. There was, however, one occasion when Gilles turned to his younger brother for help. In the spring of 1434, when Gilles simply did not feel like joining his cousin La Trémoille in the campaign to raise the siege of Grancey, he asked his brother to go in his stead. Gilles, by that time, was fully in the toils of his murderous vocation and would not tear himself away from its pleasures. René went, and not being "so good a soldier as his brother. . . . The campaign was a failure and Grancey surrendered to Philippe le Bon on 15 August 1434." [5] René, one guesses, was not too happy to have proved his mediocrity. Still, he joined Gilles at Orléans where he was ecstatically playing at being producer, director and, quite possibly, actor in *Le Mistère du Siège d'Orléans.* One wonders just how René felt in that extravagant atmosphere in which Gilles was forever the center of attraction. It was, says Benedetti, "the only occasion . . . that the two brothers are recorded as having been together." [6]

René, one hastens to add, was never one of Gilles's cronies, sexually or criminally. He was merely mean and sly and greedy. Once, while Gilles was still living, he instigated members of his family to take legal action to prevent Gilles from squandering his enormous wealth. Then, twenty years after Gilles's death, René was the prime mover behind the *Mémoire des Héritiers,* which sought to persuade the duke of Brittany to restore various lands sequestered by the duke after Gilles was executed for his crimes. The *Mémoire* pulsates with acrimony as it describes Gilles as being both a madman and a fool, the object of everyone's derision. Gilles, in the *Mémoire,* is spoken of as "insane and without sense . . . and [people] mocked and laughed at him as a madman whenever they saw him . . . he was mad, prodigal and without sense . . . [a man] of little sense and prodigal." [7] The *Mémoire* is a long, long document in which there is no trace of fraternal feeling.

GOURMAND, PRODIGAL, AND LOVER

This evil of the devil creeps in through all the sensual ap-
proaches; he gives himself to figures, he adapts himself to
colors, he abides in sounds, he lurks in smells, he infuses himself into flavors.

—*Malleus Maleficarum*

In 1432, Gilles was twenty-eight years old. He was the undis-
puted possessor of one of the greatest fortunes in France. In
money alone, his annual income surpassed two and a half million francs a year; and his capital, four and a half million. To
these holdings, one should add art objects, books, furnishings, and
tapestries estimated as being worth an additional one hundred
thousand crowns. These figures are cited by D. B. Wyndham Lewis
in 1951. Lewis cautioned that "these sums [need to be] multiplied
twice, or thrice, or for all I know, five or ten times to represent the
money of 1951." [1] What one is to make of the figures given the
inflated currencies of 1980 is anyone's guess. *Tout court,* Gilles was
vastly rich. He owned castles, keeps, and villages in Brittany, in
Poitou, in Anjou; his towns included Saint-Etienne-de-Mer-Morte,
Pornic, Princé, Chemillé, Fontaine-Milon, Grattecuisse, La Mothe-
Achard, La Maurière, Champtocé, Ingrandes, Loroux-Botereau,
Bourgneuf-en-Rais. He owned Tiffauges, Pouzauges, Chabanais,
Confolens, and much more.[2]

The Abbé Bossard, who takes nearly three densely printed pages
to catalog Gilles's holdings, says that so much wealth turned

The view from Tiffauges.

Gilles's head and lets the implication stand that Gilles's money corrupted him morally. Certainly, being rich gave Gilles the illusion that he was beyond restraint; that he had only to reach his hand out in order to possess whatever he wished. For a person like Gilles, who never entirely achieved that uneasy stasis between a child's dreams of omnipotence and the adult's experience of impotence that we call maturity,[3] money tended to obscure the fact that the real world is a place that imposes limitations. It would take Gilles the rest of his life to discover that gratifying the senses is not the same as transcending those limits, though in the years from 1432 until his death eight years later, Gilles monumentally—and, I think, suicidally—confused the two. What makes Gilles's story more complex than the usual decline into swinishness that characterizes the sensuality of the run of Gilles's contemporaries is that Gilles made transcendence itself into an act of self-gratification. He was a man who would move between the orgy and the altar, achieving ecstasies (perhaps even the same kinds of ecstasies) in both places.

This is not to say that Gilles did not eat or drink to excess. For the medieval rich, gluttony was an imperative of social rank, just as it was, for men, a mark of masculine prowess, like battlefield courage.

In an ignoble moment of his trial, in 1440, Gilles would blame gluttony for contributing to his crimes, exhorting the fathers of children to keep them from yielding to idleness and gourmandise because many evils come from those sins. He pointed out that he, Gilles, had been addicted to them both and that "an insatiable avidity for subtly flavored foods and the frequent absorption of hot wines produced in him a state of excitation which brought him to perpetrate so many sins and crimes."[4]

It is easy enough to link dissipation with crime, and there is hardly a biographer of Gilles who has not taken him at his word. Clearly, I do not believe that being a trencherman and wine-bibber is preparation for a murderous career. At the same time, one ought to note that egotistical *excess* characterized Gilles's behavior in these years. Excess for its own sake or—more accurately—excess as a form of self-display and, a little later, as a form of suicide.

Gilles, at his trial, did not specify the delicately flavored foods he was addicted to as a youth, but we can get a pretty good idea of the content of the feasts over which he presided from accounts of the typical practice of his peers. Albert Jean, in his novelized version of Gilles's life, has given us a scene in which we see Gilles de Rais consulting with his chef about the evening's dinner menu. Gilles suggests lampreys in lemon juice as a first course, then roast peacock *ornés de leurs plumages;* this to be followed by a *pâté* of wild boar spiced with coriander and stuffed with orange preserves; a salad of cockscombs, artichoke hearts, and cinnamon. Dessert was to be a tower of caramel decorated with angelica, the whole resting on a white nougat base. Gilles specifies the wine list as well: Muscadet for the lampreys; Burgundy for the red meats; and, with the dessert, Hypocras "at will." [5]

It is a not too unlikely menu. It was an age without refrigeration, and foods were likely to be highly spiced with mace, caraway seed, sage, marjoram, lavender, rosemary, and ginger to hide the lingering odor of taint in the grandiose banquet offerings the nobility (and the rich bourgeoisie) put on their tables. One can see how the idea of the trencherman as a sort of folk hero could develop when people sat down to meals of "beef, salmon and bream pies; leveret and squab tarts; roast heron, stork, crane, peacock, bustard and swan." [6] The well-stocked medieval larder included an astonishing array of creatures deemed to be edible: crows, bears, cormorants, larks, and, of course, venison took their places on the banquet tables, along with pheasant, geese, and suckling pig.[7]

"It is difficult to believe," writes D. B. Wyndham Lewis, "that the passions of the wayward were in any way restrained by a meal beginning with half a dozen or more highly spiced and seasoned meat dishes. . . . All these meats were roasted, fricasseed, grilled, devilled, and spatchcocked in a dozen different ways . . . [and were] followed by fish of various kinds . . . and a variety of elaborate pastries and sweetmeats." [8]

No wonder that Chaucer's Pardoner, himself a model of spiritual depravity, cries out against the deadly sin of gluttony—about which he also knew too much:

> There are many walking about of whom I have told you
> I say it now, weeping with piteous voice,
> That they are enemies of Christ's cross,
> Their goal is death, and belly is their god

. . . .

O stomach, O belly, O stinking gut
Filled with shit and with corruption.
At either end of you, the sound is foul.
. . . .

These cooks, how they stamp and strain and grind,
Turning substance into accident
To satisfy your lecherous desire.
Out of the hard bones, they knock the marrow,
For they throw nothing away that,
Soft and sweet, goes down the gullet.
. . . .

But surely, he that resorts to such delights
Is dead-alive while living in his vice.[9]

Because the hot wines referred to by Gilles in his "Confession" have, like his wealth and his gourmandise, been blamed for turning him into a monster, a word or two here about those wines may not be amiss. While there was plenty of good ale and old served at French meals in the fifteenth century, wine was then, as it is now, the drink of choice, though aged wines were not held to be superior until some time later. Freshly pressed and therefore rather acidic wines were commonplace, so medieval people cheerfully mingled honey, sugar, spices, or herbs in with their new wine. Some wines, called *herbés,* "were merely infusions of wormwood, myrtle, hyssop, rosemary, etc., mixed with sweetened wine and flavoured honey." [10] The infusion that interests us, however, is the wine called "hypocras"—the hot wine of Gilles's confession.

Though hypocras enjoyed a literary reputation as a wine frequently mentioned in medieval romances, and "was considered a drink of honour, being always offered to kings, princes, and nobles on their solemn entry into a town," [11] contemporary experience with such hot, spiced alcoholic mixtures suggests that in the stupendous quantities consumed by Gilles and his boon companions it must have rendered them supremely and meanly drunk. No doubt, the resultant hangovers were correspondingly fierce.

Hypocras could be red or white. The red was made with "a red wine of a Spanish complexion mulled with cinnamon, mace, white ginger, cloves, nutmeg and sometimes musk." [12] For the white, we have a recipe that comes down to us from de Taillevant, Charles VII's chef, who tells us to make it as follows:

In a mortar, grind half an ounce of cinnamon, a quarter of a clove, an ounce of vanilla and four ounces of white sugar. Slowly add five litres of very light wine. Allow the mixture to steep for fifteen days. Strain through a flannel bag, put in bottles, cork and keep in a cool wine cellar.[13]

Red or white, it was not the hypocras that turned Gilles into a monument of evil, though it may be that, if there is indeed *in vino veritas,* Gilles, with the help of his glowing wine, moved more rapidly through the windings of his own dark maze. The Minotaur who crouched at its center, however, was no invention of the wine.

Gilles was not mad—but one does not need to be mad to be acutely, even appallingly, unhappy. With Jeanne dead, and King Charles's armies temporarily disbanded, Gilles had become a *jeune homme désoeuvré*—a young man without work. More than that, he was assailed now by a lassitude of the spirit well beyond ennui. He was young, rich, good-looking. He had the sensibility of a poet, the eye of an artist and the spiritual hankerings of a mystic . . . and the sexual energies of a satyr. What, with such talents, was he to do? Michel Bataille writes, "Then, if, in this world, there is [for him] neither love, nor politics, nor dignity, nor war, what remains? For the humble, there is work, poverty, chagrin, daily toil. For others, there is a calming stupidity that is an armor against the insults of life. For some, there is piety. But for Gilles? . . . sainthood or crime." [14] Or, I would suggest, an unspeakable merging of the two.

And yet, to choose infinite depravity, to choose to go "beyond the actual, beyond all nature and all possibility [to] a world of senseless, atrocious ecstasies" [15] requires a state of mind that is bleaker than ennui, but one that is not quite as paralyzing as despair.

Anomie. The Grand Néant. A passionate uncaring. The mood of the abyss. The basilisk gaze of the moon shining benignly, indifferently down on human upheaval. Anomie. A cataleptic state of the soul. A stagnation of mind in which feeling has to be invented—or, at best, remembered. A dank neutrality of expectation, as if, in a dark corner, one lay askew—one's own discarded puppet. A state of experience in which the patience with which inevitability succeeds itself becomes an unimportant substitute for hope.

Julio Cortázar in his story "Axolotl" gives us hints of that condition. In that story, the narrator-protagonist describes how he is drawn to the Axolotl, those strange lizards in their tank, and to their "secret wish: to abolish time and space by an intense immobility. . . . Every fibre of my being responded to that gagged suffering, that rigid torture at the bottom of the water . . . [where] One feels time less if one holds still." [16]

In the grip of that despairing torpor, the mind is defenseless against an invasion of images of suicidal consolation, of impossible eroticisms, or of revenge. Images as appalling and seductive as those fragments of Christ's body that, when stitched together, form the soul-devouring tatterdemalion whose name is Satan. Those fragments are made of the world's memories of crimes committed, or torments imposed, or lives shattered: They are lumps of distention and contraction; whole troops of unformed teratomas. A Brueghel crowd of creatures, looking with the same bleakness into our eyes with which we look into theirs. To the sufferer from anomie, nothing in those images is forbidden or insane.

Gilles, his soul pierced by the darts and arrows of his contradictory natures, achieved before too long that state that Foucault describes as preceding—or far beyond—madness; a condition in which "madness and non-madness, reason and non-reason are inextricably involved: inseparable at the moment when they do not yet exist, and existing to each other, in the exchange which separates them." [17]

The impossible tension between such forces inside the real skull of a rich and very powerful young man might have made an artist of Gilles—or a saint. Instead what we got was a man dedicated to a different sort of grandeur: a hero of iniquity.

What was Gilles de Rais doing while Jeanne d'Arc was enduring her long torment? What was the effect on him of her agonizing end?

Let us remember that Gilles saw Jeanne for the last time at Saint-Denis, before the gates of Paris on September 8, 1429. Gilles was not with her when she was taken before the walls of Compiègne. What he knew of her imprisonment, her trial, and her death was as much or as little as rumor brought to him.

We do know something of what Gilles did in the interval between Jeanne's capture and her death. Early in 1430, he went off on a more or less private military mission in the service of La Trémoille who, just then, was engaged in a quarrel with Yolande d'Aragon, the regent of the duchy of Anjou. On La Trémoille's orders, Gilles occupied Sablé, from which he then set off to take the Château-l'Hermitage, which was commanded by the veteran soldier Jean de Bueil. De Bueil spotted Gilles's men, sounded the alarm, and the castle was saved—though de Bueil himself was taken prisoner in the melee. Gilles, in his grandfather's forthright manner, then had de Bueil chained and flung into a prison tower. Later, de Bueil was ransomed and released. Much later still, he returned to retake Sablé. To round out the tale, one should add that de Bueil was an eager accomplice in de Richemont's plot to assassinate La Trémoille at Chinon in 1433. La Trémoille, being a very fat man, survived the attack because the assassin's dagger failed to reach a vital spot.

In 1430, Gilles quarreled with his grandfather over Gilles's sale of the château of Blaison. A man as land-greedy as de Craon must have been bitterly affronted at the idea that his grandson would dare to sell land at all; but there is some feeling that there was more to de Craon's unhappiness than his irritation over a real estate transaction. It has been suggested (see page 21) that de Craon had caught a glimpse of Gilles with one of his male lovers, and the sight so horrified the old man that he died of the shock.[18]

Finally, we know that sometime in 1431 Gilles was involved in the kidnapping of Yolande d'Aragon as she was approaching the town of Ancenis on the Loire. She was in her own territory—still in Anjou—when Gilles de Rais, followed by a company of his men from Champtocé, swooped down on her train, kidnapping her, and looting the baggage.

After she was released, Yolande evidently held no grudge against Gilles or his grandfather because she permitted these two to serve as go-betweens in negotiations she was conducting with the slippery Jean V, duke of Brittany, to create an alliance between the duchies of Anjou and Brittany, which just then were at daggers drawn. The means to such an alliance, the marriage between François of Brittany, Duke Jean's son, and Yolande herself, was agreed upon at Champtocé on February 22. That marriage took place on November 22, 1432, just a week after de Craon's death.

There are those, like Georges Bataille, who are impatient with the notion that there was any friendship between Gilles and Jeanne. "There is nothing to it but supposition, without any greater foundation than the naivete of certain recent authors who, speaking of Gilles de Rais, wish to oppose to his odious aspect, one that is charming," [19] snaps G. Bataille. And Benedetti, more laconically, writes, "There is no evidence that Gilles showed the slightest concern for her fate," though he adds, "Whatever grief or pain he may have felt never reached the surface." [20]

I think, with M. Bataille, Albert Jean, the Abbé Bossard, and D. B. Wyndham Lewis, that there was plenty of pain and grief for Gilles. Wyndham Lewis thinks that "it is not impossible . . . that Gilles' immediate reaction was a paroxysm of fury and despair, impelling him to shake his fist at impassive heaven and strip himself violently of every vestige of the influences absorbed from Joan's intimacy." [21] Silence and pain are frequently together in the human heart; and there is something shabby in the requirement that lawcourts and neighbors make that remorse must be visible before it can be believed. In Gilles's case, all kinds of emotions, including love, had been kept concealed for years. If, as is likely, Gilles had been playing the double roles of Jeanne's friend and La Trémoille's spy, then Jeanne's grisly death must have sent Gilles reeling with guilt. Robert Jay Lifton has pointed out that guilt was the characteristic feeling of the survivors of the A-bombing of Hiroshima and Nagasaki: "Most survivors [he writes] focus upon one incident, one sight, or one particular *ultimate horror* with which they strongly identify themselves and which left them with a profound sense of pity, guilt, and shame." [22] The only way such survivors have been able to deal with the grief is to   close off" their feelings; to cut the connections between appalling stimulus and overwhelming response. To the bystander, such survivors who have "closed off" may seem to be perfectly normal, but, as Lifton discovered, they pay dearly in their inner lives for that appearance of calm.

Let us return now to the question of Gilles's friendship with Jeanne d'Arc.

There is, in Huysmans's *Là-Bas,* a brusque dialogue between Durtal and Des Hermies who have been talking about Gilles:

"You think, then," says Des Hermies, "that the Maid of Orleans was really responsible for his career of evil?"

"To a certain point. Consider. She roused an impetuous soul, ready for anything, as well for orgies of saintliness as for ecstasies of crime. . . . There was no transition between the two phases of his being." [23]

Huysmans enjoys extreme statement. It is certainly extreme to make Jeanne d'Arc the first mover of Gilles's bloodlust. The lines connecting Jeanne to Gilles are various, but they do not, in either direction, represent cause and effect. And yet, Durtal's words, taken as a metaphor, have "to a certain point" some truth in them. Jeanne's death snapped some last threads of restraint in Gilles. From the point of view of his soul, "Gilles had lived for many months in intimate association with the Maid, and for over a year in proximity of the aura of miracles that surrounded her. . . . He had heard her make incredible promises and fulfill them, and when she had fulfilled them she would take neither thanks nor tribute, saying she had accomplished all by the help of her voices." [24] But Jeanne touched Gilles's spiritual life in other ways too. In her presence, the simple ferocity of the soldier had been transformed into a holy gesture. She was God's mascot, and riding beside her, he had been able to feel the bloodlust of the battlefield transmuted into a prayer of glory. What he had received from Jeanne was the renewed conviction that God could be reached. Now that she was gone, that conviction wavered and he became a lacuna of yearning.

Various of Gilles's biographers—among them, M. Bataille, Vizitelly, D. B. Wyndham Lewis—unable to bear the notion that Gilles's honor is impugned by his silence about Jeanne's capture and death, cling to the supposition that Gilles made an attempt to rescue Jeanne from her imprisonment at Rouen. This curious defense of Gilles's honor requires of the biographers that they divide their Gilles in two: the first, Gilles de Rais, knight-at-arms, *chevalier sans reproche,* marshal of France, and companion of Saint Jeanne d'Arc; the second, Gilles de Rais, the Devourer of Machecoul, the Beast of Extermination. But Gilles did not one day step across a line dividing two such selves. He did not spring fully grown, fully monstrous out of his own honorable forehead. Like any human monster, he evolved slowly, and was evolved, out of the flesh he inherited, the experiences that molded him, and the will that, with his eyes wide open, he exercised. It is harder to understand such a Gilles, but he is the one we have before us.

Now, for the tale of the rescue raids. Michel Bataille tells it best in his *Gilles de Rais*. Bataille has it that in December of 1430, Gilles de Rais showed up in Louviers, a French-held town, ten or fifteen miles from Rouen where Jeanne was imprisoned. There, he joined the hard-bitten La Hire ("If God were a man, he would be a brigand") in the planning and execution of a series of raids to free Jeanne. These conjectural raids give M. Bataille occasion for shaping some fine, cruel prose that captures the malign indifference to their fellow humans that soldiers must develop if they are to practice their craft. The raiding parties, made up of Gilles's Bretons and La Hire's Gascons, make their forays in a winter-deadened terrain so harsh in its aspects that it appears to have been created by the spell of a vindictive magician. It is a country of dense fogs, of treacherous marshes and killing cold. Wherever the raiding party moves, it finds, or leaves, burned villages, overturned carts, and rotting cadavers.[25] The raiders, more interested in plunder than whether *La Pucelle* lives or dies, are ferocious by habit and because of the character of the men they follow: "the enigmatic, haughty Gilles de Rais who would soon sink into crime and the savage master brigand, La Hire." [26]

From time to time, as occasion requires, one of the men throttles an English sentry with his bare hands. "Others of the mercenaries prefer to work with the knife. It is quicker, but it also [in one sense] takes longer because the sight of blood seems to have neither beginning nor end. [It is] a mysterious work of Nature, like giving birth in a woman. The blade searches the throat, and the killer must master his nerves not to recoil from the shock of terror as, behind him, he hears the mad cavalcade of a million men. But it is nothing more than the [sound] of the precipitous rhythm of his own beating heart. . . . Then, the blood flows, tepid, fascinating, insipid. . . . The killer is conscious that he is now isolated in a silence as total and immense as a snow-filled plain." [27]

The raids, as M. Bataille conceives them, took place at intervals over many months, but nothing came of them. Invariably, the English replaced their sentries; invariably there were too many

English troops to make Jeanne's rescue possible, and the raiders learned that "they had come for nothing. All that they had done was for nothing. The English had been killed, for nothing. Jeanne would never be rescued." [28]

It is a moving story, lyrically told, and it does honor to Gilles. The only trouble is that there is no proof any of it ever happened. Gilles *was* in Louviers in the winter of 1429. We know, because there exists a document that shows that on December 26, at Louviers, Gilles borrowed eighty gold crowns from one of his soldiers, Rolland Malvoisin, so that he might buy "a black horse, saddled and bridled, to give to his dear and well-beloved squire, Michel Machefert, captain of the men-of-arms and bowmen of his company, directly they arrived at Louviers, to induce him to come with him on that journey." [29] Unfortunately, a single black horse given to a well-loved friend at the Christmas season does not make a raiding party.

Gilles, after his grandfather's death in 1432, led a restless, but continually splendid life. Gilles had been rich enough in his own right, but now he became many times richer, and with a feverish verve, he went to work to destroy the great fortune that was now his. If the sale of Blaison in 1429 had angered the dying Jean de Craon, Gilles's pell-mell expenditures now must surely have set the old man's corpse whirling in its grave. Gilles spent money as if he meant, by sending up a shower of gold coins, to represent his inward torment to the public gaze. By day, streams of gold; by night, torrents of blood. He spent with a sort of mythic grandeur, as if he had determined that his wealth and his life were a single secret thing, hidden, like the life of the ogre in the fairy tale, inside an egg that must be kept hidden from the hero of the tale. In his case, Gilles was the hero and the egg, and the danger of destruction rested in him.

Gilles, armed with his wealth, set about creating around himself the ambience of an emperor. He rode at the head of a complete military establishment that included thirty stalwart knights who were his personal bodyguard. These, in turn, were followed by two hundred men-at-arms, wearing his livery. These men were entitled to three uniforms a year and were supplied with all of their equipment, their horses and weapons, their room and board. Each of these men had "servants of their own [and] had no need to look after themselves, they were all cared for at the Marshal's expense and all were richly paid." [30]

The men-at-arms looked after his body; for his soul's sake, Gilles was surrounded by an ecclesiastical establishment that would have done honor to a major cathedral. That hierarchy included "some five and twenty or thirty clerics, who, like his military retainers, lived splendidly at his expense. There was a dean, Messire de la Ferrière; several chanters; an archdeacon, Messire Jourdain; a curate, Olivier Martin; a treasurer of the chapter, Jean Rossignol; a schoolmaster; and canons, chaplains, coadjutors, and clerks, in addition to numerous choir-boys." [31] It was all done for the greater glory of God, though Gilles, the master of the display, was surely in the foreground, preening . . . and paying. Wherever he went, his clerical entourage also went with him, his fee'd priests preceding him, chanting prayers, and his costly armed men following behind.

Nor were the churchmen like Chaucer's poor parson who made do with small recompense. These folk "lived on the fat of the land wherever it pleased *Monseigneur le Maréchal* to halt. . . . At home and in the towns where he sojourned, he arrayed them in long sweeping robes of scarlet, and other fine cloths . . . they wore surplices of the finest tissue, 'with amices and choir-hats of badger lined with minever, such as the canons of cathedrals have, and as if they had really been of great estate and great science.' " [32]

Gilles was as lavish with decor as he was with his clerics. The oratory of his Hôtel de la Suze in Nantes was finely painted. Its windows were of costly stained glass "and the walls were covered with cloth of gold." Waste, squandering, self-display. Despite the flamboyance of the gestures, there was incoherence in the messages Gilles was sending out. The world took him at face value. It assumed he meant to be seen, to be noticed, to be admired. The tradesmen, once the message was out that Gilles de Rais bought anything magnificent at whatever price was asked, assumed that he had chosen to become their great national resource and flocked to him with wares to sell: "His chasubles, copes and other church ornaments he possessed were considerable, and always they were immensely costly and made of the rarest materials." [33] Gilles scorned imitation and distrusted modest prices. His cloth of gold had real gold in it. The robes his priests and choirboys wore were of the finest silks, velvets, furs. And always "they cost triple what they were worth." [34] No wonder the merchants loved him—a man who, the moment a thing pleased him, turned to his paymaster with the command, "Pay." Gilles could be charged (and was) sixty to eighty *écus* an ell for cloth of gold for which anyone else in France could pay twenty-five. His panic-stricken heirs, listing all these extravagances in the *Mémoire des Héritiers,* cry out in anguish that Gilles once paid fourteen thousand *écus* "for three copes of cloth of gold that were not worth more than four thousand." [35]

Spending, spending, spending. "Candlesticks, censers, crosses, osculatories, servers, chalices, pyxes and reliquaries." Waste, piety, self-display. Reverie and penitence by day. Gourmandise and drunkenness in the evening. And at night, another passion: orchestrating the shrieks of his victims who could not, though they pleaded often for that grace, be permitted to die until their young torturer with the God-stricken eyes exhausted himself in their flesh.

We read of hand lanterns and altars, of *ciboires* and reliquaries, of diamonds and rubies, of miniature enamels and of the sonorous organs perplexing the heavens as Gilles made his continuous nervous journeys from one of his towns to another. Then we remember the nighttime orgies in which Gilles made his appalling pilgrimages toward Satan—and God—toward flesh and the spirit, punishment and forgiveness, Jeanne d'Arc and Gilles de Rais. Torment upon torment. Immediately, however, only his victims died.

There is a way of seeing those nighttime sacrifices as a long, high-styled tantrum in which the grown-up, but perpetually childish baron, who has everything he wants to play with, chooses to hack away at the limits of the impermissible. It *is*—however horrible—a major ambition. For Gilles, as with any other of the heroes of iniquity, the compelling motivation is to deny the indifference of eternity. Or, positively put, to enter into contention with God. The message to Permanent Consciousness is "Stop me," or what is more likely, since the speaker is in a sweat of pride and self-loathing, "Stop me if you dare." [36]

In 1434, Gilles was involved spasmodically in the official duties of a marshal of France when he went to Sillé-le-Guillaume, at King Charles's command, to be part of a military force that would do battle with the English there. As it turned out, "the whole enterprise was a waste of time and money. The two armies lined up, looked at each other and rode away in opposite directions. The most impressive feature of the occasion was the resplendent turn-out of Gilles' men." [37] It was from Sillé-le-Guillaume that Gilles sent his younger brother, René, to represent him in La Trémoille's effort to raise the siege of Grancey. René, we have already noted, did his best at Grancey, but the city capitulated to Philippe le Bon, and René, crestfallen, followed Gilles to Orléans, where, for Gilles, an amazing new period in his life was about to open.

Before dealing with Gilles at Orléans, where the pace of his spending almost transcends the capacity of the chroniclers to record it, let us pause here to offer a possible corrective to the view of Gilles's spending that is shared by most of Gilles's biographers, including myself. Generally, Gilles's profligacy has been treated as symptomatic of Gilles's state of mind during the years in which crime, display, and financial ruin appeared to be his chief occupations. But, at the risk of weakening a little one's grasp of a psychological "handle" on Gilles, it should be pointed out that most of what we know about Gilles's money dealings comes to us from the nearly endless catalog of financial misbehavior that René de la Suze put together in the *Mémoire des Héritiers* nearly twenty years after Gilles's death. The very mildest description of the *Mémoire* is that it is a grasping, self-serving document in which the exaggeration of Gilles's behavior is the chief aim. The *Mémoire* was intended to persuade Francis I, the duke of Brittany, that Gilles had been a madman and a fool so that various of Gilles's sequestered estates would be returned to his heirs.

But even when there is other, independent, evidence confirming Gilles's grandiose expenditures, it is necessary to see his profligacy in the context of a medieval world in which expensive self-display was endemic. Pomp and spectacle, processions and rituals in a gorgeous mixture of sacred and profane were the very texture of the Middle Ages, giving allegorical meaning to the contrasts between high and low, rich and poor, powerful and weak. Whether they were warriors or clerics, rich merchants or guildsmen, people who had wealth delighted in displaying it. The tendency to think of the world as a continually speaking allegory had its expression in all sorts of display, not only processions and spectacles. Gilles de Rais's Europe loved what was bright and shiny. "This fondness for all that glitters reappears in the general gaudiness of dress," writes Huizinga, "especially in the excessive number of precious stones sewed on the garments. . . . Transferred to the domain of hearing, this partiality for brilliant things is shown by the naive pleasure taken in tinkling or clicking sounds. La Hire wore a red mantle covered all over with little silver bells like cow-bells. At an entry in 1465, Captain Salazar was accompanied by twenty men-at-arms, the harness of whose horses were ornamented with large silver bells." [38] And Chaucer, in a wickedly sly description of his Monk, says of him that "when he rode, men might hear / His bridle [bells] jingling in a whistling wind as clear / And as loud as does the chapel bell." [39] That same monk, who had taken vows of poverty, chastity, and obedience, wore gray fur-trimmed sleeves and, to fasten his hood, used a gold "curiously wrought" pin. The Wife of Bath, who was a member of the weavers' guild, is described as wearing ten pounds' weight of finely textured kerchiefs, scarlet hose, and gleaming, brand-new shoes.

Charles V, a great accumulator, owned one of Europe's largest libraries—12,200 volumes. "Within the precincts of [his] palace were a tilting ground, a tennis-court, baths, colonnades, cages for bears and lions, and aviaries for exotic birds. . . . His collection of jewellery and precious stones, and above all of specimens of the goldsmith's art were probably the finest in Europe." [40] The Duke de Berry, Charles V's younger brother, was an avid château builder who "lived for possessions, not glory. He owned two residences in Paris . . . and built or acquired a total of seventeen castles in his duchies of Berry and Auvergne. He filled them with clocks, coins, enamels, mosaics, marquetry, illuminated books, musical instruments, tapestries, statues, triptychs painted in bright scenes on dazzling gold ground bordered with gems, gold vessels and spoons, jeweled crosses and reliquaries, relics and curios. He owned one of Charlemagne's teeth, a piece of Elijah's mantle, Christ's cup from the Last Supper, drops of the Virgin's milk . . . and enough gold-fringed vestments to robe all the canons of three cathedrals at one time." [41] And Racinet writes that "luxury did not consist of wearing foolish and expensive clothing. The ideal was to appear daily in something new." He quotes the poet Michault as saying, "Be one day in blue, another in white, still another in grey. Today, wear a long gown like a Doctor of Philosophy, tomorrow you'll need something trimmed and narrow. Above all, don't let your clothes get worn. Let them be given you in the morning. Give them away in the evening and order new ones at once." [42]

But, argues the *Mémoire des Héritiers,* Gilles lived "not according to the condition of a Baron, but according to that of a Prince," [43] and the pomp he maintained was the mark of a notorious prodigal who was out of his mind as well. To this, the duke of Brittany says a firm no. The duke points out that Gilles de Rais, while he was a marshal of France, had been "of great counsel to the king"; he had held high office, and had been a lieutenant general of Brittany, "that which could never have been if he [Gilles] had been a notorious prodigal and if he had not been reasonable and [able] to manage for himself and for others." [44] Moreover, says the duke, Gilles, in support of his king, had military expenditures in "times of war and divisions," which it comported with his honor as marshal of France to make. The duke scoffs at the charge that Gilles was foolish and maintains that "the said deceased Gilles de Raiz spoke perfectly well and properly and his words appeared to be sensible." In any case, Gilles, says the duke, was not especially extravagant. Even the two hundred and fifty men at his back were not excessive, since "there was not a court in this realm which had more revenue than that of Gilles." [45] Finally, says the duke, spending money is good for the realm "otherwise the ordinary people will have nothing around them; and furthermore, money, by its nature, desires to be dispersed and distributed in various places." [46]

THE THEATER OF BLOOD

And when I was eighteen, I had the reputation of being a great scholar in the Torah. But one day it dawned on me that man cannot attain to perfection by learning alone. I understood what is told of our father Abraham; that he explored the sun, the moon, and the stars, and did not find God, and how in this very not-finding the presence of God was revealed to him. For three months I mulled over this realization. Then I explored until I too reached the truth of not-finding.

   —The Yehudi to Hanokh, later rabbi of Alexandria. In Martin
   Buber's *Tales of the Hasidim: The Later Masters*

There is one person who, had he been permitted to talk, might have illuminated the mysteries surrounding Gilles de Rais. That was the priest, Olivier des Ferrières, who heard Gilles' confession on the twenty-seventh of March 1440, behind the altar of Our Lady in the Church of the Holy Trinity at Machecoul.

It is hard to think one's way into Olivier des Ferrières's mind that morning as he heard his parishioner whispering on his side of the confessional, while the morning sunshine poured through the rose window of the chapel. He was hearing a confession that, if it did not actually destroy the priest's faith in a compassionate God, surely tested to the limits his vow to keep the secrets of the confessional as he agonized between his pity for the victims and his fears for those who were still in danger from the penitent kneeling before him.

When Gilles's confession was over, he went to the altar to take communion, but there was a line of people there—"parishioners of low condition who, when they saw so great a lord approaching, moved to get out of his way." [1] But Gilles, still glowing from the effects of his confession, would not hear of their moving and "commanded" them to stay where they were. And so, in the midst of his embarrassed or fearful peasantry, Gilles opened his mouth and received the host, his face radiant with an inner light.

Gilles de Rais confessing to a country priest!

"Bless me, father, for I have sinned."

"How have you sinned, my son?"

"Father. My life . . . my soul is bathed in guilt."

"Tell."

"Must I tell?"

"If you would be shriven."

"It is the children. The children in the choir. Their innocent
    faces. Their clear, pure voices; their hands, palm to palm,
    their eyes lifted to Heaven. I have desired them."

"Desired?"

"The praying children. In the way of flesh. To enclose them.
    To embrace them. To drink their prayers, mouth to mouth."

"Yes?"

"There is more, father."

"Yes?"

"Father . . . I am a murderer."

"A murderer?"

"Yes. The child . . . Guillaume de Barbier . . . the ap-
    prentice . . ."

"Yes?"

"I have breathed delight in his dying sighs."

"No!"

"I have stared into the dimming eyes of decapitated children.
    Must I tell more. . . ?"

"Is there more to tell?"

"Heaven help me, father, there is more."

"Then . . . Heaven help us . . . tell."

Victor Hugo, describing the fall of Satan in his *La Fin de Satan,* tells us that a single feather of Satan's wings remains hovering at the lip of the chasm down which he has been thrown. Though he falls through aeons of time, Satan continues to catch glimpses of that feather, still there in Paradise, still within the perimeter of

God's glory. For Hugo, the image is a literary device that allows him to arrange an ultimate reconciliation between God and Satan. The feather is a sort of promissory note of salvation. Sometimes, as one tracks Gilles de Rais through the purlieus of his behavior, one gets a glimpse of him, like Satan, throwing pathetic backward glances toward God even as he rushes himself downward on the way to hell. As if, with more impudence than Tamerlane, one could draw a tightrope across the chasm that divides the light and the dark, then dance upon it, juggling crosiers, albs, pyxes, censers, candelabra, chalices, crucifixes . . . and the glazing eyes of dying children. As if vows to make a pilgrimage to Jerusalem or to enter a monastery could turn the blood of children into holy water. As if skill was a sufficient substitute for pity. As if the ability to time a child's anguish to keep pace with his own increasing sexual excitement so that the boy's death cry and Gilles's orgasm were reached simultaneously could elicit God's admiration. As if, as more and more frequently happened, Gilles's tears and lamentations—interspersed between intervals of murder and rape—might, because they were as intensely felt as the murders, weigh in Gilles's favor at the Seat of Judgment.

It was not madness—though, like any ecstasy, it was beyond reason.

"What fellowship," asks Saint Jerome, "can there be between light and darkness? What agreement between Christ and Belial. . . . We ought not to drink both from the chalice of Christ and from the chalice of demons." [2] "Unless," Gilles would say, "the two elixirs, the foul and the fragrant, taken together give us pleasure." For the sensualist Gilles, even self-destruction was an ecstasy. Even the destruction of the soul. Because the ecstasy toward which Gilles launched himself, time after time, was the perfect fusion with divinity (whether sublime or infernal) that would blot out consciousness.

That ecstasy, when it is sacred, fuses the self with God, but even then, it is not an experience lightly or frequently to be undertaken. "I should account him blessed and sacred," says Saint Bernard, "to whom it is given to have such experience rarely, now and then, or even once, and swift in its going, lasting scarcely a moment of time. For to lose himself as it were, as if he had ceased to be, and to have no consciousness of himself at all, and to be emptied of himself and almost annihilated is a matter of heavenly conversation, not of human affection." Even then, with God as the goal, the mystic may find himself, once the moment of union is finished, overwhelmed by a postecstatic malaise, crying "Unhappy man that I am, who shall deliver me from the body of this death!" [3]

If, then, we think of Gilles's lust for the annihilation of the self as a movement downward, as a thirst for union with Belial—even while the light of grace is dazzling the eyes—we may get some sense of the swings of mood through which Gilles was now living. Worst of all, he had so convoluted his feelings that even the miseries of guilt and sin and remorse had been twisted into forms yielding pleasure. They had erotic power.

> Spende and God shall send
> Spare and perpetual care
> No penny, no ware
> No goods, no care.
>
> —Go penny go.
>
>   —A Medieval English Adage

Theater, more than the other arts, satisfies the lust to imitate God. Everyone connected with a staged work takes a hand at creating lives not their own. The playwright, the producer, the director, the actors and actresses, the set designers, stagehands, carpenters, and prompters can all experience an instant charge of immortality as the word is made flesh. The theater permits one to *be* as many people as the performance displays. Moreover, theater has everything that real life has: love, hope, death, hate, danger, disaster, boredom, nobility, squalor. At the same time, the life we see in the theater differs from our own by being soothingly under control. However deadly to Othello's hopes Iago may be, the disaster of the play crashes down on Othello, not on us. We may leave the theater glowing with insights about false friends and true wives, but when all is said and done, we do not cast a backward glance to see if Iago is following us home. Even blood and thunder dramas in which people are shot, maimed, have their eyes gouged out, are hanged in the arbor, or exit pursued by bears frighten us momentarily, until someone whispers, or we remember, "It's only a play."

Gilles came to Orléans in September 1434, bringing with him the whole of his vast entourage of soldiers, clergy, henchmen, servants, pages. Where was this assembly of nobles, knights, priests, and hangers-on to stay? We know where it did stay, because there is a surviving account book kept by a notary of Orléans that lets us know just what "ruinous expenditure" might mean when it applies to Gilles. From the account book, we learn that Gilles's clerics were housed at the Shield of Saint George; his cantor at the Sign of the Epée; his men-at-arms at the Black Head; his captain of the guard and his counselors were housed at the Great Salmon; his armorer at the Cup; his brother, René, at the Little Salmon; his knights at the Image of the Holy Marie-Madeleine; his horses and wagons and those belonging to his brother were accommodated at the Round Stone; the horses belonging to the vicar of his chapel were taken care of at the Sign of the Metal Polisher; his provost and his trumpeter had rooms in the home of Jeannette la Pionne; his manuscript illuminator stayed at an inn named the God of Love. Still others, named and unnamed, were dispersed to other inns: the White Horse, the Savage Man, and the Shield of Orléans.[4]

The enormous bills for lodging, feeding, and serving such a multitude were sent of course to Gilles. But they were only the beginning. The pace of ruin would accelerate soon. In October 1434 the restless Gilles went off to Montluçon where he stayed until December. When he left for Montmoreau, he was presented with a hotel bill for eight hundred and ten gold *reals*—and could only pay four hundred and ninety-five. To content the hotelkeeper, Guillaume Charles, Gilles left behind a couple of his serving men, Jean le Sellier and Huet de Villarceau, as a gage against the unpaid three hundred and fifteen gold *reals*.[5]

Still in December 1434, back in Orléans, Gilles dictated a power of attorney whose strangeness has been a frequent subject of comment. On December 28, he handed over to his young cousin, Roger de Briqueville, the right to conduct business in Gilles's name. "According as it seemed right to him, he was [empowered] to sell his master's castles and lands in Brittany." [6] Then, de Briqueville was authorized to negotiate the marriage of Gilles's daughter, Marie, who was all of four years old at the time. It is as if, in relationship to money, Gilles had decided to throw up his hands. He still had the energy to spend—as we will shortly see—but it was entirely too fatiguing to have to think about where the money was to come from, and if de Briqueville was willing to take on the management of such trivia, all the better for him.

On the twenty-sixth of March, still in Orléans, Gilles signed another document, which, since we know that he was already well embarked on his nighttime career of torture and murder, jangles the nerves with its sinister ironies. In Machecoul, Gilles established a religious institution to be known as the Foundation of the Holy Innocents. The document insuring its future reads:

> Whereas, the noble and powerful Lord, Monseigneur Gilles, Lord of Rais, Count of Brienne, Lord of Champtocé and Pouzauges, Marshal of France, did, not long since, for the welfare and salvation of his soul, and in order that his deceased father, mother, relations, friends and benefactors might be held in the memory of the Holy Innocents at the spot called Machecoul-in-Rais, which is in the Duchy of Brittany; and whereas, in this said Foundation, he did make and ordain a curate, dean, archdeacon, treasurer, canons, chapter and college, and did order and provide revenues and possessions for their livelihood and necessaries, . . . and whereas, the said Lord did have and still has a full intention and firm resolve to maintain the said Foundation, as he has shown, and does each day show, by his deeds, now he, desiring with all his heart that the said curate, dean and chapter shall, after his death, remain in good and peaceful possession of the revenues and possessions thus assigned to them, and shall be preserved and defended from all oppression, hath given first the castle and the castellany of Champtocé to the King of Sicily and Duke of Anjou [Louis III] . . . from whom they are held in fief; and, secondly, one-half of all the lordship, barony and land of Rais to the Duke of Brittany [Jean V] in order if Madame Katherine de Thouars, wife of the said Monseigneur de Rais, or Mademoiselle Marie de Rais, his daughter, or any other relatives, friends, heirs, or claimants . . . should, by whatever title or manner or for whatever cause, deny and prevent the said Foundation, then that they, the said Lords, the King of Sicily and Duke of Anjou, and the Duke of Brittany, shall help, sustain, and defend the members of the said Foundation in order that they may enjoy it fully and peaceably.[7]

The list of future protectors of the foundation goes on. If the duke of Anjou and the duke of Brittany should refuse to look after the foundation, then his properties are to pass on to the King of France; if the King should refuse, the Emperor (Louis of Bavaria) is designated; if the Emperor will not accept, the Pope (Eugenius IV) is named; and if, finally, the Pope will have nothing to do with the matter, the Knights of St. John of Jerusalem and of St. Lazarus are chosen, each of these Orders to hold half the gifts.[8]

The document trembles with the hysteria of confused intentions, only one of which is clear: that in Gilles's mind there exists a terrified hope that messages to God may reach their destination if only Gilles can create a living monument that will plead for him, should his own acts of contrition prove inadequate to move God's pity: "Considering that neither he [Gilles] nor any other human creature can requite his Creator for the benefits derived from His grace and benevolence, and that it is a necessary thing to acquire an intercessor, by the help of whom, one may, in continuation of temporal welfare, attain to the glory of spiritual prosperity." [9]

It is a pathetic bargain: to create a chapel of devout children whose voices chiming into eternity will praise God sufficiently to move His compassion for Gilles de Rais who, in this life, even as he was signing the document, was being supremely destructive to his spiritual prosperity.

The Foundation of the Holy Innocents! A beatitude of insult to the children. A mocking altar to Satan, designed to be a delectation to his loins. Usually only the children in the choir of the Holy Innocents were safe from his killing, though not from his amatory embraces. Because, as Poitou would testify, "he appreciated [their art] and because [the boys] vowed to keep his affairs secret." [10]

The Holy Innocents. The ambiguous prodigality.[11]

The first massacre of biblical holy innocents is, of course, the one ordered by the pharaoh in Egypt as a means of keeping down the population of his Jewish slaves: "And the king of Egypt spake to the Hebrew midwives. . . . And he said, 'When ye do the office of a midwife to the Hebrew women, and see *them* upon the stools, if it be a son, then ye shall kill him; but if it be a daughter, then she shall live.'" [12] But the Hebrew midwives were unwilling to follow orders and saved the boy children. Finally, "Pharaoh charged all his people, saying, 'Every [Hebrew] son that is born ye shall cast into the river, and every daughter ye shall save alive.'" [13] It is to avoid that death that Moses' mother made for him "an ark of bulrushes, and daubed it with slime and with pitch, and put the child therein."

In the Christian tradition, it is the second Massacre of the Innocents that is commemorated on December 28. The story is told in The Gospel According to Saint Matthew, where we read that when the star appeared in the heavens, which the wise men from the East interpreted as announcing the coming of a new king of the Jews, Herod "privily called the wise men [and] inquired of them diligently what time the star appeared. And he sent them to Bethlehem and said, 'Go and search diligently for the young child; and when ye have found *him,* bring me word again, that I may worship him also.' " But the wise men were warned by God in a dream "that they should not return to Herod," so "after they had found the child Jesus and worshipped him; and when they had opened their treasures, [and] presented unto him gifts: gold, and frankincense, and myrrh," they went secretly home and did not return to Herod. "Then Herod, when he saw that he was mocked of the wise men, was exceeding wroth and sent forth, and slew all the children that were in Bethlehem, and in all the coasts thereof, from two years old and under. . . ." [14]

There is a short thirteenth-century Latin play, "[The Service for Representing] The Slaughter of the Innocents," that was performed on the festival of the Massacre of the Innocents (December 28), in which we follow the white-garbed child victims as they move across the stage singing praises to God. Not very far into the play, when Herod is informed that the wise men have escaped to their own countries, Herod, "as if demented, having seized a sword [makes as if] to kill himself, but [is] finally prevented" by his followers, who tell him, "Determine, my lord, to vindicate your wrath, and with the sword's point unsheathed, order that the boys be slain; and perchance among the slain will Christ be killed." Herod then hands his sword over, saying, "My excellent men-at-arms, cause the boys to perish." The boys are promptly killed, after which, say the stage directions, "let Rachel be led in, and two comforters; and standing over the boys let her mourn falling at times to earth, saying

> Alas, tender babes, we see how your limbs
>   have been mangled!
> Alas, poor children, murdered in a single frenzied
>   attack!

Alas, one whom neither piety nor your tender age
restrained.[15]

It is all bathos, on the face of it, but one must keep in mind that
for Gilles de Rais the image of the massacre of the innocents was
not a literary device intended to provoke the pious tears of church-
goers. It was a cruel emblem whose meaning to Gilles one would
give a lot to know. In his own nighttime massacres of the innocent,
what role did Gilles believe himself to be playing? Pharaoh?
Herod? The putative killer of some suddenly renascent Christ? Did
he, in some remarkable act of the imagination, believe himself to
be playing the part of the children he slew?

Or did he, remembering Jeanne d'Arc, hear her voice raised in
"lamentation and weeping, and great mourning, [like the] voice of
Rachel weeping for her children, and would not be comforted because they were not." [16]

Gilles's spendthrift sponsorship in Orléans in 1435 of *The Mystery
of the Siege of Orléans* [17] was a culminating *acte gratuit* reflecting his
longtime interest in theatrical presentation. The *Mémoire des Héritiers* complains that even before Orléans, Gilles employed compa-
nies of players who put on daily performances of the theatrical fare
medieval audiences craved. Indeed, the quality of his resident
players was so high that Gilles is said to have lent them to envious
nobility who begged for a chance to preside over moralities, farces,
moresques, soties, and mystery plays of their own.[18]

The mystery play was the most popular, perhaps because it was
the most spectacular of medieval stage productions. Like the great
Cecil B. De Mille film productions of our own day, the mystery
plays were occasions for vivid, if not elegant, display. The themes
of the mysteries were taken from the Bible or from secular history,
so that one has on the one hand such plays as *The Mystery of Adam,
The Mystery of the Passion;* and *The Mystery of Great Troy, The Mystery
of Orléans,* on the other. Such plays, endless in their length—20,000
to 50,000 verses—and requiring as much as a week to perform, were
hardly literary vehicles in which dramatic conflict or character are
developed with any subtlety. Rather, audiences were offered grandeur, spectacle, color, movement and stories perfectly familiar to
them: ". . . pious legends, stories of saints and martyrs. . . . As for
[their style] it was what it could be, given not only the imperfec-
tion of the language, but also the poverty of imagination of the
poets." [19]

Normally, the great mystery plays were financed as cooperative ventures with the costs shared by the municipalities in which they were given, by the local clergy, and by civic-minded private citizens. The actors, usually local volunteers eager for a chance to dress up and parade about and declaim before the eyes of their fellows, were expected to pay for their own costumes. The audiences, too, paid for their pleasures, sometimes a great deal. Even the poor paid a one-franc admission price for their standing room, while the high-ranking clergy or the nobility, who sat in tiers of benches built specially for them, paid as much as eighty-five francs.[20] Gilles, however, when he undertook the sponsorship of *The Mystery of the Siege of Orléans* was to change all that.

Gilles's cumulative stays in Orléans, from September 1434 to August 1435, were probably the most financially costly of his life. In less than a year, he spent between 80,000 to 100,000 gold *écus* which, speculates Georges Bataille (1959) amounted to "hundreds of millions, perhaps a billion of our money." [21] This was the epoch in which, wherever Gilles moved, he took with him not only his men-at-arms but also his Chapel of the Holy Innocents, complete with the sort of sweet-voiced choristers fifteenth-century painters loved to depict as angels with that realism that makes it possible for us to tell which of them were sopranos and which were altos.[22] Music transported Gilles. Especially the music of boys' voices, singing or in pain. Jean Rossignol, an exceptionally gifted chorister of his chapel, received a gift of land from his appreciative master, and both of his parents were sent money presents as well. Rossignol, whose name means "nightingale," appreciated Gilles in turn and became one of his more devoted lovers as well as a pander to Gilles's deadlier lusts.

It is not surprising that Gilles's overweening presence in every aspect of the production and staging of *The Mystery of the Siege of Orléans* has been seen as the expression of an avid ego. The equivalent of millions of dollars were spent on the production. He paid for the construction of the great scaffolds that served to stage the play. He paid also for the more than a hundred and forty actors who made up the cast. He paid for the five or six hundred people who had walk-on or crowd-scene parts. Gilles costumed them all, insisting that what they wore, whether the gilt armor of knighthood or the rags of beggars, must be authentic and made of the finest materials. The stage ecclesiastics whose costly dress and paraphernalia might be worn only for moments in the play were nevertheless given new clothing and accouterments for each successive performance. Nor could what they carried or wore be made of any inferior stuff. Copes, robes, chasubles, dalmatics were all authentic, though they might be worn by lowly carpenters or shoemakers playing exalted parts. The Abbé Bossard can hardly contain himself. He writes:

> And certainly, the Marshal de Rais had too great a love for what is most beautiful in the way of ornaments . . . the documents are explicit on this subject. Nothing was missing in the way of stage decor . . . each member of the cast had his own costume, according to his role and his rank . . . even beggars, valets, scoundrels—in despite of historical and dramatic verisimilitude—were no less well dressed than kings or great folk. Because for [Gilles] , a mystery play was not only a display of great events, he considered it above all as a demonstration of wealth. . . . Gold, crimson satin, silver, velvet, jewels, cloth of gold or cloth of silver, expensive armor, costly accoutrements, fine embroideries, silk, all the marvels of the arts were scattered in profusion. . . . The middle ages, its civilization still at a gross stage, was indiscreetly magnificent. . . . [And] The Marshal de Rais undertook to pay the immense costs required by such representations out of his own wealth. And such sums.[23]

Emile Gabory insists that all of this expenditure was *only* in the service of Gilles's enormous ego. "Was it not enough," he writes, "to intoxicate an impressionable, vain and feeble mind, to be, at the age of twenty-five, rich and liberal enough to scatter unheard of sums of money in a few months, and share the delights of one's own sensations with an entire populace?" [24] Gabory is echoing Bossard's charge that Gilles was overwhelmed with a "great desire to dazzle the mob," [25] but what Gilles was doing had more corrosive implications than either self-display or crowd-pleasing.

Very soon, when the details of Gilles's crimes are made clearer, it will become impermissible for the reader to have even the slightest reflex of sympathy for him. It is easier in the real world to *say* that one is prepared to "hate the crime and not the criminal" than to abide by that too abstract distinction. Gilles's murders were atrocious, and there will be no effort made in these pages to plead extenuation of any sort for him. He became unspeakable, a monument to all that is cruel; and he deserved no better end than the one to which he came. But, since the aim of this work is to insist that people like Gilles are a crystallization out of the general human essence; that they along with us are equal members of the human species, it may not be amiss to remind the reader that Gilles, in Orléans, was entering what was probably the most tumultuous, grief-stricken, and terrifying epoch of his life. The world would see Gilles in Orléans seized by a fever of spending and self-display. And surely Gilles was in a fever; and certainly fountains of gold spewed from his coffers. But what we ought to keep in mind as we watch Gilles prancing and spending is that he was engaged in an intricate ritual designed, minute by minute, to contain his demons. It was, let us remember, only three years since the death of his grandfather, whose great accumulation of wealth Gilles was dissipating. Jean de Craon's wealth! Left to Gilles, to whom the tightfisted old river pirate did *not* leave his sword of manhood, leaving it instead to his whey-faced younger grandson, René. There is an animus in Gilles's spending that is at once suicidal, vengeful, and ritualistic. The clatter of gold on its way to the merchants and hangers-on has the vehemence in it of Gilles's youthful *je-m'en-foutisme* as he dares his grandfather to interfere from the other side of the grave. "So much for your sword, old man. So much for your sword."

There is a similar vitality expressing itself in the tenacity with which Gilles attached himself to *The Mystery of the Siege of Orléans*, which played daily for nearly five months. There is dream management here, as Gilles takes on the responsibility of displaying an idealized Jeanne d'Arc ideally raising the siege of Orléans assisted by her idealized, noble, and chivalric good friend Gilles de Rais.

Dream management. The manipulation of symbols. The correction of reality. The rewriting of bad memories. Telling lies.

And something else. By 1434, when Gilles came to Orléans, he was fully engrossed in his career as a torturer-murderer of children.[26] He had crossed over that line on the other side of which the human takes on the aspects of the demonic. This is no metaphor of Gilles's psychological state. The trial transcript makes it clear that by 1435 Gilles had already made "many and various evocations and conjurations of evil spirits" in various of his residences, *Orléans included*.[27] Gilles, with the full consent of his will, had set out to find Satan.

There is some reason to think that the apparently mindless extravagance of Gilles's expenditures may have been related to what

Gilles had learned from his occult studies. If, as I think, Gilles was literally and magically invoking the spirit of Jeanne d'Arc by his involvement with *The Mystery of the Siege of Orléans,* then Gilles's requirement that all the costumes in the play be brand new becomes something more important than self-display. In one of the *grimoires*—one of those manuals of instruction in the demonic arts that, it appears, Gilles had studied—he would have learned that a "vital requirement [for the magician] is that everything used must be 'virgin.' The magician must either make his instruments or 'magical weapons' himself from previously unused materials, and this is preferable, or he must buy them brand new and especially for his operations. The virtue of a thing which is virgin is that its innate force has not been dissipated by use, but, beyond this, to use any object which is secondhand or has been employed for nonmagical purposes is to risk terrible dangers." [28]

The main point here is that at Orléans Gilles mounting *The Mystery of the Siege of Orléans* was simultaneously involved in a variety of frenzies: exacerbating his grandfather's disapproving shade; pacifying and glorifying the spirit of Jeanne d'Arc; tormenting himself in the mood swings between the grandeur and the glory of the daytime performances of the play and his nighttime performances in pursuit of Satan.

For all these, the play was a marvelous scape-toy. A vast plaything, whose huge scaffoldings extended for the length of many city streets; whose backdrop was the sky and the earth meeting at the horizon. The play, which had God perched on the highest scaffold looking down approvingly at the comings and goings of gorgeously dressed persons whose costumes and gestures were all paid for and prescribed by Gilles de Rais. The play, each day reinventing a handsome Jeanne d'Arc (played by a boy, naturally) moving toward her destiny in the company of her faithful and devoted companion, Gilles de Rais.

For nearly five months, after May 8, the anniversary date of the raising of the siege, the play was performed daily. Daily, Jeanne d'Arc could be seen riding across the stage garbed in splendor, as the real-life Jeanne, at the close of her career, had been. Gilles had witnessed the changes, filled with allegory, in Jeanne's choice of clothing. He had heard of the red dress she wore at Domrémy; and he had seen her at Chinon when she appeared before Charles VII dressed as a boy with "a black doublet with hose attached, a short frock of dark gray material, her black hair cut straight round, with a black hat on her head." [29] He had watched her, as she moved farther and farther toward her apotheosis, yielding to the temptation to shine. More and more eagerly, she took to wearing the expensive gifts that came her way: white armor, cloth of gold, red capes, velvet cloaks, purple silks. Now, as the patron of *The Mystery of the Siege of Orléans,* Gilles was responsible for dressing the stage Jeanne as sumptuously as the one he remembered: the Maid of Orléans, the stocky, strangely graceful androgyne who "when she was not in armour dressed as a horse soldier with shoes laced behind the foot, tight-fitting doublet and hose, and small hat on her head [and who] wore magnificent clothes of cloth of gold and silk well trimmed with fur." [30]

In the bright and shiny world of Orléans in 1435, the whole world was invited to see a brighter and shinier version of the lifting of the siege the city had endured until 1429. And all the world came because, to see this mystery play, neither the poor nor the rich were required to pay admission. Gilles bore the cost of everything. Not only was the populace admitted free, but it was also fed at Gilles's expense. "During the entire period of these exhibitions," writes Emile Gabory, "the town of Orléans was converted into one vast banquet; everywhere there were tables in the open air, in the streets and in the public squares. Hypocras and hydromel flowed in torrents from precious drinking urns; the most sought-after venison, the best of viands and the most succulent of fish furnished out the colossal orgy, which was recommended each day." [31]

The play *The Mystery of the Siege of Orléans* has 20,529 verses. In its nineteenth-century printed version, it is 509 quarto pages long, and it makes interminable reading, which is not surprising, since spectacle, not complexity of character or plot, was the anonymous author's goal. In Orléans, after all, everyone knew how the siege had ended.

Whether, as has been speculated, Gilles occasionally played himself in *The Mystery of the Siege of Orléans* is not particularly important. What matters is that wherever he appears in the play, his role is glorious and honorable. There is no whisper anywhere in the action of the play about Gilles as La Trémoille's creature, spying on Jeanne. Not a word about Gilles's disappearance from Jeanne's side after the debacle before Paris. Nothing about his silence during her long captivity, or about his inertness during her trial and execution.

Instead, Gilles is importantly present whenever in the play Jeanne d'Arc appears on stage. Whatever he does is noble, good, and kind. Whatever he says is high-hearted and true. Charles VII tells Jeanne, in the play, that she

> will have the Marshal de Rais
> And Ambroise de Loré
> A valiant gentleman
> Both of whom I expressly command
> To lead you wherever you please
> Anywhere at all, whether near or far.

The Maid thanks the king and gives him advice:

> King, always be humble and gentle
> Toward God: he will immediately care for you.

Upon which the Marshal de Rais says:

> Lady, what will it please you to do?
> We are very close to Blois.
> Perhaps you would care to retire
> There for two or three days to rest;
> To inquire where the English are
> As well as to refresh your men
> Or would you prefer to go
> On to Orléans at once?

The Maid replies:

> My Lord, I shall be pleased
> For us to go to Blois
> To wait there for our people.

And Gilles, anxious to serve Jeanne, says:

> Madame, we will accomplish
> Your will at once.[32]

When various of the war chiefs are perplexed about which route to take toward Orléans, the stage Gilles points out that the road via Beauce is infested with the English. Gilles's advice is to go by way of Sologne.

Always, in the play, the emphasis is on Gilles's alertness; his devotion to the Maid. When "the English retreat, Rais is the first to propose pursuit; and it is he who with much eulogy of Joan supports the Duc d'Alençon's proposal that the Loire country should be cleared of the English prior to the march on Reims." [33] Gilles's role is always to be "near [Jeanne], ever evincing the greatest devotion to her person." [34] And Jeanne, appreciative of his care, calls Gilles "Noble, valiant, gentle prince." [35]

"Noble, valiant, gentle prince." It was something for Gilles, whatever it cost him, to get to hear these words daily. What if it was dream-rewriting? Self-delusion? Self-stupefaction? Truth is a human hunger easily overwhelmed by the yearning for happiness. For the time being, Gilles could afford paying the expensive piper for his exquisite tune: "Noble, valiant, gentle prince."

CHAPTER EIGHT

THE ALEMBICS OF SATAN

There is no true work of art in which the Demon is not a collaborator . . . the artist cannot succeed without the aid of God's monkey.

—Marcel Schneider

Hegel, distinguishing between mysticism and magic, says that for the magician, "there is no question of worship or of reverence for a spiritual being, for what has an absolute objective existence of its own. The process is rather the exercise of lordship over nature—the sway of the magician over those who do not know.

—Joseph Hone

Gilles de Rais was fifteen years old when Nicholas Flamel died in Paris, eighty-nine years old and full of good, Christian works. Flamel, a kindly, tenacious, and inquisitive alchemical researcher, who claimed to have found the philosophers' stone, seemed, so far as his character was concerned, to have deserved it. His affection for his childless wife of many years shines through his account of his alchemical researches, as does his civic decency. Whether Gilles de Rais actually knew Flamel's work is uncertain, though Huysmans takes it for granted that "there is no doubt that Gilles had acquired [Flamel manuscripts], for he was an avid collector of the rare. Let us add that at that epoch the edict of Charles interdicting spagyric labors under pain of prison and hanging, and the bull, *Spondent pariter quaes non exhibent*,[1] which Pope John XXII fulminated against the alchemists, were still in vigor. These treatises were, then, forbidden

115

and in consequence desirable. It is certain that Gilles had long studied them." [2]

Flamel's own story of how he came to make the philosophers' stone has no smell of the demonic about it. It is, in every respect, a pious Christian narrative. Flamel tells us that he was living in Paris where he earned his living as a scrivener—a copyist of manuscripts. In the course of his professional labors, he frequently had access to manuscripts that dealt with arcane matters and he became early interested in such documents, especially those having to do with alchemy. Though he was but a stumbler in Latin, his head was steeped in esoteric texts, but for a long time to no purpose. Then one night, he had a vision in which "the mystical Bath-Kôl appeared to him under the figure of an angel, bearing a remarkable book bound in well-wrought copper, the leaves of thin bark, graven right carefully with a pen of iron. An inscription in characters of gold contained a dedication addressed to the Jewish nation by Abraham the Jew, prince, priest, astrologer, and philosopher." [3]

The apparition promised Flamel that one day the scrivener would understand the secrets the book contained. "Flamel eagerly stretched out his hands to take possession of the priceless gift, but book and angel disappeared in an auriferous light. The scrivener woke to be ravished henceforth by the divine dream of alchemy." [4] But the dream was brighter than the reality, and many years passed with no further indication that Flamel was indeed to be singled out for alchemical good fortune. Then one day, "God . . . Who never forsakes the righteous generation, or suffers the children of the just to beg their bread, nor deceives their expectations . . ." [5] made His move. Flamel bought a gilded book "very old and large, which cost me only two *florins.*"

"It was not made of paper or parchment, as other books are, but of admirable rinds (as it seemed to me) of young trees. The cover of it was of brass; it was well bound and graven all over with a strange kind of letters, which I take to be Greek characters, or some such like." [6] Though Flamel could read the Latin text, he could make neither head nor tail of the strange letters, and even less of the marvelous drawings that appeared on every seventh leaf of the twenty-one-page book:

Upon the first seventh leaf was depicted—1. A Virgin. 2. Serpents swallowing her up. On the second seventh, a serpent crucified; and on the last seventh, a desert or wilderness, in midst whereof were seen many fair fountains whence issued out a number of serpents here and there.

Upon the first of the leaves was written in capital letters of gold, Abraham, the Jew, Priest, Prince, Levite, Astrologer and Philosopher, to the nation of the Jews dispersed by the wrath of God in France, wisheth health.

After which words, it was filled with many execrations and curses, with this word MARANATHA, which was oft repeated against any one that should look in to unfold it except he were either Priest or Scribe.[7]

Flamel did look in and discovered that his two florins had purchased a manual that taught in a most secret fashion how to make the *prima materia,* or the philosophers' stone. The secret was on the fourth and fifth leaves of the book, but "though it was singularly well and materially or intelligibly figured and painted, yet by that could no man ever have been able to understand it without having been well skilled in [the Jewish] Cabala." [8]

The secret lurked in the pictures. But what was Flamel to make of scenes that showed a young man with wings at his ankles holding a caduceus in his hand toward whom "there came running and flying with open wings, a great old man with an hour-glass fixed upon his head, and a scythe in his hands, like Death." [9] Or of the picture of a red, white, and blue flower, with golden leaves growing on a mountaintop surrounded by griffins and dragons? There were other pictures that need not detain us, but, "On the last side of the leaf was depicted a king with a falchion, who caused his soldiers to slay before him many infants, the mothers standing by, and weeping at the feet of their murderers."

Altogether, the series of scenes, including the last representation of the Massacre of the Innocents, was a coded instruction manual for the creation of the philosophers' stone. Poor Flamel had learned enough to know that he held that great secret in his hand, but not enough to be able to read it.

Flamel, however, was as tenacious as he was pious. He worried at the document for twenty-one years "in a perfect meander from the verity; in which space of time I went through a thousand labyrinths or processes, but all in vain; yet never with the blood of infants [as the picture showing the Massacre of the Innocents seemed to imply], for that I accounted wicked and villainous." [10]

Then, with the help of a certain Anselm "a practiser of physic and a deep student in this art" and an unnamed Spanish rabbi, Flamel's piety and assiduity were rewarded. The secret of the pictures was revealed to him: "Knowing the preparations of the prime agents, and then following the directions in my book, I could not then miss the work if I would." On Monday, January 17, 1382, he turned a pound and a half of mercury into pure silver. Then, on April 25, in the presence of his devoted wife, Perrenelle, Flamel, using again a pound and a half of mercury, "transmuted [it] into almost as much gold, much better, indeed, than common gold, more soft also, and more pliable. . . . I had truly enough when I had once done it; but I found exceeding great pleasure and delight in seeing and contemplating *the admirable works of Nature within the vessels.*" 11

The congenial scrivener who refused to shed innocent blood for the sake of his experiments became immoderately wealthy. He and his wife, Perrenelle, gave their money "to works of charity and mercy." Flamel tells us that "after the death of my faithful companion, whose loss I cannot but lament all the days of my life, she and I had already founded, and endowed with revenues, fourteen hospitals, three chapels, and seven churches, in the city of Paris, all which we had new built from the ground." 12

I have summarized the story of the kindly Nicholas Flamel in good faith, but I must add Arthur Edward Waite's comments that "hostile criticism has endeavoured to destroy the testimony which the history of Flamel affords to the reality of transmutation. . . . The alchemical testaments and treatises attributed to him are condemned one and all as spurious [by] the Abbé L. Vilain. . . . It must be granted out of hand that all the alchemical compositions which have passed under the name of Flamel are open to more or less suspicion, and some are undoubtedly forgeries. . . ." "On the other hand," adds Waite, who, like myself, is attracted to the Flamel story, "there are strong arguments for the genuineness of the *Trésor de Philosophie.*" 13

Cause and effect are more gratifyingly linked for earlier historians than they are for historians today. Thus, Michelet, writing in the nineteenth century, has no trouble telling us how Gilles turned vicious. Michelet writes: "The fifteenth century, for all its two or three great discoveries, is yet, I take it, a tired, outworn, exhausted century, lacking in ideas.

"It starts grandly enough with the Royal *Sabbath* of St. Denis, the mad, wild, gloomy festival Charles VI gave in the Abbey of St. Denis to celebrate the reinterment of Du Guesclin.[14] For three days and three nights Sodom caroused over the tombs of the dead. The mad king, not yet the imbecile he afterwards became, forced all the kings, his ancestors, their dry bones dancing in their coffins, to share his revel. Grim Death, whether he would or no, was made a pandar and added a horrid spur to the wanton pleasures of the Court. . . . The young nobles on their side were just as shameless, and exposed their persons in an equally disgusting fashion. Whilst women wore Satan on their brows in the twin-peaked cap, knights and pages displayed his symbol on their feet in those pointed shoes that turned up like so many angry scorpions. Under the guise of animals, they disported themselves in brazen travesty of the basest lusts of beasts. It was there Gilles de Retz [*sic*], himself a page at the time, first learned his monstrous vices." [15]

Today, we are likely to think that vices are a response to inner hungers. That they are not, in any case, taught by example. Still, as in the story of Gilles's involvement with alchemy and satanism, we are sometimes taken aback by the way external events are in collusion with one's hungers.

Money and power have been the stated goals of alchemists and necromancers, but as we turn to an account of Gilles's meddling in those arts, we ought not to overlook the degree to which he found them psychologically attractive as well. The alchemical view that the world's metals bear a hierarchical relationship to each other forming a ladder of perfection surely moved Gilles as an allegory of his own "trying out." A man who used stages of corporeality to test his relationship to God would be sympathetic to a science whose mystical aim is to discover the discipline of the spirit by means of which the baser human elements are purged. Regeneration of the soul—not gold as such—is the alchemist's passion. Waite writes that "the mystical and mysterious instrument of preparation in the work of alchemy is the conscience, which is called by a thousand misleading and confessedly incongruous names. By means of this instrument, quickened into vital activity under a sense of the presence of God, the matter of the stone, namely, Man, is, in the first place, purged, to make possible the internal realisation of Truth." [16]

Radix malorum est cupiditas—cupidity is the root of all evil, says Chaucer's glib-tongued Pardoner, a man who like Gilles was a sensualist of imminent damnation. Paradoxically enough, though Gilles was not himself an acquisitive person, one might with reason blame money for turning him to alchemy and the black arts, those twin passions of inquiring and greedy medieval minds. In Gilles's case, his pursuit of the philosophers' stone and especially his quest for Satan form a painfully comic chapter in his otherwise tragic life.

Money! The evil root. He had acquired the habit of high spending and he was incapable of giving up that gratification just because he was running out of cash. If spending made it possible for him to live as if exhilaration were the only mood, then there was but one thing to do: spend.

As a consequence, he quickly learned three more of the essential skills of the profligate: borrowing, pawning, and selling real estate. "He borrowed from anyone who would lend him [money]," writes the Abbé Bossard.[17] Gilles became a feckless pawner, pledging for trivial sums objects that he had paid fortunes to possess. Worse than that, he "rarely saw any profit [from what was sold]; everything was handled by his servants and friends and, if some cash did finally reach Gilles, it flowed away from him like water." [18] He pawned jewels or works of art. He pawned his famous volumes of Valerius Maximus, his Saint Augustine, and his Ovid. Nothing, indeed, was safe from the pawnbroker, not even his horse, Cassenoix (Nutcracker); not even his silver head of Saint Honoré.

Ruin, not spending, is the prodigal's secret goal, and Gilles moved off toward ruin at a gallop. From selling or pawning portable property, he shifted to the sale of real estate. He sold towns, villages, manors, manor houses, castles to anyone who would buy, and, again, at knockdown prices. Gauthier de Brussac, a military commander, purchased Confolens, de Chabanez, de Châteaumorant, de Lombert; Jean de Marseilles bought various lands in Anjou; Guillaume de la Jumellière, a fellow nobleman, bought other Angevin lands; Hardouin de Bueil, bishop of Angers, bought both land and timber rights. Among the unbusinesslike contracts, however, we have to note a series of apparently profitable dealings with Jean de Malestroit, bishop of Nantes and chancellor of Brittany. The bishop bought "the lands and castles at Prigny, Vüe, Bois-aux-Tréaux; the parish of St.-Michel-Sénéché, and a great number of other lands situated in de Rais territory." [19] The bishop, says Bossard,[20] paid an enormous sum for the lands he acquired—a fact he may have remembered in 1440 when he initiated the proceedings against Gilles de Rais that brought the baron finally before the bar of justice. The presiding judge at that trial would be Jean de Malestroit, bishop of Nantes.

That danger was yet to come. For the time being, Gilles had more to fear from his family, which had become terribly uneasy about the torrents of money flowing from Gilles's coffers.

From their point of view, Gilles, despoiling himself of his grandfather's wealth, was at the same time robbing his heirs. Besides, Cathcrinc, his wifc, had brought him a considerable dowry, which Gilles seemed perfectly capable of spending along with his own wealth. One has to presume that Catherine and Gilles's brother, René, as well as other members of the family, expostulated with Gilles—to no effect, because "in their despair, they carried their griefs to the foot of the throne," [21] begging Charles VII to do what he could to prevent the disaster looming over Gilles's estates. Charles, convinced that the family had a point, issued a number of *Lettres Patentes,* which were read publicly by town criers in Orléans, Tours, Angers, Champtocé, Pouzauges, and other towns and villages where Gilles had domains: The substance of the letters was that Gilles was forbidden to sell land; and it was forbidden for anyone to make contracts with him. It was an interdiction more or less effective in French territory, but the duke of Brittany, having good and sufficient reasons of his own, chose to ignore Charles's edict. As a way of cozening Gilles, Jean V appointed him baron lieutenant general of Brittany; after which, ignoring Charles VII's edict, he continued to acquire various of Gilles's properties.

While the royal edict hardly clipped Gilles's wings, he could not entirely overlook the fact that his financial behavior was being scrutinized in a way that could prove a threat to him in other areas of his life. If he did not alter his behavior, it is because he was already in pursuit of the grand magisterium—the philosophers' stone with whose help he expected to be able to change this world's dross into an endless supply of gold.

That pursuit apparently had its beginnings in 1426 when Gilles,

in Angers, met a knight imprisoned there for heresy who lent him a book that dealt with alchemy and magic. Gilles read the book "avidly and several times." He also visited the soldier in his prison, where he discussed the book's contents with him. But, Gilles would later claim, he returned the book when he left Angers, and in any case he did not have it in his possession for very long.[22]

It was also at Angers that there transpired one of the sillier episodes in Gilles's alchemical researches. Gilles was staying at an inn called the Silver Lion when his henchman, Eustache Blanchet, the priest, brought him the news that there was a jeweler in the town who was a skilled alchemist. Gilles immediately ordered Blanchet to bring the savant to him. "No sooner said than done." Gilles gave the jeweler a silver mark and asked the man to work on it; then he shut him in a room in the inn. The jeweler was a more skillful drunkard than he was an alchemist. Made rich with the silver mark, he managed to get wine into the room in which he had been locked and promptly drank himself into a stupor, in which condition Gilles found him. The jeweler was flung into the streets with Gilles's curses flying about his head.

Undaunted by that episode, Gilles sent out emissaries to find him more reputable teachers than the Angers drunkard. One by one, the experts came to Tiffauges, where Gilles had set up a laboratory. There they worked for a while with Gilles beside them. One by one, they left. There was no dearth of expertise: "Princes," writes Gabory, "were swamped by evocators, magicians, astrologers and mountebanks of every stripe and kidney. Many of them were Italians, who claimed to be versed in the occult sciences. . . . All the cities of the Breton peninsula were overrun with these greedy adventurers. Aside from their more or less avowed practices, they engaged in the sale of poisons, and when required, they gave instruction in their use." [23] Gilles had no interest in poisons, but he labored alongside his teachers, deploying for the sake of the gold he believed they would bring him the rapidly dwindling supply of gold that he still had, but experiment after experiment produced nothing but frustration or ingenious excuses.

As happened with a certain sorcerer named de la Rivière who, one night, put on a great show in a wood near Tiffauges where he

Ruins of Gilles's castle at Tiffauges.

went to summon the devil for Gilles. While Etienne Corillaut (Poitou), Henriet Griart, and the priest Blanchet huddled with Gilles at the edge of the wood, de la Rivière, dressed in white armor and carrying a sword, moved in among the trees. A long interval passed during which Gilles and his friends heard nothing but the croaking of frogs and the wind rustling in the branches. Then Gilles, worried at de la Rivière's too long absence, led his men into the wood. There, they came upon the sorcerer, stumbling about, haggard and aghast. "A leopard," he whispered. "Satan . . . in the form of a leopard. Silent . . . still . . . A leopard, stalking. Satan . . . Satan."[24] Gilles and his men, as terrified as de la Rivière, fled with him from the wood. It was another disappointment for Gilles though perhaps not for the magician, who was paid twenty *reals* for his labors.

The pace of the invocations quickened. On one occasion, Gilles and his cousin Gilles de Sillé participated in a ritual conducted by an unnamed magus. While de Sillé, who was afraid to join Gilles and the sorcerer in the magic circle, cowered near a window pressing an image of the Holy Virgin to his heart, Gilles, as terrified as his cousin, tried desperately to remember some holy words that would defend him from the Great Adversary he was paying so much to summon. At last, he remembered "a prayer to Our Lady which begins with *Alma.*"[25] The magician, outraged at his employer's equivocation, ordered Gilles from the circle. Gilles, grateful to be dismissed, left the room and was followed by his equally fainthearted cousin. A little while later, these two heard the noise of blows repeatedly raining down on the magician. When they flung the door open, Gilles and de Sillé found the magus bruised and bloodied from head to foot, all but unconscious. The man was so badly hurt that he believed himself to be dying.

Not surprisingly, the sorcerer recovered his health and moved on.

The charlatans continued to replace each other, but, still, neither money nor demons appeared at the end of Gilles's exhausting sessions with them. De Sillé, who procured sorcerers as well as victims for Gilles, met a couple of witches who sent back two important messages. The first was that Gilles would never succeed as a magician so long as his soul was attached to the Church. The other message, more ambiguous than the first, was to the effect that Gilles would come to a bad end unless he "abandoned or ceased to do a work he had begun, or which he intended to continue." [26] These cautionary messages had no effect on Gilles, and he continued to track Satan and the philosophers' stone.

Then, in 1439, François Prelati came into Gilles's life. Prelati leaps up at us from the pages of the trial transcript. He is vivid, brilliant, beautiful, and sly. He is charming, assiduous, and false. Before ever there was such a literary genre as the Gothic novel, Prelati in the flesh, stood there, in the fifteenth century, modeling the complete Gothic villain. In the hands of the great masters of eighteenth-century fear literature like Matthew G. Lewis, Horace Walpole, and Ann Radcliffe, such villains were invariably tall, dark, vibrant, handsome, and sexually overendowed Italians whose destiny it was to pursue pale, frail, decorous virgins through the dank corridors of ruined castles with intent to commit rape—or worse (incest, for example).

According to Prelati himself, he was a native of Montecatini, near Pistoia. He became a priest at a very early age, receiving the tonsure from the bishop of Arezzo himself. He was something of a prodigy who mastered poetry, magic, and alchemy before his twentieth year.

He was twenty-one years old and living in Florence when he met Eustache Blanchet, that other wicked, but very dreary, priest who sometimes served Gilles as a factotum. Blanchet was in Florence hunting for sorcerers to send home to Gilles. Prelati instantly charmed the older priest, who devoted much time and a considerable amount of his master's money in getting to know the suave Italian whom he treated "with wine and feasts in abundance." [27] One guesses from what transpired later that Blanchet fell more than half in love with the dashing Prelati. Meantime, Blanchet was on his master's business, which, on a bibulous occasion, he pursued. "Do you have," Blanchet inquired, as if it were a matter of only the mildest interest, "any understanding of the alchemical . . . and the . . . demonic arts?"

François, who could think circles around the lumbering Blanchet, understood that he was not being asked an idle question. Firmly, he replied yes.

"Would you," the stolid French priest asked the mercurial Italian, "would you be interested. . . . There is in France a great lord, a

Breton . . . a certain Baron Gilles de Rais . . . who is most anxious to have in his household a savant instructed in those . . . occult sciences. Would such a post be interesting to Signor Prelati?"

"As it happens," Prelati replied ambiguously, "I have a cousin in France, a cousin named Martilis who lives in Nantes. It has been on my mind to make a visit to my cousin." [28]

It was not long before the two priests were riding together to France. In Prelati's saddlebag there reposed a thick and curious volume of forgotten lore stuffed with alchemical and thaumaturgic instructions. When Gilles de Rais was apprised of their coming, he sent his servants and henchmen Griart and Poitou to meet the travelers and to conduct them with speed to Tiffauges. When Blanchet finally introduced Prelati to the baron and described the younger man's forbidden skills, Gilles "greatly rejoiced." [29]

Gilles and Prelati were to work together for a year and a half. Gilles, we should remember, in 1439, already many times a murderer. Prelati, so far as we know, had no greater crimes on his head than those of which he boasted: He was a poet, an alchemist, and a necromancer who had many times called up Satan to his service. But Prelati was quickly aware of the sort of man Gilles was. It would not be long before he threw out hints that more than arcane language and fragrant smoke might be necessary if they would wring obedience from the powers of hell. Blood, he hinted. Blood might be required. Gilles, already in love with Prelati past all saving, glowed. He knew about blood.

The two set to work at once. Gilles, who was dazzled by Prelati's "agreeable commerce" and elegant Latin, was charged with new hope, but when their initial tentatives at calling up demons ended in failure, Gilles complained, "Why is it the devils never come when I call?" Prelati studied his master, then said he would go to the heart of the matter by asking the devils themselves. And off he went to perform certain rites and invocations which, lo and behold, produced a demon. Conjured to explain why Gilles had such bad luck with the denizens of hell, the demon replied that Gilles had a bad reputation among the damned. He was known as a man who promised to give the infernal creatures much, but—he did not keep his word. Prelati's imp went on to say that if Gilles wished to converse with himself, for example, he, the imp, would be glad to appear if Gilles would sacrifice a cock, a hen, a pigeon, or a dove.

Such small bloodlettings would be all right if Gilles expected very little in the way of help. For something of importance, Gilles ought to offer the demon "a member of a young boy." [30]

It was not long after this that Gilles came to Prelati's room bearing the hand, the heart, the eyes, and the blood of a youth, which Prelati, criminally incurious about the source of these gifts, offered to a demon—who ignored the courtesy and refused to appear. The child's remains were wrapped in a napkin and buried in hallowed ground, though why the remains of a child slaughtered for Satan's sake should need to be buried in sanctified soil is not clear.

The demon Prelati and Gilles sought most assiduously was named Barron, an old familiar of the young Italian's. Barron had appeared to Prelati in Florence ten or twelve times, and always in the form of a handsome young man. Gilles, who had a handsome young man before him, was enchanted. He and Prelati drew magic circles, burned aloes and myrrh. They recited formulas, one of which went, "I conjure you, Barron, Satan, Belial, Beelzebub, by the Father, the Son and the Holy Spirit; by the Virgin Mary and all the saints to appear in person, so that you may speak to us and fulfill our desires." [31] Once, Gilles wrote a letter to Satan that he entrusted to Prelati to deliver. Gilles wrote, "Come at my wish, and I will give you everything you want—except my soul and the diminution of my life." Not much of an inducement for a devil, one would think, but Gilles was always something of a pettifogger in relation to Satan. Prelati, in any case, had to return the letter when the addressee failed to appear when summoned by one more invocation.

According to Prelati, Barron still visited him from time to time, but never when Gilles was present. Once, Barron sent Gilles a gift—some black dust, which, at Prelati's suggestion, Gilles had enclosed in a silver case that he might wear as an amulet to bring him luck. Then, one day, when Gilles was at Tiffauges, but not at Prelati's side, the Italian summoned Barron and the demon came, inquiring testily, "What now?" "In my master's name," Prelati replied, "give us money." Suddenly the whole room glowed and Prelati, overjoyed, discerned a quantity of gold ingots giving off a great light. Prelati rushed to call Gilles, who asked, his heart in his mouth, if he might be permitted to see the great wonder. "Yes," Prelati said.

Together, they made their way back to the scene of the transmutation, but Prelati, who was first, cautiously opened the door and was horrified to see "a vigorous great winged serpent about the size of a dog" inside the room. Gilles, the famous warrior, when he learned what was on the other side of the door, turned tail and ran, followed, at a more leisurely pace, by his friend Prelati.

Later, armed with a crucifix in which there was embedded a sliver of the true cross, Gilles was ready to confront the winged serpent in the gold-filled room, but Prelati cautioned him against it, saying it was not wise to use the blessed cross in such infernal matters. Gilles set the cross aside and waited for Prelati to reconnoiter the room. According to his own account, Prelati went in, the gold continued to glow, but when he reached out to touch it, the glittering mass turned into a pile of fine, but perfectly ordinary dust. For Gilles, it was one more adventure that ended in defeat.

There is another occasion that deserves our attention. The story comes to us from Blanchet's testimony at Gilles's trial. Blanchet, who had come to detest Prelati—and was roundly detested by him in return—told how he was sent for in haste one day to come to the castle at Tiffauges. When Blanchet arrived, he found Gilles pacing a corridor of the castle, sobbing his heart out. "He's dead. Prelati is dead," Gilles groaned. He told Blanchet that he had heard terrible sounds coming from Prelati's room—blows, shrieks, yells. "I'm afraid to go look. I can't. . . . Please . . . Blanchet, my friend. You go."

Blanchet, who was not particularly courageous, did not wish to venture into Prelati's room either. He contented himself with climbing up to a window opening from which he called to Prelati, "François, François."

There was no reply. Then Blanchet heard a low groaning, which he reported to Gilles. A moment later, a pale Prelati himself staggered from his room. He had been beaten. The devil, he reported, had beaten him.

Prelati looked a mess. He was bruised and scratched and bloodied. The anguished Gilles put him to bed, where he promptly came down with a high fever. For seven days and seven nights, the Lord Baron de Rais stayed at Prelati's bedside, tending his dear mountebank with his own hands, forbidding anyone else to enter the room.

The story as Blanchet tells it smacks of jealous pique. Blanchet, after all, had been excluded from the evocation tête-à-têtes between Gilles and Prelati because Prelati deemed him an untrustworthy prattler who would betray their secrets.

Gilles, then, as alchemist and Satanist, makes a pretty shabby figure: part bumbler, part dupe. He had bad luck with his alchemical guides; and he was frightened out of his wits by his tentatives toward Satan. But even his ridiculous adventures into the arcane managed to be touched by blood. At Gilles's trial, the vengeful Blanchet, who was the first of his henchmen to abandon Gilles, would let drop that Gilles had one day taken him into his study at Machecoul where Blanchet was shown a book the baron was writing. It was a big book with wide margins, and its pages were covered with crosses, signs, and handwriting, all in red. "The writing, [Blanchet] supposed and suspected, had been made with human blood, children's blood," the envious priest specified, "which Gilles needed in order to write books." [32]

THE WORKSHOP OF FILTHY CREATION

An atrocious silence filled the room. When Siegfried had slain the dragon, he heard the singing of birds. But when one has slain a child, no birds sing.

—Michel Bataille

There is a place in the mind where nothing exists that does not squirm. It is a place of shadows and sinister warmth inhabited by wraiths, alive with gleaming tentacles, with protean shapes, avid mouths, and serpentine coilings. For children, it is the Dreadful Place where evils they are not yet old enough to imagine lurk. For adults, it is the subconscious, where the stuff of nightmare pauses before it stalks its way into our dreams. For adults and children, fear is only half of what is frightful there. Equally atrocious is how seductive, how delicious, how commanding are the images that nerve endings, cooperating with the glands, contrive. Out of that darkness come hungers that ought not to be dreamed of: torn flesh, violated mouths, demeaning or abusive yearnings. Swirling sensation elaborating images of sensation; imagined stimuli producing unimaginable responses. Self-indulgence inventing frustration, where the self, turned hot and hasty, reaches in all directions, toward gratification, crying alternately, "More, more, more," or "Me, me, me." The place of the deadly delusion in which is confirmed the law of the damned: For the sake of my pleasure, no self has value but my own.

We follow Gilles now into that region on the day when he kills, for his sexual delectation, his first child victim.

We do not know when or how that first bloodshed was accomplished or what was the occasion. Though Gilles's prosecutor charged him at his trial with fourteen years of child murder; Gilles more accurately specified only eight. Michel Bataille has speculated that the first murder was a consequence of some untoward bit of brutality more or less accidental in which what was meant to be passion somehow got out of hand.[1] It is a not improbable suggestion. Gilles may well have told himself that that was how it had happened. Or even contrived the event to fit that explanation when one night, drinking heavily as was his wont, he pretended to be drunker than he was, seized one of the choirboys—one of his Holy Innocents—and embraced him. There followed caresses familiar to him from his relationship with his cousin Roger de Briqueville, or his servant and confidant, Henriet Griart—or from other *jouissances*. This time, some violent caress turned suddenly fierce, then bloody. Perhaps, in a paroxysm of joy, his hands closed on the child's throat; or else he drew his dagger and used it. In either case, what happened was beyond Gilles's wildest expectations. There was a leap of vitality as the child's stopped life, the flow of his blood and Gilles's ecstasy were knitted into a single thrill in which every nerve in Gilles's body felt as if it had been newly created. The child dying in his arms produced, in addition to orgasm, a rush of immanence so intense as to make him believe he was in the grip of a mystical experience that could be induced only by blood.

Until 1439 Gilles, it would seem, killed children for his pleasure only. Then Prelati, the suave Italian, came into his life and taught Gilles how to link murder with Satan. Prelati assured his master that only human sacrifice would prove his sincerity to the demon he wished to invoke. Raffaele Ciampini, in his fictional *Barba-Blu,* has a scene in which Prelati shows Gilles a book written in red characters. "You must know," Prelati tells Gilles, "that the red color comes from the blood of a woman. One night, when I was evoking demons, I heard an inhuman voice say, 'Go to the Saline cavern . . . you will find a woman there who has been slain by a wolf. Take some of her blood and with it, write your invocations.' "

Prelati went to the cavern only to discover that the woman was not dead, but only wounded. She pleaded with him to save her, offering him her body and her wealth, but Prelati, mindful of the demon's demands, waited for her wounds to take effect; however, she bled too slowly. Again, he heard a voice, saying, "Gather her blood and write your invocations with it." Then came the further instruction, "Empty her veins."

"And . . . you did?" Gilles asks.

"Yes. The demons wished it."

Gilles, attending to this bizarre tale, gets a feverish look in his eyes. His beard, by the light of the torches, gives off strange metallic blue reflections. Then Prelati tells him that using the blood of someone already dead won't do—indeed, it might prove dangerous. "I know," says Prelati, "that the blood of a child has greater value and is preferred by the demons."

To this, Gilles's reply is, "It will be done."

Prelati then warns Gilles that the demons may require terrible things of him. "You told me that you were not afraid. Well then, the moment has come." [2]

Whether Gilles's sacrifices to Satan originated in as fanciful a way as this or in some less lurid fashion we do not know. However, we do have Poitou's testimony at the trial that he had heard it said that Gilles "would not be able to accomplish what he intended [invoking demons] unless he gave or offered to the devil a foot, a hand or some other member [belonging to] a child." [3] And that Poitou came in upon his master one day and found Gilles covering with a linen napkin a glass cup containing the hand and the heart of a slain child, which he then placed on the mantel above the fireplace.[4] At this point in his testimony, Poitou has one of those hesitations about detail that strikes a reader with the force of truth—he cannot remember whether what he saw was a right or a left hand.

If there is no trustworthy record of Gilles's first murder, there is only too much evidence of the content and the manner of the others. Eventually, there would be more than anyone could remember. Estimates as to their number range from 141 to 800, but the precise number can touch neither the quality of our compassion, nor the intensity of our moral outrage. There is danger that we will anesthetize our consciousness when we report hideous events merely in terms of numbers. To a decent person, one death is bad, two are worse, three are dreadful, four, appalling, five, a tragedy, six, a disaster . . . and then . . . and then . . . ? The absurdity of such a sequence is clear. Our feelings cannot keep pace with the arithmetic. We know well the anesthesia of numbers when we try to deal with the statistics of the German death camps.

The emotional difference between 5,400,000 as opposed to 6,000,000 dead is neither imaginable nor expressible, though we have no hesitation in saying that the larger number is worse than the smaller. But to do that is only an act of courtesy to logic and no longer has much to do with our feelings. The point is, as Dostoevsky has pointed out, that one innocent death is a disaster.

Gilles's first murder, we may guess, did not have the elaboration or the refinement that he was to bring to his later homicides. As he became more skilled, and more ambitious, he organized his sessions with the children to make them serve his complex lust for cruelty, determined to make of murder an act of infinite variety.

"People," writes Dostoevsky in *The Brothers Karamazov,* "talk sometimes of bestial cruelty, but that's a great injustice to the beasts; a beast can never be so cruel as a man, so artistically cruel. The tiger only tears and gnaws, that's all he can do. He would never think of nailing people by the ears, even if he were able to do it. These Turks took a pleasure in torturing children, too; cutting the unborn child from the mother's womb, and tossing babies up in the air and catching them on the points of their bayonets before their mother's eyes. Doing it before the mother's eyes was what gave zest to the amusement." [5]

The zest, in short, is derived from knowledge—not from instinct. The delight in the pain came from expressing it as a *symbolic* act, that is to say, an act of communication; from making it—God help us—a human gesture. An act of the will; an act committed in relationship to, and defiance of, a moral code; a gesture achieved in the presence (and especially in the presence) of God. Gilles, who would be called the Beast of Extermination, was determined to be cruel beyond bestiality. And cruel especially to children whose helplessness moved him. "You see," insists Ivan, in *The Brothers Karamazov,* "it is a peculiar characteristic of many people, this love of torturing children, and children only. . . . It's just their defencelessness that tempts the tormentor, just the angelic confidence of the child who has no refuge and no appeal, that sets his vile blood on fire." [6] Children are small and brave and innocent. They move us with their smiles and dimples, with their exquisite eyes looking out on the world with wonder and curiosity; they stir our hearts hinting at all the beauty and pain they will yet discover; we see them as being *ourselves* before the enchantment of existence has yet rubbed off; they delight us because they are archetypes of the po-

tential. We smile at the darling disarray of the young—at their caps
awry, at their smudged cheeks and the sweat-plastered hair clinging to their foreheads. We love their delight in discovery, even if it
is the discovery of their own foolishness. Children are dear to us
because they forever give us a false promise about the future—it
will be better because see how beautiful these innocents are.
Surely, we tell ourselves, they will grow into something better than
we are.

I do not know why Gilles turned to the torture-murder of children. Perhaps it was their defenselessness that tempted him. Perhaps, as I have suggested, the deaths of the children were
manifestations in him of the Rage; or else those nighttime scenarios were elaborate messages to himself or to God. It is, I think a
cogent observation of Benedetti's that "[Gilles's] victims were small
beautiful children, often fair-haired and fair-skinned, like himself," [7] which allows us to speculate about what it was that Gilles
was trying to kill: some aspect of himself? some image of a childhood he never had, or had too intensely? Or, as I used to think,
perhaps the deaths of the children were messages written to God,
each one crying out "Stop me," or "Stop me if you dare." Or, as
seems to me now more and more certain, the children died because
their deaths provided Gilles with that erotic delight that comes
from the destruction of an image of exquisite guilt. The image, in
the androgynous bodies of the children, of the androgynous Jeanne
d'Arc in her boys' clothing. Jeanne d'Arc who had roused in Gilles
a swarm of conflicting physical, moral, and spiritual tensions. To
whom at the worst, he had been false and who, in any case, had
died a frightful death leaving him behind, light-struck and be-
wildered by his survival.

> this hauling up and down was repeated until
> the hangman and his helpers went to dinner.
>
> —Paul Carus

Murder became Gilles's avocation in 1432. From then until the
end of his life, paroxysm became his style as he moved from one

form of intensity to another. On horseback, followed by his armed men, he was the *chevalier sans reproche*. In his chapel, clothed in the garb of a canon of the Church, he inhaled incense and intoxicated himself with the sound of children's voices raised to heaven singing "Hail Redemptress Mother." At night, there was murder, which, however explosive his ecstasies, satisfied him only momentarily after which a new hunger gnawed in his brain. He swung from event to event; from mood to mood. From blood to music; from prayer to murder.

To the degree that he could tolerate the paradoxes of his existence, he was a not untypical medieval man. For Gilles's contemporaries, as has been observed, paradox, melodrama, vivid contrasts characterize the uneasy tension that arched between their flesh and spirit. Huizinga says, "As for the great lords, the basic unsoundness of their life of arrogant pomp and disordered enjoyment contributed to give a spasmodic character to their piety. They are devout by starts, for life is far too distracting. Charles V of France sometimes gives up the chase at the most exciting moments to hear mass. Ann of Burgundy, the wife of Bedford, now scandalizes the Parisians by splashing a procession by her mad riding, now leaves a court fête at midnight to attend the matins of the Celestines." [8]

Huizinga tells us, too, how Philippe le Bon could be a busy father of many bastards, a gourmand, and a grasping politician even as "He was in the habit of remaining in his oratory for a long time after mass, and living on bread and water four days a week, as well as on all the vigils of Our Lady and the apostles." [9] The contradictory behavior of such folk as Philippe le Bon, Charles V, and Ann of Burgundy are examples of what Huizinga has called "a romanticism of saintliness" whose characteristic is oversimplification. For Philippe le Bon, the passion of adultery did not need to be resisted if it could be compensated for by the passion for living on bread and water. It was a mechanistic mean, not an organic one; the *forms* of good and evil—not their essences—were made to balance each other.

In Gilles's case, I suspect there was not so much a polarity of experience as there was an interpenetration of essences. When he sat listening to the choristers of his Foundation of Holy Innocents, he was entirely uplifted by the sight of ranks of lovely heads tilted upward gazing toward God with their clear brown or blue eyes. Yet, even as his heart throbbed with their spiritual loveliness, his arms and loins ached for them. The purity of the children, the possibility of his own purity were insensibly transformed to messages of lubricity, and he longed to do what we know from his trial that he did: "[He] exercised his libidinous unnatural ardors, first taking his virile rod in his hand, stretching, rubbing, and agitating it, after which he introduced it between the thighs of the said children, and, in that manner rubbing the said rod over the bellies of the said children, delight[ing] and excit[ing] himself until the sperm, criminally, and in other ways improper, spurted on the bellies of the said children." [10]

One guesses that Gilles, in the years of his crimes, lived in a stupor of sensation that often imitated clarity. That he rose from his prayers illuminated, then signaled to one of his henchmen—to Henriet Griart, to Roger de Briqueville, to Gilles de Sillé, or to André Buchet—and made his way to his chamber where another order of exaltation was awaiting him.

One thinks of the children . . . always from poor families . . . who had been caught or bought or enticed or hired . . . and who, for the longest time, must have believed that their fortunes had been made. They had been noticed by the lord of the manor. They waited . . . children from homes in which there were seven or eight or ten other little ones; always too many mouths to feed. They lived huddled in smoke-filled country huts that were cold in winter, hot in summer and, at all times, richly verminous. They ate little, or badly. They were dirty and wretched, and ragged. Nevertheless—so God had contrived it—they had managed to become beautiful, which is why they were here, in the lord baron's anteroom, dreaming of a better destiny. Of warmth and roast meat and fine clothes and bits of pocket money. Of ponies to ride. Of being the envy of all the other children left behind in the squalor that was called home. They waited, these chosen ones who would be—according to the lord baron's servants—trained to be pages.

The word *page* occurs frequently in the accounts of the abduction of the children. Almost as frequently as the word *beautiful* describing them. For the medieval poor, there were really only two ways their sons might escape from their poverty. They could enter the Church, or, if they were lovely and personable, they might attract the notice of the lord or lady of the manor who would take them from their parents to be trained as pages. For the poor, the word *page* had the true ring of hope in it, and it was especially cruel of Gilles's accomplices to hold that promise out to the parents of his victims.

The first of the murdered children we know about was a twelve-year-old whose family name was Jeudon, and who lived in Machecoul. The boy had been apprenticed to a furrier named Guillaume Hilairet. Hilairet and his wife would testify at Gilles's trial in 1440 that they lent the Jeudon boy to two of Gilles's henchmen: Gilles de Sillé and Roger de Briqueville, who wanted him, they said, to run an errand. When, much later on the same day, de Briqueville and de Sillé were asked where the child was, they shrugged their shoulders and suggested that the child had perhaps been taken by thieves who had carried him off to be made a page of somewhere. That was all the comfort they could give the furrier and his wife. The boy was never seen or heard from again.

Slowly, the terror spread as the children of the poor disappeared. The terror, writes Thomas Wilson, "made its appearance in one place on one day and at another place the next day. . . ; it was here to-night and far away in the morning; it ravaged the country, spreading terror, and leaving in its track not simply fear and mourning, but the torture of insanity and death. . . . All that the terror-stricken parents and family knew was that their child was here to-day, and now he or she was not. . . ; now it was gone, gone as completely as though swallowed by the earth." [11]

Some of the tales of the lost children are inextricably mixed with the trivia and stupidities of ordinary life. As in the story of the credulous son of one named Georget, who, not getting on with his father, asked his mother for his share of a tiny inheritance that would come to him through her, and was given "one silver marc [*sic*]," which he put in a small box and carried with him into Gilles's household for safekeeping. The box (but not the silver mark) was returned to the boy's father. The boy himself was not heard from again. [12]

There is one tale that, if it did not have such a desperate ending, has in it a chiming undercurrent of mirth. The story, in all the legalese of a deposition taken at Gilles's trial, follows. The speaker is Peronne Loessart, a mother residing at La Roche-Bernard . . . who deposes that two years ago, the said Sire de Rais, returning from Vannes, came to lodge in the said Roche-Bernard, at the inn of the said Jean Colin, and spent the night there. The deponent lived at that time facing the inn of the said Jean Colin. She had a son [Robin], a ten-year-old schoolboy, who was invited by one of the Lord de Rais' servants, by the name of Poitou. This Poitou came to speak with the said Peronne asking her to [permit] the child to stay with him. That he would dress [the boy] very well, and would give him great advantages. It would be advantageous for the said Poitou as well to have the child. To which the said Peronne replied that she could wait for such [promised] advantages and that she would not take the child out of school. In response, the said Poitou affirmed and promised and swore that he would keep faith and would send [the boy] to school and that he would give to the said Peronne one hundred *sous* for a dress. Trusting to that promise she permitted him to take the child with him.

A while later, Poitou brought her four *livres* for her dress. Upon which she remarked that there were twenty *sous* missing:

which he [Poitou] denied, saying that he had promised her only four *livres*. She said, then, that now she knew that he would not keep his other promises, since already twenty *sous* were missing. To which he said that she should not be upset—that he would give her other presents, both for her and for her child. He then took the said child to the home of Jean Colin.

The story is carried forward now by Jean Colin and his wife, and by Olive, his wife's mother, who depose that

the said Colin sold to the said Poitou a small horse for the sum of sixty *sous* as a mount for the said child. And the said women report that on the evening when the said mother handed over the boy to this Poitou, he brought him [the boy] to the inn belonging to them, the witnesses, saying to the Lord's other servants that the boy was his page; and they [the servants] said the boy would not be his [for long], and that the said Lord would keep [the boy] for himself. And that morning, when the said Lord was taking his leave outside the said inn, the women heard the boy's mother praising the boy to the said Lord, in Poitou's presence and the boy's; upon which the said Lord said to Poitou that the child had been well chosen; to which Poitou replied that there had been none but the boy to choose, and the said Lord answered that he [Poitou] had not made a mistake because the boy was as lovely as an

View toward Machecoul.

angel. A little later, the boy went off riding the said horse with the said Poitou and the companions of the said Lord. And the said Colin declares that two or three months later, at Nantes, he saw another [boy] riding the horse, which surprised him. And the witnesses named above assert that, since then they have not seen the said child nor heard of his whereabouts, except that, when they have asked the said Lord's servants about [the boy], some replied that he was at Tiffauges, while others said that he was dead; that in crossing one of the bridges at Nantes, the wind had blown him into the river.[13]

It is an artless story fit for breaking hearts. It is all "Once upon a time, there was a poor mother . . ." mixed with shrewd peasant details of greed: the mother's greed for a hundred *sous* with which to buy a dress; Poitou's greed in giving her less than he promised; the greed of the great Lord Gilles de Rais eyeing the boy who was "lovely as an angel." And the pride of the child riding the horse for which the lord had paid sixty *sous*. And off they went toward Machecoul—where, it was said, "They eat children there." [14]

Then comes that chilling encounter with the horse in Nantes, where the animal is seen being ridden by another boy, who was, no doubt, as beautiful and as angelic as Robin. Robin, who was . . . where . . . ? Tiffauges? Or, was he dead, as had also been asserted? Could a boy really be caught up by a wind and thrown into the river?

If Gilles's victims were not given to him or sold by their parents to be pages, he could get them from an endless source closer to hand. There were always beggar children who came daily to cluster before the gates of his castles for the alms he dispensed with so liberal a hand. Like the ragamuffins who went off together from Coueron to Machecoul: One was the son of the departed Jean Bernard; the other, a ten-year-old, was the son of Jean Meugner. They left home "because of the charity that was given [at Machecoul] according to custom, and with the intention of getting alms." [15] Only the young Meugner returned from that journey. The last that was seen of the ten-year-old Bernard was when he went off to seek a lodging for them both. Meugner waited three hours for his friend—who was never seen again. Nor was the eight-year-old Brice boy, an orphan, "very handsome and named Jamet," who was the son of a poor man; he also went begging never to return.[16]

In the depositions made by parents or by friends of lost children, the phrase "and was not seen again" echoes like a mournful chord. And the tales of loss take on a formulaic pattern: The child is reported missing; he is wept for; later, someone remembers that there was one or another of Gilles's servants in the vicinity. According to local rumor, for one child lost in Machecoul, there were seven lost in Tiffauges.[17] Sometimes four are reported missing at once. One mother, a certain Ysabeau, wept for the loss of two of her children. One boy, Bernard le Camus, sent down by his uncle from Brest to study French, encountered Gilles's men, Poitou and Eustache Blanchet, who engaged the fifteen-year-old in conversation. That evening "toward ten o'clock, the boy left the house, without taking his coat nor his hood . . . [but] saying to the houseman that he was leaving, and [after asking him] to put away the cups, he left the house. Since which time, they had not seen the lad nor heard what became of him." [18]

Always, the deponents speak of grief, though it is notable that one of the stranger aspects of Gilles de Rais research is the frequency with which one comes upon scholars who are willing to believe that medieval parents were sanguine about losing their children. Thomas Wilson, for instance, writes:

> Did the parents recover from it? Yes, they became accustomed to it. Human nature can become accustomed to anything. Their fate seemed better, not because it was better, but because, not getting worse, they got used to it and were able to stand it better. . . . They felt themselves incapable and incompetent to war against this mysterious supernatural force; hence they resigned themselves to the affliction, considering it to have been sent from almighty God as a punishment for their sins.[19]

If the depositions show anything, it is that the parents were grief-stricken *and* helpless. Here and there a deposition gives us glaring evidence that fear, not stoicism, kept parents silent: "[Macé] Sorin and his wife, having listed the disappearance of five children, then say that the son of Georget le Barbier, their near neighbor, was lost since Easter without anyone knowing his whereabouts. They have heard of these losses, and still others, and heard great lamentations *but one dared not talk too much* about them" (italics added).[20]

André Barbe, a shoemaker at Machecoul, giving testimony

about the disappearance of the Jeudon child, says that "he had heard complaints also of the loss of other children in the vicinity of Machecoul. He adds that one dared not talk of it to the people [belonging to] the chapel of Gilles de Rais or other of his people. Those who complained risked being imprisoned or mistreated if their complaints were reported." [21]

"No one," writes the Abbé Bossard, "dared voice a complaint. There was wailing—but in secret; it was talked of, but in hushed voices; there was accusation, but with wary looks. Who dared raise a voice against a great lord? The master was not kind to his enemies." [22]

No. There was plenty of grief, but it was the grief of the poor and the helpless, which is why, in the depositions, it takes on such a numb tone. Especially when the depositions describe the basic hunger and innocent hope that sent the children to Gilles's gates or into the arms of his procurers. There is the story of the beggar boy who stood in one of two lines of begging children before the castle gate at Machecoul. When it came his turn to receive alms, he was invited into the château on the kindly premise that the child had failed to get any meat in the first distribution of food. And he was not seen again. And there is the story of the thirteen-year-old who had been taken into the castle to be made a page. He came home one day, glowing with news for his mother: He had been allowed to clean the great Sire de Rais's room and had been rewarded with one of the round loaves of bread that had been baked for the baron, which—see—the boy had brought home. Then the lad went back, "and that was the last they had seen of their son." [23]

Sometimes, the children were turning the spit in one of the fine houses where Gilles and his entourage stopped. Sometimes, they disappeared from the meadows where they were tending the cattle. One was last seen playing at pelota; another, an eight-year-old, had been left at home to tend a year-old sister while his parents went off to dig a field. When they came back, there was only the fretful baby. Another was last seen picking apples; others, on the way to the fair, throwing balls to each other.

"Some children," writes Roland Villeneuve, "were snatched up off the streets; on their way to church; on their way to buy bread; or carrying a message to the château. They had the ill luck to please the Baron." [24]

The Estonians, when they wished to raise a wind, strike a knife into a house beam in the direction from which they desire the wind to blow, while at the same time they croon an old-time canzonet. The underlying idea is that the gentle wind will not let an innocent thing, even a beam, suffer without coming swiftly and breathing softly thereon to assuage the pain.

—*Malleus Maleficarum*

There is a perenially glossy literary notion that links literary greatness with the presence in the writer of some great character flaw. Norman Mailer, for instance, working himself up to praise Henry Miller, observes that it is "as if Henry Miller contains the unadvertised mystery of how much of a monster a great writer must be." [25] In fact, that mystery has been frequently flaunted, especially since the triumph of the romantic movement when the dark poetic figures whom Byron and Goethe dramatized (Manfred, Cain, and Faust) stood for the appalling cost to the poets of their art. It has been reiterated in our century by Thomas Mann, André Gide, and Jean Genêt.

With Gilles, the matter is reversed. Not the artist as monster, but the monster as artist. It is an idea one would like to deplore, but it obtrudes itself tenaciously into the biographies, and it raises a difficult question. Can one, outside the pages of Kafka's "The Penal Colony," be an artist of torture? And if so, what does the word *artist* mean?

It means first that the victims were chosen for their beauty, "because," writes M. Bataille, "aesthetics, however depraved, still governed the matter, and there was no pleasure in killing ugly children." [26] Further, it means that Gilles took great care to *arrange* the pain and death of his victims. The difference between the ordinary carnage that sends a murderer to prison or to the gallows and the acts of Gilles de Rais is that his were not committed under the impetus of rage or jealousy or revenge or gain. There was nothing spontaneous about Gilles's murders. They were invariably performances for which a stage had to be set; to which, however tiny, an audience was invited. And the theater piece had to be reconceived again and again. Always, the performances were stylized, unified, choreographed, designed.

The dramas had their order. However a child was enticed or stolen by the accomplices, once he arrived at the castle he was greeted warmly. Somebody saw to it that the boy (usually the victims were boys, though, rarely, girls were taken) was cleaned, bathed, reclothed. His hair was combed, his nose wiped. Then, no doubt feeling he was in an amazing and beautiful dream, he followed an accomplice toward the great lord's bedroom. One cannot write the dialogue for such scenes with any certainty, but one can make reasonable guesses at what transpired.

It was a gentle game at first. There was a friendly interplay between Gilles and the child as Gilles set the boy at ease. The idea for Gilles was to take time. He loved the children's faces; their slim forms; their exquisite voices. Like any practiced lecher, he meant to delay his gratification. Meanwhile, there was pleasure to be had in watching the child grow used to his good fortune. To see him swagger about as he accepted first sweetmeats, then caresses, as if he deserved them both. To see the look in his face changing from self-confidence to the impudence, the innocent arrogance of a favored child.

Then, some chitchat. "You're a very pretty lad. Has anyone ever told you that? Very pretty. Come here . . . let me look at you . . . there . . . that's it . . . now turn around." From small talk to caresses that, at first, appeared to be directed at the boy but that became increasingly exciting to Gilles. Then pinches, graspings, heat—Gilles turned avid. The child was violated. Then, the rape accomplished, "the said Gilles de Rais suspended [the child] with his own hands, or [had him] suspended by others, he lowered, or caused to be lowered, cajoling [the child], pretending he had been only playing with [him], assuring [him] that he intended no harm, nor to wound [him]; that, on the contrary, he had only meant to play with [him] . . . and in such fashion he kept [him] from crying." [27]

It was a process of deceiving and undeceiving; a slow engulfing of a child in mortal pain. What excited Gilles's ardor was the movement from surprise to unbelief, from unbelief to terror, from terror to reassurance in which the child was, as it were, cajoled into innocence once again, and the way that the boy, despite his memories and the marks on his body, allowed himself to believe that what had happened had not really taken place. Because, how could it have? How could a lord dressed in ermines and silks, who spoke so well, and from whom there wafted the fragrance of such fine perfumes, do . . . what had been done?

The game was to torment more than the flesh; to make a parody of love, in which every caress, every enthusiasm that usually leads to pleasure was taken to its logical absurdity in the flesh. Lovemaking—it is a truism—means getting close to the loved one; getting to *know* the beloved. Gilles, dallying with his children, achieved undreamed-of knowledges, intimacies, ecstasies of union in which he most literally, and mortally, entered into them. Gilles, at his trial, would confess that

> he took, or caused to be taken, for his ardor and sensual delight a great number of children—he did not know how many for sure—with whom he committed the vice and the sin of sodomy; and he says and confesses that he emitted [his] seed in the most culpable fashion on the bellies of the said children as much before as after their deaths; to which children sometimes he, or sometimes his accomplices (specifically, the above mentioned Gilles de Sillé, Messire Roger de Bricqueville, knight, Henriet [Griart] and Poitou, Rossignol and Little Robin), inflicted various kinds and manners of torment.[28]

The sexuality, for Gilles, tended to be the preliminary act. Griart would testify that "the said Gilles, the accused, exercised his lust once or twice on the children. That done, the said Gilles killed them sometimes with his own hand or had them killed." [29] The trial transcript records the variety of ways the children were killed. Again, it is Griart who is cited: ". . . sometimes they were decapitated, and dismembered; sometimes he [Gilles] cut their throats, leaving the head attached to the body; sometimes he broke their necks with a stick; sometimes he cut a vein in their throats or some other part of their necks, so that the blood of the said children flowed." [30]

And, as the children were dying, Gilles, the artist of terror, the skilled Latinist who read Saint Augustine; Gilles, the devoted companion of Jeanne d'Arc, squatted on the bellies of the children, studying their languishing faces, breathing in their dying sighs. "And [Griart] deposed having heard the said Gilles, the accused, say that he took more pleasure in the murder of the said children, and in seeing their heads and their members removed, and watching them languish, and seeing their blood flow than [he did] in knowing them carnally." [31] Sometimes, he yielded to the temptation to do both: "While they were languishing, he committed with them the vice of sodomy in the manner above said." [32]

One would think that the deaths of the children would have ended the theater piece Gilles was playing out, but Gilles's appetite for sensation was not yet appeased. Sometimes he opened the body cavities so he could view the interior organs; sometimes he coupled with the cadavers while they were still warm. "Often he loved to gaze at the severed heads and showed them to him, the witness [Griart] and to Etienne Corrillaut, otherwise called Poitou, asking them which of the said heads he showed them was the most beautiful, the head just then severed, or the one decapitated on the previous day. And he often kissed the head which pleased him the most, and delighted in it." [33]

There is a cruel housekeeping that is required to maintain Gilles in his passion. There were knives and daggers, poniards, sticks, "other crushing implements." [34] There was a sword called a *bracquemart* that was especially useful for decapitations; there were hooks, pulleys, and ropes. When, finally, Gilles was exhausted, the accomplices Poitou and Griart cleaned up.

They sweated and panted. They laid the fire with enormous logs for which a great deal of kindling needed to be gathered; and the flames once taking, they sat with their master and watched as the bits and pieces of what had been children and now was meat yielded to the flames until another metamorphosis was achieved and all that was hopeful and beautiful, all that we understand as lovely in youth was divided between the ashes that were yielded to the earth and the smoke rising to an indifferent sky.

CHAPTER   TEN

THE ACCOMPLICES

I saw the star supposed, but fog o' the fen,
Gilded star-fashion by a glint from hell;
Having been heaved up, haled on its gross way,
By hands unguessed before, invisible help
From a dark brotherhood, and specially
Two obscure goblin creatures, fox-faced this,
Cat-clawed the other, called his next of kin.

—Robert Browning, *The Ring and the Book*

Gilles de Rais has been our central mystery: "This warrior who had been overwhelmed with honors, this young Marshal who paraded in gleaming armor astride his brilliantly caparisoned horse, this generous patron, acclaimed by the multitudes to whom he offered the most romantic and edifying spectacles and the most luxurious banquets, was like the whited sepulchres mentioned in the New Testament. His was the cruelest and most corrupt soul of all. He was surrounded by lewdness, cruelty and decay." [1] And we have circled round and round Gilles in an effort, not so much to penetrate his mystery, but to discern it more clearly. Then, just as Gilles seems to be emerging from the mist of detail and speculation that surrounds him, another mystery, in its own way more unsettling, obtrudes itself: Gilles had accomplices. As many as sixteen!—two of them priests, two of them women.

Gilles, who tormented children to their death, had help. This fact shakes every effort to make a single, systematic explanation of Gilles's behavior, because, just as we have worked out the configuration of details that might help us to understand Gilles, we find ourselves dithering in the presence of a dozen or more people whose life stories are beyond recovery. People like the priest André Buchet who helped Gilles find necromancers and who, on one occasion, brought him a pretty little nine-year-old boy from Vannes. Gilles destroyed the child in his usual fashion, and the holy man was rewarded by a gift of a horse worth sixty gold *reals*.[2]

What shall we do about people like Buchet, who was one of the less bloody of Gilles's accomplices? About Henriet Griart, and Etienne Coriaullt, also known as Poitou? What about the horrid woman La Meffraye? What about Gilles's cousins, Roger de Briqueville and Gilles de Sillé? Is it required of us to establish that they lost parents or were raised by cruel grandparents? Or were shattered by their contact with someone whose innocence they needed nightly to destroy? If Gilles was sane, shall we say that his accomplices were insane?

Or is it really true, as I believe, that there is no need for so much strenuous searching to explain Gilles's accomplices, since what they did was to obey that instinct for collusion, that hunger to be an accomplice that lies buried not far below the surface of everyone's consciousness. There is a sensuous yielding up of the self to another's will; a joyful abandonment of one's identity that people in mobs, in armies, or in fascist societies experience. The self is always swarming with contending responsibilities, guilts, hungers. One of the most powerful of the many temptations to abandon consciousness is to yield it up to someone else's will. It hardly matters what that other will requires. Murder or madness, salvation or damnation are of equal weight. What matters is to be an assistant *something*. An assistant saint or an assistant torturer. In either case, obedient, relieved of personal responsibility: "He told me to do it, so I did." The deed is almost beside the point. What counts is permission and opportunity, and the act is shamelessly embraced.

It is a horrid enough notion, but not an especially unique one. One can see a powerful expression of it in Dierik Bouts's fifteenth-century painting "The Martyrdom of Saint Erasmus," in which we are shown Saint Erasmus trussed to a torture machine on which he lies while a string attached to his entrails unwinds them according to the motions of a crank being turned by one of his torturers. The faces of the torturers are fascinating. They show neither lust nor revulsion. Nothing but a calm impassivity. They are doing their

jobs, waiting, perhaps, for their midafternoon rest; or thinking
what they will be having for dinner when they get home. They are
torturers—that is to say, they have been employed to do what they
are doing to Saint Erasmus, but, so far as one can tell, they have no
animus toward him, and no particular affection for their task either. The point for them is not that Saint Erasmus is achieving his
martyrdom. Looking into their calm, dutiful faces, one can find no
excuse to ask grave questions like, "Why are they doing it?" The
answer is too evident: They were told by a sufficient authority to
do it, so they do.

The accomplices, Roland Villeneuve tells us, "were corrupt persons, avid courtiers, rapacious accomplices with dissolute morals
drawn to the eagle of Laval [Gilles] by the bait of easy gain or the
satisfaction of forbidden delights. . . . They . . . came from various
walks in life: nobility, clergy, low folk from the countryside from
which would be recruited two sinister sorcerers. None of them
shrank before crime—except perhaps Blanchet—if it would help to
satisfy the passions of their master." [3] But that is a judgment after
the fact. What matters is that before they were corrupt, they were
well-bred courtiers, priests, scholars and knights who, when Gilles
asked their help to commit shattering crimes, found themselves
able to give him what he needed.

Gilles, as we now have him, is a creature of the documents, bits
of paper passing from hand to hand. But when he was actually
readying himself for murder, he must have felt how supremely
lonely the crime would make him. I am haunted by his problem:
how to find someone with whom to share his growing passion. I
think, Did he review his friends in mind, wondering in which of
them to confide? I try to imagine, for instance, the conversation in
which he approached Gilles de Sillé:

GILLES: [*to de Sillé*] Do you want to hear a secret?
DE SILLÉ: [*perhaps drunk*] Why not?
GILLES: [*caressing de Sillé*] Promise not to tell?
DE SILLÉ: It's important, is it?
GILLES: Very important. You must promise.
DE SILLÉ: [*petulantly*] All right then. I promise.
GILLES: You have to swear.
DE SILLÉ: What the hell.

GILLES: Swear.

DE SILLÉ: All right then. I swear.

GILLES: By Christ's body.

DE SILLÉ: By Christ's body.

GILLES: I swear never to reveal . . .

DE SILLÉ: [*curious and eager*] I swear never to reveal . . .

And so on, until Gilles, looking deeply into de Sillé's eyes says something.

De Sillé, uncertain that he has heard his cousin rightly, says, "What?"

Gilles bends forward and whispers into de Sillé's ear. There is a long thick silence during which de Sillé slowly understands that Gilles is not joking. He risks a nervous smile and says, "But what do you want me to do?"

Again, Gilles whispers. De Sillé breathes quickly; his hands tremble; his eyes glitter as he catches a glimpse of the abyss into which Gilles has plunged. Then, his eyes glowing with anticipation, de Sillé turns to Gilles and says, "Yes . . . yes . . . I will." [4]

The question is, how can anyone risk such a conversation! What sickly joke would Gilles have to claim he was making if the accomplice—as we imagine *we* would—throws his hands up in terror and runs from the room. To call . . . whom?

The mock dialogue with de Sillé does not dispose of the problem by any means, because de Sillé was one of Gilles's bed partners, readier presumably to be sympathetic to his lover's confession. What of the other accomplices with whom Gilles had no sexual relationships? What about Buchet, the priest? What about the woman, La Meffraye?

Michel Bataille speaks of the accomplices with horror. They were, he says, "more scandalous than he. . . . This monster had the excuse of his monstrosity. Those who, avid for financial gain, kept him provided with prey . . . had less excuse. To behave like a monster because one is one, is horrifying enough, but isn't it baser still when one has all of one's reason, to share the view of a monster only to get money out of him? To push him, to encourage him, to excite him, to lead him farther and farther into monstrosity for the sake of his fee, that is baseness itself." [5]

M. Bataille's horror, while it is moving, obscures the point by inventing a Gilles who was merely a monster who was aided by men who were not. As if Gilles were a pure atavism and his accomplices were immoral men. As if Gilles were frightful and yet true to his nature, while the accomplices were cold moneygrubbers. Let me urge that there is no moral abyss between Gilles and his accomplices; that the word *monster* gets in the way of our understanding of the real issue, which is the human readiness, given permission and opportunity, to do the most appalling things. The only difference between Gilles and the accomplices is that he went at the torture-murder of children *primarily* for his pleasure, while the motivation for the behavior of the accomplices varied from individual to individual. For Etienne Coriaullt and Henriet Griart, obedience to Gilles seems to have been the chief factor. Coriaullt (Poitou), in the ingenuous language of his deposition, says that "following the orders of the said Gilles, and hoping to merit his gratitude, he brought Gilles a young and handsome boy from La Roche-Bernard to . . . Machecoul and delivered him to Gilles who committed on him his abominable crimes of lust; to the point at which the boy had his throat cut, like the others above mentioned." [6]

There is a certain pathos that hangs over the story of Poitou, who was brought into Gilles's household as a boy of twelve as an intended victim. He was saved at the last minute when Gilles de Sillé, Gilles's cousin, who had been an excited witness to Gilles's proceedings, stepped between Poitou and Gilles's dagger. De Sillé pointed out that Poitou was an exceptionally good-looking boy who would make a handsome page. It would be a pity to waste the child on a single night's pleasure. It was an argument that could have been made for any of Gilles's victims, but Gilles, for whatever reason, put his dagger away and Poitou lived to become one of Gilles's most devoted followers, his bed companion, his servant, and an energetic purveyor of victims, some of whom he slew with his own hand.[7]

The young Henriet Griart is not easy to distinguish beneath the surface of the equable prose of the trial transcript. Unlike Poitou, he had not stared death in the face in Gilles's bedroom. He was, rather, only a simple servant for whom personal devotion to Gilles transcended any other kind of consideration. If any of Gilles's helpers resembled the gratefully employed torturer of Dierik Bouts's

"The Martyrdom of Saint Erasmus," it is surely Griart. This stolid young man served as Gilles's chamberlain for five or six years—until Gilles's arrest—and was a ready purveyor of children for his master. At need, he served as executioner of those children whom Gilles was not interested in killing. He was, like Poitou, pressed into service as an assistant torturer from time to time. He was, one guesses, a slow thinker, but thickheaded as he was, it finally came to him that the life he had been leading in Gilles's employ was not good. He had been loyal, lustful, or murderous on command, but after his arrest and as he was being led to prison, he thought briefly of committing suicide. But, illuminated by his experience as an assistant to Gilles in his master's invocation of demons, Henriet Griart concluded that the devil was enticing him to suicide and he abandoned the idea. If any of the accomplices was a man of *moyenne sensibilité,* it was Griart. He was not passionate nor especially wicked; he was a drinker without being a drunkard; he was not especially erotically driven though he participated in Gilles's debauches. Like Poitou, he followed Gilles to the gallows, thinking, perhaps, as he had heard Gilles say of himself, that he had been born under an unlucky constellation.[8]

Gilles's cousins, Gilles de Sillé and Roger de Briqueville, though they did not finally share Gilles's fate on the gallows, shared his secrets, his bedroom pleasures, and, on various occasions, his crimes. These two have been described as cowards, flatterers, scoundrels, and parasites. But it is worth remembering that they were both young knights, trained in the courtesies of medieval war and peace.

There is little to know about de Sillé beyond his presence at Gilles's orgies and that on occasion he was, like Blanchet, sent hunting for necromancers whom Gilles might consult; and that, dressed in a disguise, he moved about the countryside inveigling children for his master. M. Bataille, in his *Gilles de Rais,* has a chilling, but by no means verifiable, scene in which Gilles de Sillé is shown galloping about the countryside in search of victims. He rides into a village, reins in his horse, then sits in his saddle, dangling a pouchful of coins. The villagers stare sullenly. "Nobody moves. Sillé swings the money pouch more and more slowly . . . . Finally, a heavy peasant woman hitches up her skirts with both hands and moves off with great strides toward her farm." Minutes later, she returns, bringing with her a boy whom she has quickly and roughly cleaned up. "The child carries a stick and a knotted, blue-and-white kerchief [containing his things] . . . Sillé lets the money pouch swing one more time, then lets it drop. It falls into the mud at the feet of the woman, splattering her apron. The peasant woman bends and, without even wiping it, thrusts it into a pocket under her skirts. Then, with no word of goodbye to the urchin, she turns on her heels and is gone. The transaction has been brought to its close, without a word being spoken . . . The peasants regretfully disperse . . . Innocent blood will flow anew tonight in the high chamber of Messire de Rais' tower." [9]

Roger de Briqueville is more complicated than de Sillé. De Briqueville's father, a nobleman of Normandy, fled that province when the English invaded it and took refuge in Brittany, where he and his family were reduced to poverty. The de Briquevilles were kin to Jean de Craon, and the old warlord took Roger into his own household, raising him side by side with Gilles. The role of poor relation, then, is the one that de Briqueville plays very early, but it is clear that he played it very much to his own advantage. Over the years, partly because of his sexual intimacy with Gilles, and partly because Gilles had no interest himself in managing his estates, de Briqueville acquired awesome power over Gilles's land and money, managing "the castles, woods, ponds, fields, meadows, vineyards, jewels, furniture." [10] De Briqueville, like nearly a dozen other accomplices, scoured the countryside for lovely children. Years later, he would deny that he knew what Gilles would do with them, but, writes the Abbé Bossard, "Roger de Bricqueville was ignorant of nothing, absolutely nothing—either of Gilles' pleasures or his crimes. He took part in them, and one of the heaviest parts." [11]

The women who served Gilles—probably because they *were* women—seem not to have been admitted to his innermost counsels. There is no evidence, for instance, that any of them ever witnessed a murder. One of the women, of whom almost nothing is known, was Etiennette Blanchu. The other is the notorious Perrine Martin, who was nicknamed La Meffraye.[12] More than any of the other accomplices, La Meffraye has come down to us as a nearly mythical figure, the evil crone of a fairy tale. Between fifty and sixty years old, she dressed habitually in gray, but wore a black hood and a black veil over her ruddy features. Her technique was to "approach little children looking after the cattle [in the fields] or who were begging. She flattered and caressed them. She enticed them to the castle of the Sire de Rais, and they were not seen again." [13] Her favorite terrain was the region around Nantes. Her skill at attracting the young was great enough to make the Abbé Bossard marvel: "it was not only children seven or eight years old whom her words enchanted, but also nubile women, youths and young men." [14]

They were—the accomplices—a bad lot, but none of them was quite as bad as Gilles. "Compounded of mire and blood, these [people] toyed with life and chastity and death. . . . But the hero himself, the conductor of this dreary retinue, what was he, since he surpassed them all? The vilest, the cruelest, the most atrocious of men." [15] The Abbé Bossard, whose natural aptitude is for exaggeration, is, in this summary of Gilles's character as it relates to the children, understating the case.

CHAPTER ELEVEN

THE FACE OF
THE BASILISK

Be quiet or I shall show you my original shape.

—A Tamil proverb

There is a brooding description of Antonin Artaud's face written by the American editor of Artaud's *The Theater and Its Double*. Saillet writes, "His face and his poetry were instinct with that disturbing gentleness of soul torn between heaven and hell, a soul that can find the meaning fulfilment of its perfection only in its own disaster." [1] One is not sure that the description is moving because of what it says of Artaud, or because it has an uncanny resemblance to an occasionally glimpsed portrait of the rest of us.

It is a pity that there is no portrait of Gilles de Rais that might give us such an opportunity, as Saillet has with Artaud, to discover how Gilles's features may have reflected his crimes. Gilles, then, would have to look like the calculating devotee of pain that he became. We ought to see in Gilles's eyes the flaming power of an unappeasable sexual appetite, and in his features, as in Oscar Wilde's Dorian Gray, the full cost of the debauches that made Gilles's name a byword for cruelty. If nothing else, his face ought to be marked with the struggle in him of that coincidence of opposites in which God and the devil sanctify and taint each other.

There is no authentic portrait of Gilles and, even if there were, there could be nothing in it to make us guess at his crimes. Anyone who has had the slightest experience with criminals—even criminals whose crimes are horrifying—knows that there is nothing in their features from which we can guess their acts. Horrid men and

women leave their marks on their victims. Their own faces, all film
and physiognomic lore to the contrary, give no clues of what they
have done, or can do.

What did he look like, our murderer with the glitter of a fool of
God in his eyes? Bernard Shaw, who also did not know, takes the
easy way out and describes him in his play *Saint Joan* as a young
man who lacks natural joyousness and who wears his beard dyed
blue, as if the description in the folktale of Bluebeard were sufficient authority for that beard. There *have* been portraits made of
Gilles. Two were made just after Gilles's death and have become
attached to the trial transcript that is to be found in the Bibliothèque Nationale:

> One [of them] (Manuscript Latin, N° 17 663) shows him standing,
> without a beard, in Renaissance clothing *in foro ecclesiastico* before the
> Bishop of Nantes, the prosecutor, and a court clerk. The other (Man-
> uscript Français N° 23 836) . . . shows [Gilles's] execution and carries
> the rubric "Criminal trial of Messire Gilles de Bretagne [*sic*] Baron de
> Raiz, Marshal of France, who was executed on the 26th of October,
> 1440." [2]

There is, too, a nineteenth-century portrait made by the painter
Ferron, which, says Roland Villeneuve, "is a pure fantasy." [3]
There have been pictures in various biographies of Gilles (includ-
ing this one), but they are all fanciful works. As is, for instance, this
description of Gilles by Paul Lacroix, the so-called Bibliophile
Jacob, a notoriously unreliable popularizer of history:

> The Lord de Rais' [features] did not betray, at first glance, that vicious
> nature, and those atrocious ways that have been attributed to him; he
> had, on the contrary, gentle, coaxing features which were not
> shadowed by his small moustaches or his trimmed, dovetail beard.
> That curious beard that resembled no other [in the world] was black—
> though his hair was blond—but, under the influence of various lights,
> took on a nearly blue gleam . . . which is what gave to the Sire de Rays
> [*sic*] the surname of Bluebeard.[4]

There have been still more fanciful explanations for the name
Bluebeard. Albert Jean suggests that it comes from Gilles's horse,
because the villagers who learned to fear Gilles spoke of his *"barbe
bleue,"* his blue horse, from the way Gilles's jet black horse struck
blue lights as Gilles rode by.[5]

Imaginary portrait of Gilles by Ferron.

Vizitelly has given us a portrait of Gilles that is a candid composite of details derived from various historians. Gilles, in his telling, was "a well-built man, of majestic stature, with an engaging countenance; in his youth . . . handsome and graceful . . . Gilles, so tradition asserts, had fair hair with dark eyebrows and a black moustache and beard; his sunken eyes were blue . . . his lips thin, and his cheeks pale." [6] It is a fair enough speculation, to which a couple of commonsensical notions may be added. His prowess in battle suggests that he was physically strong. What we know of his bouts of heavy eating and drinking as well as of the emotionally exacerbating nature of his sexuality makes one suspect that Gilles's youthful fitness was considerably eroded as he plunged deeper into his debaucheries. Beyond these guesses, the only authentic portrait of Gilles we will ever have is the one his misdeeds will fashion in our minds.

I'm dirty, Milena, infinitely dirty—which is why I make such a fuss about purity. No people sing with such pure voices as those who live in deepest hell.

—Franz Kafka, in *Letters to Milena*

Those authors who have made novels of Gilles's life are able to provide us with clearer, though by no means truer, answers to the question "Why did he do it?" than the documents on which historians must rely. Raffaele Ciampini's *Barba-Blu* shows us the young Gilles slowly being taught lessons in sadism and masochism, first as a bloodthirsty hunter in the field who pits himself against a buck and kills it in single combat when no fighting man of his grandfather's men-at-arms will take up the challenge; then as a groping youth whom women corrupt. We are shown Gilles, in his eleventh year, following his old nurse into one of the castle rooms, where the woman, stretching herself out on a sofa, opens her low-cut dress and whispering urgently to him, "whether it was with the freedom of a nurse, or with malign intent, bares her still attractive breasts

to the open air." [7] Later, Gilles has a more complete sexual experience with Isabella, a laundress in the de Craon household. Gilles,
we are told, is embraced by Isabella, from whom his inexpert caresses evoke short, anguished moans. She drags him to a divan
where Gilles longs to bury his fingers in her hair, to shake her, and
to bite her neck covered with its blonde down." [8] Years later, after
his purifying experience as Jeanne d'Arc's battle companion, Gilles
learns to detest Isabella; just the same, desire sends him back to her
nightly, though in her embraces he "feels himself drowning in a sea
of lukewarm milk fragrant with the perfume of roses. Her embraces teach him that woman's hands are "instruments liberating
[in him] delirious music. Love was a suave and terrible [thing] and
did nothing to assuage boredom." [9]

One young woman, Ciampini tells us, is not enough for Gilles.
Soon there are others: Anna, "who abandons herself without a
word, merely gritting her teeth in her frenzy. . . . Margherita, small
and blonde who emits submissive cries. And there was Maria . . .
and Laura . . . and . . . Lisetta, the eleven-year-old whose mother
offered her for money, and Gilles bought her out of irritability and
with a mixture of curiosity and horror. There were all of the
women of the district, young and old; and the old taught him
terrible things, rousing in him the instinct for cruelty." [10]

Little by little, Gilles learns more and more about sexual cruelty
until one night, "Maria—the one who emits breathless sighs, and
who looks as if she is suspended between life and death, ready at
any moment to die," says to Gilles, " 'Will you do what I ask you
to?' "

"Speak," says Gilles.

"But I can tell you won't do it."

"Speak."

"Do you know how to hurt me?"

"Certainly," replies Gilles. "While I kiss you."

"No," the woman says. "Not that way."

"Biting you?"

"No. It isn't that either." [11]

To end the guessing game, Maria takes a small knife from her
pocket, and though the idea is at first repugnant to Gilles, she
teaches him to wound her with it as she cries, "Cut me. Cut me."
When he plunges the tiny weapon into her thighs, she becomes
delirious and urges him on, crying, "Harder. Harder."

It is Maria who teaches Gilles his true vocation. Once inducted into the mysteries of blood, he becomes its passionate devotee. "After that, Gilles saw no other [woman] than Maria." [12]

In Edward Lucie-Smith's novel *The Dark Pageant,* we are given several scenes in which the psychodynamics of Gilles's sexual murders are prepared for. Lucie-Smith provides Gilles with a noble foster brother, Raoul de Saumur, who is the narrative voice of *The Dark Pageant.* From him, we learn that the boy Gilles had "a rough, impatient cruelty with animals. He would stick spurs into a horse, then harshly rein it back, just to feel the beast writhe between his legs." [13] Later, there is an episode in which Gilles is hauled before his grandfather who inquires, " 'Did you do this?' [de Craon] nodded to one of the soldiers, who moved forward and teased open the bundle with the toe of his boot. What I [Raoul de Saumur] saw within made me gag back the bile in my throat. Two newborn pups lay inside it. One had its belly ripped open. The guts had been pulled out of the slit, and trailed glistening from the body. The blind eyes of the other had been roughly put out, perhaps with a pointed stick." [14]

The puppies episode lets us know that Gilles was early a sadist, but Lucie-Smith also gives us a scene in which we see that Gilles had a masochistic streak in him as well. As Lucie-Smith tells it, Gilles is the sexual aggressor as he pursues Pierre Cardinal, the captain of Jean de Craon's guard. Cardinal is described as so attractive to women that "when he washed himself, on summer mornings, in the castle courtyard, they would cluster in the doorway to see him do it." Nevertheless, one hot summer morning, Raoul de Saumur comes upon Gilles and Cardinal,

> and a strange sight it was. Gilles was trussed face downward on a wooden bench like those we sat on in the dining-hall, with his hose lowered and trailing round his calves. Across his buttocks and thighs were a number of fresh weals. Standing over him was the captain of the guard, stripped to the waist and sweating profusely, with a familiar leather strap in his hands.
>
> "Again!" said Gilles. With a kind of groan, Pierre swung the belt and brought it crashing down with the full force of his arm.

The beating culminates when Cardinal abandons his strap and throws "himself on top of the prostrate figure before him."

"Too soon, Pierre, too soon," was what I thought I heard Gilles murmur as he accepted the assault.[15]

Raoul de Saumur, in *The Dark Pageant,* describes the adolescent Gilles as reticent in matters of sex. "[Gilles] and I continued to share a bed. . . . During the summer months just before my sexual initiation, he and I had begun a series of fumbling experiments with one another's bodies. These took place . . . in the small hours when one or other of us would stir in semi-wakefulness with an adolescent erection. What had taken place was never acknowledged by either of us in the morning." [16]

Lucie-Smith's speculations are as reasonable as they are clinical. Adolescent homosexual groping is no doubt the initiation experience for many homosexuals. And the sorts of masochistic and sadistic experiences described by Ciampini and Lucie-Smith are also possible. But, such episodes, even if we knew that they had happened to Gilles, would by no means be predictive signs that he would grow up to become a torturer-murderer.

Clinicians have tried for years to identify such predictive signs of violent behavior, and though various characteristics have indeed shown up on lists made by psychiatrists, it is dangerous to draw conclusions based on them. Some of the so-called predictive signs, for instance, include enuresis in childhood, fire-setting, and cruelty to animals. This triad "is well known and widely utilized by clinicians in the prediction of dangerousness," writes Bernard Diamond in "The Psychiatric Prediction of Dangerousness." [17] Still other clinicians have identified such predictive signs as childhood injury and violent adult behavior; temper tantrums, intense and recurrent fantasies of revenge, loneliness, withdrawal, isolation, and even "speech and spelling errors." To this list may be added "a childhood history of maternal deprivation, poor father identification, or both . . . and brutalization by one or both parents." [18]

Dr. Diamond says that

this corresponds to my own clinical experience with both mentally ill and supposedly healthy persons who have committed or attempted murder. I would even say that the conclusion of the clinicians cited by Goldstein represents the sum total of our present scientific knowledge concerning predictive factors of murderous violence.[19]

But, having said this much, Dr. Diamond warns us that it would

be dangerous to conclude—even from such clinical experience—
that one can *predict* the future behavior of people who have shown
such behaviors in their past.

> Yet I have repeatedly found some, and sometimes all, of these predic-
> tive factors in individuals who have never committed even the slightest
> harmful act, let alone assault or murder. And I have examined offend-
> ers who have committed the most extraordinarily brutal acts of great
> violence and lethality who possessed none of these factors.
>
> I know of no reports in the scientific literature which are supported
> by valid clinical experience and statistical evidence that describe psy-
> chological or physical signs or symptoms which can be reliably used to
> discriminate between the potentially dangerous and the harmless
> individual.[20]

Clinically speaking, then, we are left with thoughtful guesses
about what might have made Gilles do it. Morally and spiritually,
we are free to exercise the best intuitions we can muster.

In the course of his trial, in 1440, Gilles would be asked by one of
his judges who it was that induced him to his crimes and taught
him the manner of their doing. Gilles's answer was that everything
he had done was dictated by his own imagination "and without
the counsel of anyone and for [my own] pleasure and fleshly delight and not for any other intention or goal." [21]

Charles Lemire, a nineteenth-century biographer of Gilles, is
pleased to think otherwise. He would put the blame on literature.
We know that Gilles had inherited from his grandfather a small
but priceless number of books: a manuscript of Valerius Maximus;
two copies of Saint Augustine's *The City of God*, one in Latin, the
other in French; and a sumptuous volume of Ovid's *Metamorphoses*
on parchment, bound in purple leather, ornamented with copper
nails, and closed with a silver gilt clasp.[22] In addition to these
treasures (about which we know because Gilles had occasion to
pawn them), there was also a volume of Tacitus and a copy of
Suetonius' *Lives of the Caesars*. It is Lemire's view that Suetonius'
Lives is the culprit volume that taught Gilles his murderous trade,
and Lemire gives us a confident account of what happened. Gilles,
he says, especially treasured the Suetonius, which he turned over to
his official reader (and chamberlain), the university educated
Henriet Griart. Gilles showed Griart

certain passages and invited him to read the text. It was the chronicle of the life and customs of the Roman Caesars. The book was embellished with handsomely painted pictures showing the misconduct of these pagan emperors. There [in the book], one could learn how Tiberius, Caracall[a] and the other Caesars took special delight in the massacre of children.

Listening to [Griart read], Gilles's caressing feline face was transformed. It took on a ferocious aspect and his eyes flamed. He did not fear to assert that he would imitate the said Caesars. That same night, he began to do so, following the lesson and the pictures of the book.[23]

Lemire is a bit mechanical in blaming Suetonius, but many of Gilles's biographers, including some recent twentieth-century writers, are drawn to the notion that Gilles was hurried on to his acts by what he learned in *Lives of the Caesars*. While I have a great respect for the power of the written word, I am a long way from believing that Gilles was led down his particular path to damnation by the reading of a single book. I would wonder, for instance, why Gilles was not saved for virtue, since he possessed not one, but two copies, of Saint Augustine. Did they count for nothing? It will be objected, of course, that the Suetonius does indeed describe the emperors' lubricities and crimes in somewhat sweating detail. But Suetonius' little history book had been around for more than twelve hundred years without, so far as I know, ever having created any other monster.

Be that as it may, in Suetonius, Gilles would have read about the pathetic exploits of Nero, the self-besotted emperor who fancied himself a singer, an actor, and a poet, but who has left us chiefly the record of his misdeeds. His practices were certainly "lustful, extravagant, greedy or cruel." [24] Nero was many times a rapist—of boys or women. According to Suetonius, Nero conceived a sexual passion for his mother with whom "[some say] he did, in fact, commit incest every time they rode in the litter. . . ." [25] Perpetually inventive, Nero was a poisoner, a torturer, and a scoundrel. Says Suetonius:

Nero practiced every kind of obscenity, and at last invented a novel game: he was released from a den dressed in the skins of wild animals, and attacked the private parts of men and women who stood around bound to stakes. After working up sufficient excitement by this means, he was despatched—shall we say?—by his freedman Doryphoros.[26]

When Nero had his mother killed, he "rushed off to examine [her] corpse, handling her legs and arms critically, and, between drinks, discussing their good and bad points." [27]

Nero came to the bad end he deserved when, at the age of thirty-two, he was declared a public enemy by the Roman Senate. Nero's death was as squalid as his excesses had been vicious. In the course of an idiotic day of stumbling and fumbling toward death, muttering that he was "Dead! And so great an artist!" he finally made the suicide attempt he owed to his dignity as emperor. But he could not manage even that well, and required the help of his scribe, Epaphroditus, before he died, at last, his eyes "glazed and bulging from their sockets." [28]

It is hard to think that Gilles, if he read his grandfather's copy of Suetonius with any attention, could find much that was imitable in Nero's career. It may be that he found Suetonius' accounts of Nero's brutality fascinating—it was bizarre enough. But Gilles—if one can be fastidious in these matters—was more interested in a sort of closet drama of terror, not in the public squalor that characterized Nero's excesses.

The case for a model is a trifle better when we come to Gaius Caligula. Gilles would have read in his Suetonius that Caligula habitually committed incest with his three sisters in turn. That he was arrogant, violent, disrespectful, and, of course, cruel. On one occasion, when Caligula was looking over his accounts and discovered that feeding the arena animals was expensive, he gave the order to feed the beasts with condemned criminals instead of cattle. On another occasion:

> He watched the manager of his gladiatorial and wild-beast shows
> being flogged with chains for several days running, and had him killed
> only when the smell of suppurating brains became insupportable. A
> writer of Atellan farces was burned alive in the amphitheatre, because
> of a single line which had an amusing double-entendre.[29]

So it went. Disembowelings, poisonings. Reflex murders; casual rapes, seductions (of men and women). Most of all, what Gilles was to share with Caligula was his nearly inexhaustible taste for inflicting pain. Like Caligula, he seemed to be possessed of torrents of sexual energy. Caligula

> had not the slightest regard for chastity, either his own or others', . . . Valerius Catullus revealed publicly that he had enjoyed the Emperor, and that they quite wore one another out in the process. Besides incest with his sisters, and a notorious passion for the prostitute Pyrallis, he made advances to almost every well-known woman in Rome.[30]

Suetonius ticks off Caligula's physical appearance as follows:

> Height: tall
> Complexion: pallid
> Body: hairy and badly built
> Neck: thin
> Legs: spindly
> Eyes: sunken
> Temples: hollow
> Forehead: broad and forbidding
> Scalp: almost hairless, especially on the poll [31]

Hindsight makes good physiognomists of historians, and Caligula, in Suetonius' snapshot, does not appear to have been charming. In any case, the argument that Gilles de Rais modeled his behavior either on Nero or on Caligula is fanciful. Such people as Gilles do not require models for their behavior. Perversion and bloodlust, if they are to be delighted in, must have the stamp of the personal fantasies that generate them. With or without Suetonius, Gilles would have proved equal to his destiny.

In 1439, nearly eight years after Jeanne d'Arc died in flames, crying "Jesus, Jesus, Jesus!" a shabby miracle stirred the red haze of prayer, death, wine-swilling, satanic invocation, and orgasm that Gilles's life had become. He clawed at the children; he was in ecstasies at mass; he doted on Prelati; and he dreamed of going on a pilgrimage to Jerusalem where he would repent of all his sins. Then, one day at Tiffauges, he looked up and there stood Jeanne d'Arc.

She was alive. Jeanne d'Arc, come to life. His Jeanne, returned from the dead. Spirited miraculously out of the flames so that she might return again to save France . . . to save Gilles. The impossible hope coming true: Destiny was offering him a second chance. Jeanne, come to forgive him for his silence and inertia during her imprisonment and trial. If she could be redeemed from the flames at Rouen, why might he not be saved from his catastrophe? Why not? They would be comrades-in-arms again. High-hearted warriors riding into battle with the genial light of God's smile shining down upon them. Instead of bedroom slaughters; instead of the wearisome incantations to indifferent demons; instead of the endless stirring of pots of mercury that resolutely would not turn to gold.

If she could be redeemed, why not he?

Her name was Claude des Armoises and she was the best known of several false Jeannes who appeared in France claiming to have survived the blazing faggots of Rouen, claiming to have been saved by God so that she might complete her mission in France. Claude des Armoises showed up at La Grande-aux-Ormes in 1436, where she persuaded several people to recognize her as Jeanne d'Arc. The dean of Saint-Thiébault of Metz chronicled the event: "Nicole Louve, a knight, gave her a horse whose price was thirty francs and a pair of hose, and the lord Aubert de Boullay a hooded cape, and sire Nicole Grognat a sword. And the said Maid leapt upon the horse very skilfully and told sire Nicole Louve several things by which he understood well that she it was who had been in France." [32]

For a while, this "Jeanne d'Arc" enjoyed considerable prestige. She was given money and jewels. In Luxembourg, "she was constantly with Madame de Luxembourg . . . and the count [of Warnembourg] loved her greatly, so much so that when she wanted to go he had made for her a beautiful cuirass for her armor." [33] Claude des Armoises so intrigued the citizens of Orléans that they spent considerable money to pay for sending messengers to and from the heroine. One such messenger, Coeur-de-Lys, billed the Orléans municipal council for "bread, wine, pears and green walnuts . . . and for drink[,] for the said Coeur-de-Lys . . . was very thirsty." [34]

Petit-Jean, one of Jeanne d'Arc's brothers, was among those who welcomed Claude des Armoises. Though the young woman is said to have resembled Jeanne d'Arc amazingly, it is difficult to believe that Petit-Jean was deceived into thinking she was his sister. One guesses that he sensed there was profit to be made by allying himself to the imposture. Certainly, Claude des Armoises, for a while, did well financially. On July 18, 1439, she was a guest of the city of Orléans where she was given a *vin d'honneur* and on "August 1st the town made her a present of two hundred and ten pounds *parisis* 'for the good which she did the town during the siege.' " [35]

It was shortly after this that she showed up at Gilles's castle at Tiffauges. Gilles, for a brief while, was dazzled with her. It has been suggested that Gilles actually armed the young woman, but the matter is not certain. In any case, Claude des Armoises bade farewell to Gilles and made her way to Paris, where, the Bourgeois de Paris tells us, "this great mistake of believing her to be the Maid sprang up again, so that the University and the Parlement had her brought to Paris whether she liked it or not and shown to the people at the Palais on the marble slab in the great courtyard. There a sermon was preached about her and all her life and estate set forth." [36] A very uncomplimentary sermon in which, among other things, the "Maid" was charged with being no maid at all.

After Paris, Claude des Armoises seems to have made her way to Rome, where, dressed as a man, "she fought as a hired soldier in the Holy Father Eugenius's war and twice committed homicide in this war. She turned soldier again in Paris and formed part of the garrison." [37]

As for Gilles, he sank back into his red, red haze.

CHAPTER TWELVE

ARRESTED

I should be very much obliged if you [Watson] would slip your revolver into your pocket. An Eley's No. 2 is an excellent argument with gentlemen who can twist steel pokers into knots. That and a toothbrush are, I think, all that we need.

> —Sir Arthur Conan Doyle, in "The Adventure of the Speckled Band"

Frenzy, almost by definition, is of short duration. Gilles, by a remarkable manipulation of stimuli, had managed to live *au bout des nerfs* throughout nearly eight years. War, blood-rites, prayer, gourmandise, music, and remorse had kept him in ecstasies; but somewhere along the way, he had learned that ecstasy is not the same as pleasure, though pleasure is one of its components. Ecstasy, rather, is a *raideur*, a rigidity of the self in the senses straining to be freed of them, and therefore always exhausting. For the saint, the exhaustion is experienced as memory of a union with God; for the sexual criminal, the spent moment marks the beginning of a new dismay; for lovers, there is warmth and sleep. For Gilles, whose ecstasies were tangled snatches of all three, it must have seemed often that only death would get him off the atrocious wheel on which he was bound.

Otherwise, how explain the quality of collusion in his behavior in the period preceding his arrest. He knew very well that his life was under scrutiny; that the duke and the bishop had designs on his property; nor can it have escaped him that the populace had long ago identified him as the region's ogre.[1] Or so it has seemed to those who have commented both on the meekness with which Gilles submitted to arrest at his castle in Machecoul on September

15, 1440, and on the bizarre circumstances that led to it. Albert Jean, echoing the Abbé Bossard says that

> Gilles de Rais, on September 13, 1440, behind the ramparts of Machecoul—any more than Robespierre before the Commune of Paris on the evening of Thermidor—did not succumb to any physical weakness, but to a rupture of the will. For one as for the other, the moment of the soul had been sounded; the sublime moment toward which their entire destiny had been preparing, from the time of their first breath.[2]

As habitual ecstasy turned out to be insufficient to sustain his life, Gilles became a man for whom even the deaths of the children were now bad theater; sad re-creations of moments that had once been bright and alive, with blood spilled in the service of the imagination, or the self-consciousness of achieving the forbidden. But what had begun as passion had subsided into habit and, latterly, had dwindled to reflex and now, like Dostoevsky's Stavrogin, having crossed over into the desert of the absolutely forbidden, Gilles found himself condemned to vices that gave him no joy.

It may be, too, that Gilles was oppressed by the very immunity that for so long had shielded him. Protected by power and wealth, there was no reason why he could not have gone on to prey on the children of Brittany and Anjou as the Beast of Extermination he had become. The Abbé Bossard writes:

> One is astonished at once that Gilles de Rais' crimes were able to exist for so long a time without early arousing the attention of justice, whether ecclesiastic or civil; without there being raised in the four corners of the land a cry of reprobation; without there appearing, at last, a judge to avenge the weak. . . . But when one considers the mystery in which Gilles' life was enveloped . . . and the fear of a population decimated by an enemy everpresent everywhere in the land at once, and, just the same, invisible; and the fear that his name and power inspired; . . . one is less surprised.[3]

There is every reason to think that Gilles's crimes were as well known to the authorities as they were to the parents of the victims. Not, perhaps, that either parents or authorities knew the manner of the children's deaths. Though even that may have been better known than our documents tell us. Medieval architecture did not provide much in the way of personal privacy. Moreover, Gilles's various households were run by huge staffs of people. It is very hard to believe that all the traces of Gilles's complex crimes could

escape notice for so many years; or that those who knew what was happening, and were sworn to secrecy, would keep such an oath, once sworn. The sheer terror of it might have required a confidant.

Nor is it to be believed that the crowd of boys who served in the choir of the Holy Innocents, and who were regularly sodomized by their patron, would not develop among themselves a colorful folklore of what their life was like. Nor that some of that gossip would not have found its way outside the walls of the various castles.[4]

The Abbé Bossard writes:

> Nothing could hide such crimes, neither impious oaths sworn on the Evangel, nor the shadows of night, nor the streams into which the ashes of the victims were thrown, nor the blazing fireplaces, nor ditch-water, nor marshes. All clever precautions failed.[5]

The country people, anyhow, were no longer in any doubt about who was causing their torment. Of Machecoul, it was said, "They eat children there." And, though the phrase was not yet invented, the Beast of Extermination had been identified. He was Gilles de Rais.

How little good it did simply to know, we can tell from the following episode. Some weeks before Machecoul was to be delivered to René de la Suze, Gilles ordered Gilles de Sillé and Robin Romulart to clear some forty bodies away from the base of a watchtower where they had been buried. It was slow, ugly work; not, one would think, of the sort to attract bystanders. Nevertheless, Roger de Briqueville, for whatever reasons of his own, conducted two noblewomen, La Dame de Jarville and Thomin d'Araguin, to a peephole where they took their fill watching the macabre proceedings. That they told no one what they had seen is hard to believe. Gilles de Sillé, anyway, complained bitterly to Robin and Poitou, "Was it not sneaky of Messire Roger de Bricqueville to let Jarville and Thomin d'Araguin see Robin and me through a crack when we were removing the sacks of bones, knowing full well what we were doing?"[6] The Abbé Bossard wonders whether the ladies were themselves mothers, in which case they must have experienced a terror "like that which overwhelmed

Ruins of Gilles's castle at Machecoul.

Bluebeard's wife when, curious and trembling, she penetrated into the forbidden chamber and saw the seven dead wives hanging along the wall." [7] Mothers or not, it is not possible that the women kept what they saw to themselves. But what was there to do? Who, without support from some very high place indeed, would charge the lord of the land with the destruction of children?

Gilles knew all this, which is why one aspect of himself contrived to give the people what they needed: a friend in high places who could dare to confront the Baron de Rais.

It had, however, to be done Gilles's way. One could hardly expect him to write a letter to an appropriate officer of church or state, confessing his crimes and begging to be arrested. No. Flair was Gilles's other *métier;* violence and ego, his style. For the time being, he went right on with his reflex murders until the world presented him an opportunity for an absurd display of violence.

Here, we need to remember that Gilles's ruinous financial dealings had not gone unnoticed by Jean V, the duke of Brittany. The duke had been maneuvering for some time to acquire various of Gilles's lands at bargain prices. Then, in 1438, he employed a certain Geoffroy le Ferron as a cat's-paw. Le Ferron purchased the château at Saint-Etienne-de-Mer-Morte from Gilles, and put his brother, Jean le Ferron, a tonsured priest, in charge of the place.

Gilles, then, for mysterious motives, decided to back out of the transaction on the grounds that one of his own cousins, the Lord de Villevigne, was interested in buying Saint-Etienne. The trouble was that Geoffroy le Ferron believed that a contract was a contract, and would not give back what he had paid for.

What happened then is more characteristic of the younger, impetuous Gilles than the nearly stupefied man he had become. He leaped to arms in the spirit of

> Some friend must now perforce
> Go forth and bid my boy
> To saddle up my wooden horse
> For I must conquer Troy.

The ridiculous expedition to Saint-Etienne-de-Mer-Morte only makes sense if we see that Gilles was seizing an opportunity to bring his miserable career to a stop, though it is notable that rash as the expedition was, Gilles took time out to consult his satanic helper Barron to find out whether he might encounter an ambush on his way.[8] Barron replied that the coast was clear.

Gilles, putting himself at the head of a band of seventy men, then marched off to Saint-Etienne. It was the fifteenth of May 1440.

Arrived at Saint-Etienne without mishap, Gilles found the town silent—with most of the population in the village church. Jean le Ferron, as priest, was naturally there too, celebrating mass with the others.

> Near him, not far from the choir, stood Guillaume Hautrays who had come in the name of the Duke of Brittany to enjoin the inhabitants against paying all fines and taxes to Gilles de Rais.[9]

In the silent town, Gilles had no trouble disposing his men for an ambush. They were, of course, all armed "but many of them wore capes and cloaks by way of disguise." [10] Inside the church, the congregation was on its knees when

> all at once Gilles de Rais, bareheaded, and carrying a dagger [*jusarme*], burst into the church, followed by his retainers, helmeted and armed with their swords. The Marshal hastened to the spot where Le Ferron was kneeling, and shouted in a terrible voice:
>
> "Ha! *Ribault!* Thou hast beaten my men and practiced extortion on them! Come—come out of the church, or I will kill thee quite dead!"
>
> Jean le Ferron, on his knees, pale with terror, could only answer: "Do with me as you please." [11]

The poor priest, not quite Thomas à Becket, yielded all that there was to yield. He gave up possession of the château and supposed the matter would end there. But he was dealing with Gilles de Rais who could elaborate rage with the same fixity of purpose with which he attenuated pain. The priest was hauled off in chains to the dungeons of Saint-Etienne-de-Mer-Morte where he was joined later by his brother, Geoffroy le Ferron, as well as by Hautrays and Rousseau, the duke's tax collector and sergeant-general, respectively.

In an age as violent as the fifteenth century, this bit of thunder and lightning was not, on the face of it, more serious than, say, Gilles's kidnapping of his wife, Catherine, had been. Gilles's bad luck was that his outburst chanced to offend three powers at the same time: Charles VII, Duke Jean V, *and* the Church.

> It was an open revolt in violation of the oath of fidelity he had sworn to the Crown; it was a violation of Breton law which forbade any of its nobles to take up arms without express permission of the Duke . . . finally, by a piece of good luck, this rebel against the state, this flaunter of Breton law, had become a rebel against the Church.[12]

It was a formidable set of enemies. And yet, one cannot help noting that, as the various machineries were set in motion against Gilles de Rais, the question of the tortured children of the poor was not of any interest to the three offended powers.

At first, the gathering retribution moved slowly. The duke slapped Gilles's wrist with a fine of 50,000 *écus* of gold—a fine that was never paid. Michel Bataille argues that "the Duke did not *wish* [*sic*] him to pay. He meant only to shake him up, then to lead him, if he could, to a new outburst, after which he would be sure of him." [13]

Gilles, convinced that one more discussion with the duke would produce an understanding, set out for a meeting with him at Josselin. But first, faithful as ever to his continually unfulfilled hopes in the help of the devil, he asked Prelati to invoke Barron once more to learn if the trip to Josselin would be safe. Prelati, out of Gilles's presence, invoked the patient imp and brought back the good news, "Yes. Gilles would be safe." [14]

Gilles set forth from Machecoul, but his misgivings about the duke were severe enough that he needed further satanic reassurance. Prelati was required to contact Barron once more. At Nantes, Prelati made a further invocation (again, out of Gilles's presence). The answer was that Gilles would be safe. One would have thought two reassurances would be enough and yet, even as Gilles and his men were approaching Josselin, he felt he needed to ease his anxieties, and the biddable Prelati cast his spells. For the third time, Gilles was sent the message that he would be personally safe in his dealings with the duke.

And, he was. For the simple reason that the duke was by then perfectly aware that his cousin, the bishop of Nantes, was preparing his own response to Gilles's forward behavior at Saint-Etienne-de-Mer-Morte. Even as the duke played host to Gilles, the bishop was pursuing an ecclesiastical "inquiry" about Gilles. The Abbé Bossard suggests that the duke was more than aware—that he was, in fact, a party to the inquiry.[15]

It was now July of 1440, and, says Huysmans

during this time the priest [the bishop] hastens his redoubled investigations. He delegates commissioners and procurators in all the villages where children have disappeared. He himself quits his palace at Nantes, travels about the countryside, and takes the depositions of the bereft. The people at last speak.[16]

It is utterly unbelievable that Gilles or someone of his crew did not learn of the bishop's inquiry. Under the circumstances, one would suppose that Gilles would impose a reign of caution on himself. Instead, by an act of self-deception far beyond folly, Gilles, on his way back from his visit to the duke, paused one night in an open field to sacrifice three more children. Later, at Vannes, there was a final murder. The details of that crime, if we can block out for a moment that a child's life was snuffed out, are the stuff of which the coarsest of low comedies are made.

Gilles was staying in a house owned by a certain Lemoine. André Buchet, a sweet-voiced chorister, just then in the service of the duke's chapel, who knew Gilles's tastes, brought him a ten-year-old boy, the son of Jean Lavary; and Gilles, not quite for the final time, committed the child to his embraces. But the usual little drama had to be interrupted before the climax, since the Lemoine house was not one in which one could dispose of a murdered child. The company, then, left and made their way to another nearby house owned by one Boetden. Here, various of Gilles's knights were quartered, and here Gilles could indulge himself in the final stage of his fantasy. The child was beheaded and the head burned in Gilles's bedroom fire. The body, for whatever reasons, was not burned. Instead, in a bizarre replay of a scene from Chaucer's "The Prioress' Tale," the body, bound with the child's own belt, was taken and thrown into the household cesspool. The headless corpse, however, would not sink, and Poitou, "with much difficulty," [17] had to climb into the muck where, with infinite labor, he tried to get it to stay down. Unlike the child in "The Prioress' Tale," this poor victim did not miraculously sing *Alma Redemptoris*

Mater out of the mire. Here, Buchet, the sweet-voiced singer, stood above the horror and called encouragement to the beslimed Poitou.[18]

Meanwhile, the secret inquiry regarding Gilles proceeded with all deliberate speed. At the end of July, the bishop secretly published a "writ of defamation," a curious document that seems quite opposed to what we think of as fair in contemporary law. The "defamation," however, had a special purpose in medieval society. It has been several times observed that Gilles was safe, despite the widespread knowledge of his crimes, because there was no one among the people daring enough to bring charges against him. In a world divided among the Church, the nobility, and the rest of humankind, there was no way for the poor or the oppressed to seek redress of grievance against the nobility except, as here, when the Church put out a call as it were for sufficient hearsay of wickedness to create a putative case. If enough smoke was generated by such a call, the presumption was that there might be a fire to investigate. In this case,

> no parent of his victims was likely to risk [making a charge]. Everyone was too fearful of Gilles, and, one must add, properly fearful of *justice*. It is here, then, that the *défamation* is necessary: it consisted of gathering whatever troublesome rumors circulated about a person, backing them up with as many proofs and witnesses as one could find, and drawing [the information] together.
>
> Finally, if one established thus that the reputation of the incriminated person was seriously in question, then justice could enter into the matter, even when no [person had laid a formal] complaint, nor had personally filed a deposition.[19]

To us in the twentieth century, this sounds very like trial by gossip, and, no doubt, there were people injured by the process. In a case like Gilles's, where the accused was a man of great wealth and power, the "defamation" was the nearest available approach to justice.

The news of the inquiry, though it was intended to be secret, must have been reassuring to the peasantry at least. What they had known and wept over without hope of consolation might now be brought into the light of day. How strong that hope was, we may conjecture from the fact that eight *menu peuple*, ordinary people (seven of them women), consented to have their names included in the list of "good and discreet persons" who had made "complaints and declarations" against Gilles. One dreads to think what their fate might have been had Gilles found a way of compounding with his accusers and lived to confront the people on the list.

The episcopal investigation lasted more than a month, but its Declaration of Infamy was not published until the thirtieth of July. The entire document reads:

> To all those who will see these present letters, we, Jean, by divine permission, and by grace of the Holy See, apostolic bishop of Nantes, give greetings in the name of Our Lord, and require of you that you shall put faith in these present letters:
>
> Be it known by these present letters that, visiting the parish of Sainte-Marie-de-Nantes, in which Gilles de Rais, designated below, often resides in the house called de la Suze; and that he is a parishioner of the said church. . . . In the course of visiting other parish churches designated below, we have encountered, first, frequent and public rumors; and then charges and declarations of good and discreet persons:
>
> Agathe, wife of Denis de Lemion; the widow of Regnaud Donete, of the said parish of Notre-Dame; Jeanne, widow of Guibelet Delit, of St. Denis; Jean Hubert and his wife, of St. Vincent; Marthe, widow of Eonnet Kerguen, of Saint-Croix-de-Nantes; Jeanne, wife of Jean Darel, of Saint-Similien, near Nantes, and Tiphaine, wife of Eonnet le Charpentier, of Saint-Clément-Outside-the-Walls, of Nantes, all parishioners of the said churches whose testimony is upheld by synodal witnesses of these churches, and other discreet, prudent and respectable persons.
>
> We, visiting these same churches, as befits our office, have examined them diligently, and by their depositions have learned among other things, as being certain, that the noble Lord Gilles de Rais, Chevalier, Lord of the said place, and Baron, our subject and within our jurisdiction, with various of his accomplices, has cut the throats of, killed, massacred in odious fashion various innocent boys, that he has practiced with these children the lewdness that is against nature and the vice of sodomy; that he has often done, and caused to be done, the horrible evocation of demons, has sacrificed to them, and made pacts with them, and perpetrated other dreadful crimes within the limits of our jurisdiction; and we have learned by the inquiries of our commissioners and procurators that the said Gilles has perpetrated and committed the crimes mentioned above and other debauches in our diocese as well as in various other places subject to it.

In regard to these crimes, the said Gilles de Rais is, was and is still [declared] infamous by respectable and honorable persons. And, to the end that there be no doubt, we have written these present letters and have affixed on them our seal.

Given at Nantes, the 29th of July, 1440.
By order of the said Lord Bishop of Nantes
"Signed: Je. Petit." [20]

The arrest of Gilles de Rais on the morning of September 15, 1440, seems hardly a scenelet in the corrosive drama of Gilles's life. It was, rather, a quiet moment in the life of a man for whom rage and the continual exercise of his own will were nearly lifelong habits. Certainly, Jean Labbé, captain of arms to the duke of Brittany, must have gone off to his assignment that day with considerable trepidation, despite the thirty mounted soldiers at his back. What, in the best of circumstances, were his thirty men to the two hundred Gilles could muster? His thirty *outside* the walls of the château at Machecoul.

It was a bright, clear day as Labbé and his men approached those forbidding walls where they paused to let the duke's herald ride forward a few paces. The herald was, we may suppose, not entirely comfortable either, but he put his trumpet to his lips and blew a blast. On the ramparts of the castle, Gilles de Rais watched the approach of Labbé's troop.

The herald tucked his trumpet back into his belt, then withdrew the parchment scroll he carried and unrolled it. Then he read:

We, Jean Labbé, captain of arms, acting in the name of Monseigneur Jean de Malestroit, Bishop of Nantes, enjoin Gilles, Count of Brienne, Lord of Laval, of Pouzauges, Tiffauges, Machecoul, Champtocé and other places, Marshal of France, and Lieutenant General of Brittany, to give us access at once to his château and to constitute himself a prisoner in our hands so that he may respond to the religious and civil jurisdictions for the triple crimes of sorcery, murder and sodomy.[21]

It may be that Gilles, on the wall, was tempted to obey the advice his henchmen gave him: to fight.[22] And yet, Gilles, the hotheaded warrior, hesitated. The Abbé Bossard gives various reasons for the hesitation: First, Gilles de Sillé and Roger de Briqueville, the two accomplices on whom Gilles most counted, had disappeared a few days before, evidently alerted to what was coming. Moreover, resistance, though it could buy the marshal time for flight, could not provide him a refuge. Most probably, says Bossard, Gilles chose not to fight because he truly believed he could somehow compound with his enemies—pay a fine, or make written promises to amend his ways.

> What had he to fear from justice that might worry the ordinary criminal . . . he was sufficiently protected, to begin with, by powerful friendships, by a glorious name and a glorious past. There were none who would dare to attack him; or to unveil his crimes. . . . Out of pride, then, for political [reasons], out of bravado, he believed it would be better to put himself into the hands of the archers [the duke's soldiers]. And this he did, without striking a blow.[23]

The decision not to resist, I have suggested, was a good deal less reasonable. In any case, the drawbridge was lowered and Gilles strode forward to greet the arresting officer, Captain Labbé, to whom he said, making a poor enough pun for the occasion, "I have always intended to become a monk [one day]: well then, here is the abbot who will induct me." [24]

The arrest, then, was accomplished with none of the outbursts of violence that the duke's men had been right to worry about. Instead, after the minimal amenities involving horses and men that the occasion required, Gilles placed himself in the midst of Labbé's troop, and the cavalcade retraced its steps toward Nantes.

Gilles—or some part of him—must have known that he was riding toward his death.

CHAPTER THIRTEEN

JUSTICE

The Passion of Christ is not prefigured only by the sacrifice of Abraham; it is surrounded by all the glories of torture and its innumerable dreams; Tubal the blacksmith and Isaiah's wheel take their places around the Cross, forming beyond all the lessons of the sacrifice the fantastic tableau of savagery, of tormented bodies and suffering.

—Michel Foucault, in *Madness and Civilization*

Gilles's twenty-four-mile ride from Machecoul to Nantes was a playlet in which everyone played singular roles. As police officers—and anyone who has ever been arrested—know, there is a curiously intimate relationship that develops between a prisoner and his guards. For the time that they are together, their lives and his are enclosed in the same frame. On the one hand, the prisoner and his guards are required to regard each other with hostility: The prisoner may try to escape; the guards will try to prevent him. Somebody may die. On the other hand, the guards and the prisoner are travelers together: comrades sharing meals, noticing the view, drinking together at rest stops, chatting the hours away as they ride to their destination.

Various of Gilles's accomplices had been arrested with him at Machecoul: Blanchet, Prelati, Poitou, and Henriet Griart. Others of his "friends, servants, former courtiers, deserted him . . ." and disappeared as quickly as they could. Gilles and his accomplices may have cast nervous glances at the boxes of evidence Labbé's men had gathered and which were now being transported to Nantes. Boxes containing "fine powder said to be the ashes of a child incinerated perhaps the day before . . . [and] a child's bloody shirt which sent off a repulsive odor." [1]

The Abbé Bossard says that when the news spread to the villages and hamlets that the troop going toward Nantes was conducting the Lord Gilles de Rais to be judged and punished for his crimes, "[people] had the same stunned feeling one has after a storm; then, it was as if the oppressed hearts were eased." [2] For Gilles, it was a journey toward a gathering storm. A journey in which Gilles was harshly reminded that honor is what defines the difference between fame and notoriety. Gilles had known what fame was. He had achieved it in King Charles's wars, and beside Jeanne d'Arc in her period of glory. He had been one of the four knights who brought the Holy Ampul from Saint-Rémy to Reims for the sanctification of the French crown. He knew the feeling of conscious pride that comes with being the cynosure of all eyes. Now, though heads were still turning to watch him ride by, what followed him were not admiring glances. Maledictions, cries of horror. Looks of fear, dismay, or contempt. Whatever eyes could do to unsettle Gilles de Rais who was still officially the lieutenant general of Brittany, but whom the populace had long ago identified as the beast of extermination; as the ogre of Machecoul, of whom it was rumored that he roasted stolen children.

A baseless charge. The truth, as we have seen, was much worse.

On the evening of September 15, Gilles and his accomplices, and his guards, rode into Nantes: "Gilles, Baron of Rais, Lord of Laval, Marshal of France, Lieutenant General of the Armies of Brittany; Gilles, the companion of Jeanne d'Arc and of the Constable de Richemont, the counselor and friend of Charles VII; Gilles, the cruelest and the most infamous of men . . . chained like a malefactor, but with a haughty brow and a disdainful look [marched] toward *La Tour Neuve*." [3] There he would live for a month. He would descend from the tower to his trial. He would ascend to it at the end of each day's proceedings. Gilles's rooms in the tower were spacious and high-ceilinged. He was in no way mistreated.

Ciampini, in his red and black rendition of Gilles's life, *Barba-Blu*, has Gilles locked into a tower room from which all light is excluded, except that which comes from a tiny opening overhead. Gilles's guards, in Ciampini's tale, mistreat him. They call him, "*Cane, cane* [Dog. Dog.]" He is fed only some morsels of black bread, and given putrid water to drink. Gilles, however, bears his ills with fortitude, devoting himself to prayer from morning till night, asking God for the boon of a fierce punishment. When he weeps, his guards mock him, saying, "Listen to that, a dog weeping. Weep. Weep. Would that you had wept before you caused the shedding of so many mothers' tears." [4]

Ciampini gives us also a scene in which Gilles speaks to the priest who has come to hear his confession. Gilles asks the friar, "Father, how can God listen to such dreadful things?" And the friar replies, "God saw you when you were doing them." [5]

If he was not in a dungeon, and he was not in chains, Gilles just the same was under confinement in La Tour Neuve. The bravado with which, standing on his own walls in Machecoul, he had been able to meet Jean Labbé must surely have dissipated in the long hours of the journey. None of the documents tells us what Gilles did or thought or said in the five-day interval between his tenancy of La Tour Neuve and his first appearance before the trial court. But for a man of his fiery temperament, the passage of days alone must have been dreadful. What does a man who has lived *au bout des nerfs* do when mealtimes are all he can expect in the way of excitement during any day?

It seems to me that Gilles, in those silent days in La Tour Neuve, was not so much taking the measure of his position as closing off against his realization of it. Even his low-grade witticism on the day of the arrest, "I have always intended to become a monk [one day]: well then, here is the abbot who will induct me," can be understood as a symptom of the shock we have discussed. From now on, Gilles would behave, most of the time, presentably enough. But we may be sure that the hot turbulence that had marked his life was now turned clammy and cold.

With delay and loneliness as his companions, and with time to consider, as well as to invent, the dangers that faced him, he became increasingly tense. After all, Griart and Poitou, who knew everything, had been arrested with him. How long, if they were put to the Question, would they delay giving dreadful answers. And what of Prelati, the handsome, dark Prelati, the Latinist for whom, in the past year, Gilles had developed some of those feelings that go with being in love? The Italian was a suave and elegant man, but was he a man on whom one could rely? And count on for what?

Romantically, one wants to believe that while Gilles waited he was visited too by the ghosts of his victims, in the way that Richard III had to confront his grisly crew. It may only be a literary hunger, or a spiritual one, that makes me want such a dark night of the soul for Gilles. They ought to have been there, the children:

Colin Avril, the boy with the lovely name—April, full of springtime, but captured in August. A slim boy with a pale face who had been "borrowed" by one of Gilles's people to serve as a guide. Then he was whisked away to the Hôtel de la Suze where Gilles enveloped him in his affections. . . .

And the nameless, guileless schoolboy from Nantes, employed by one of Gilles's men, Princé, who promised to treat the boy well and make something of him. But the promises did not, somehow, ring true to the boy's parents when they heard that Princé had a horse too fierce for their son to mount. They begged the child to come home. But the boy, still glowing, replied that the great lord had taken a liking to him . . . and after that . . . they were fobbed off with a story of a Scotsman who had been drawn to the boy and taken him away.

And another boy, thirteen years old, who had been surprised over his studies and abducted.

And the baker boy, with the smell of flour still on him.

And the ten-year-old to whose mother, Péronne, Poitou had promised great things. The urchin lovely as an angel. Pale and slim. A handsome lad.

A lad playing at pelota. A delicious beggar boy of eight. A tailor's apprentice. A furrier's boy. Begging brothers.

Or a brother and sister. Or a couple of friends. As always, once they were scrubbed up, they were beautiful with that glow of children whose bodies, not yet grown to sexual readiness, were especially enticing to him, as if by caressing that flesh at that time, as if by destroying it, he might redeem the children from the consequences of Adam's curse.

What was important was that one of the two must please the baron's taste. If the other was homely, no matter. And when the lascivious commerce was over and the preferred child had been soiled and bloodied; when its throat was cut, or it had been decapitated, Gilles turned his attention to the spurned brother or sister or friend, and killed again. Not for any carnal reason, but for a reason that has a certain sophisticated, if entirely vicious, humanity: He did not like to think that the surviving child would miss the one who died.[6]

Disappeared. Disappeared. "And after that they were not seen again." Beautiful boys. Handsome lads. Curious children, wide-eyed at their good luck. Tall, or short, or slim, or soft, but always young flesh, still breathing that rose odor of youth.

They were taken, and he had commerce with them and sometimes he broke . . . and sometimes by his order, one of his servants broke . . . cut open . . . had commerce with . . . spilled . . . wept . . . praised the heads . . . saw God in the steaming mortality . . . saw himself . . . saw nothing . . .

Ecstasy.

For the sake of our image of how the decencies ought to take over in the crises of our lives, one supposes that Gilles began now, in this interim, as he waited for his trial, to think beyond flamboyance; to think somberly of the state of his soul. About now, his sincere and anxious love of God may have stirred in the presence of his memories, and his real massacre of the innocents have become more than a mere metaphor of Christian grief. Perhaps he guessed at last that his fixation on being always in a state of grace had something of the devil's touch upon it; and recognized the paradox of what it is to lust for salvation without preparing the self to be saved.

Because "the Church has a fear of blood, according to the sacred formula, and leaves it to the secular arm to strike at the necks it has designated with an inclination of the head,"[7] Gilles would be tried twice: once in an ecclesiastical court, which would determine his crimes against the Faith; and once by a secular court, which would decide his guilt regarding his crimes against the state. The bishop of Nantes, Jean de Malestroit, was the chief officer of the ecclesiastical court. The civil tribunal, directed by the chancellor of Brittany, Pierre de l'Hôpital, assisted by Jean de Touscheronde, followed the ecclesiastical trial closely.

The Abbé Bossard, seconded by D. B. Wyndham Lewis, goes to great lengths to assure us that Gilles had a fair trial. "From the beginning of this trial to its end," writes Bossard, "one saw deployed a luxury of precautions which greatly honored the judicial process; sessions were frequent, questioning was intense; everything took place in no way as in the shadows of a ducal palace at Venice, but in the full light of day and before the eyes of a crowd. . . . Depositions were received from the most honorable people; the charges, instead of being hidden from the accused, were publicly communicated to him and frequently read in Latin as well as in the common tongue; he was confronted with his co-accused; his accomplices were called as witnesses." [8] What the abbé says is true enough—up to a point. But the trial was hardly "a work of calm truth," though paradoxically it did become a "work on the side of justice in the service of the weak, which . . . avenged [their] sufferings and their tears." [9] Gilles, let us remember, had been terrorizing the weak and the poor for years in circumstances that make it impossible to believe that his crimes were hidden from the authorities. And yet, it was not the fate of the children that led to Gilles's arrest, but his abuse of Jean le Ferron at Saint-Etienne-de-Mer-Morte. That insult to the power of the Church set the machinery of justice into motion. Michelet remarks that Gilles "would never have been either accused or judged without the singular circumstance that three powers, normally opposed to each other, seemed to have agreed on his death: the Duke, the Bishop, and the King." [10]

There was nothing disinterested about Gilles's trial. Jean V, the duke of Brittany, had been a keen observer of Gilles's rush to debacle. He—or his cat's-paws—had been buying various of Gilles's properties over the years. Moreover, the duke had other reasons for wanting to see Gilles de Rais humbled. Jean V had tolerated with ill grace Gilles's melodramatic displays of wealth and power. Gilles's Hôtel de la Suze at Nantes, for example, was more luxurious and splendid than the ducal palace. If the duke was not himself the actual instigator of the inquiries into Gilles's life after the affair at Saint-Etienne-de-Mer-Morte, he was certainly a collaborator in them. More than that, the bishop of Nantes, Jean de Malestroit, who was directing the investigation into Gilles's life—and who would be his judge—was the duke's cousin. [11] The bishop of Le Mans, Guillaume de Malestroit, another of Gilles's judges, was in his turn Jean de Malestroit's cousin. The horrified Albert Jean writes, "Malestroit and Malestroit. Two relations. Two bishops. Two judges . . . I am astonished that the Abbé Bossard, normally so attentive, has not seen it his duty to underline the suspicious, for me intolerable, implications that this familial constitution of the tribunal presents." [12]

It is clear, too, that the judges were in no doubt of the outcome of the trial. When Gilles made his first brief appearance before the court in the great hall of La Tour Neuve on Monday, the nineteenth of September, his judges—the bishop of Nantes, Guillaume Chapeillon, assisted by Olivier Solide and Jean Durand—gave him to understand that he would be charged with doctrinal heresy. Nothing at all was said about the more fearful charges made against him in the declaration read to him on the day of his arrest. That document, with its too precise knowledge of his crimes, said, "Gilles de Rais, Chevalier, Lord of the said place, and Baron, our subject and within our jurisdiction, with various of his accomplices, has cut the throats of, killed, massacred in odious fashion various innocent boys, that he has practiced with these children the lewdness that is against nature and the vice of sodomy . . ." [13] Now, Gilles, hearing himself charged only with doctrinal heresy, felt a weight lifted from his heart. When he was asked if he accepted the jurisdiction of his judges, he replied, almost eagerly, that he did.

It was a trap, and Gilles fell into it. Because he believed himself to be a good Catholic, he did not fear the charge of heresy. What he did not know was that the practice of magic also constituted heresy. Now, having accepted the right of the tribunal to try him, he had acceded to an entire proceeding that would compass him around. Gilles, unaware of the skill with which his judges had arranged his doom, was led away.

On Wednesday, the twenty-eighth of September, the judges, assisted by Jean Blouyn of the Order of Preaching Friars who participated as a member of the tribunal representing the Inquisition, heard witnesses telling over their losses. Sons, daughters, nephews, nieces treacherously taken, miserably slain. And always, suspicion pointed to Gilles de Rais. The child was last seen in the company of one of Gilles's people: Perrine Martin (La Meffraye) or a certain Poitou.

On Saturday, October 8, more accusing witnesses were heard. Gilles was not present in the courtroom. Then, at the hour of *tierce* (about nine A.M.), Gilles appeared in court for the second time. Now, Guillaume Chapeillon charged Gilles verbally with the whole list of his crimes: murders, perversions, violations of secular and ecclesiastic law. It must have been a stunning blow, but the trial transcript only tells us that Gilles, "verbally, and not in writing, appealed from the judgment of the Bishop and the Vicar of the Inquisition." [14] The appeal was peremptorily denied on the ground that it was "frivolous" because presented orally and not in writing. At the same time, the judges assured Gilles that they did not want to overwhelm him with any evil intentions.

Gilles did confess that one item, among the forty-two listed in the charges against him, was true: "He confessed to having received the sacrament of baptism and having [therefore] renounced the devil and all of his pomps." [15] Then the prosecutor Chapeillon, in a final tilting of his lance, offered to swear an oath that he, Chapeillon, would tell the truth. Was Gilles ready to take a similar oath? Gilles said no. Once, twice, three times and four, he was asked and urged, but Gilles would not swear. Patiently, the judges put off his next appearance to the following Thursday, October 13, and the court was adjourned.

What did Gilles hope to gain by refusing to take the required oath? Nothing that one can see—unless it was a reflex of his grand manner asserting itself. By now, he knew that he had been tricked by this panel of learned doctors of law and theology. Perhaps refusing to swear was his way of maintaining his sullen dignity as the judges, in their clerical garb, pushed him genteelly toward an abyss that was visibly opening beneath him.

The designated Thursday arrived when Gilles was to make his third appearance before the court, but the session was devoted instead to hearing still more witnesses against him. Gilles would cool his heels in La Tour Neuve until the following Friday, October 21. Meanwhile, men and women in a long line continued to make their appearance in the courtroom complaining "sadly and in tears of the loss of their sons . . . pleading for justice." [16]

J. K. Huysmans, in whose bizarre novel *Down There* the life of Gilles de Rais serves as *obbligato* to the decadent fiction, has a typically luxuriant and breathless description of Gilles's court as theater.

> The room in which the Tribunal sat was crammed, and there were multitudes sitting on the stairs, standing in the corridors, filling the neighboring courts, blocking the streets and lanes. . . .
>
> The courtroom, massive, obscure, upheld by heavy Roman pillars, had been rejuvenated. The wall, ogival, threw to cathedral height the arches of its vaulted ceiling, which were joined together, like the sides of an abbatial miter, in a point. The room was lighted by sickly daylight which was filtered through small panes between heavy leads. The azure of the ceiling was darkened to navy blue, and the golden stars, at that height, were as heads of steel pins. In the shadows of the vaults appeared the ermine of the ducal arms, dimly seen in escutcheons which were like great dice with black dots.
>
> Suddenly the trumpets blared, the room was lighted up, and the Bishops entered: Jean de Malestroit, Bishop of Nantes; Guillaume de Malestroit, Bishop designate of Le Mans; Jean Prégent, Bishop of St. Brieuc; Denis de la Lohéric, Bishop of St. Lô. Their miters of cloth of gold flamed like the lightning. About their necks were brilliant collars with orphreys crusted, as were the robes, with carbuncles. In silent processional the Bishops advanced, weighted down by their rigid copes, which fell in a flare from their shoulders and were like golden bells split in the back. In their hands they carried the crosier from which hung the maniple, a soft green veil.
>
> At each step they glowed like coals blown upon. Themselves were sufficient to light the room, as they reanimated with their jewels the pale sun of a rainy October day and scattered a new luster to all parts of the room, over the mute audience.[17]

But the court was composed of more than bishops. There was Olivier Lesou, parish priest of Bouvron, Jean Durand, priest of Blain. There was the Dominican Brother Jean Blouyn, the designated representative of the Holy Inquisition, alert for evidence of the crime of heresy; Jacques de Pentcoëtdic, official of the Cathedral of Nantes, as well as Robin Guillaumet, a public notary who

The trial transcript.

Universis presentes litteras inspecturis Johannes […] permissione divina et sancte sedis apostolice gratia […] Cameracensis Salutem In domino et fidem ipse presentibus […] In […] parrochia Egidii de Rays Infrascripto […] In domo vulgariter nuncupata de […] morabatur […] parrochiani […] ecclesie […] Et alias Infrascriptas parrochiales ecclesias visitans fama publica et frequenti […] Referente et clamosa Insinuatione Bonarum et discretarum personarum Agathe […] de lemignon […] Relicte defuncti Reginaldi […] ipius […] marie Johanne […] et […] Sancti dionisii Johannis gimbert et […] sancti […] Mathei Relicte defuncti […] heguen Sancte […] in […] Johanne […] Johannes […] Sancti Guillelmi prope Nannetas Et theophanie […] Sancti […] Sancte […] Clementis […] nuncios Nannetei […] parrochialium parrochianorum Cum testibus synodalibus ipse ecclesiarum et aliis probis et discretis viris et personis non suspectis quos tam super Infrascriptis quam aliis Nos […] ecclesias visitans Officium visitationis huiusmodi tangentibus […] examinavi feramine diligenter Comperimus ac per eorum depositiones Inter cetera nobis constitit Nobilem virum dominum Egidium […] de Rays militem dicti loci dominum et Baronem subditum universalem […] plures pueros Innocentes per se et quosdam super complices Jugulasse Interemisse et Inhumaniter trucidasse Cum viris contra naturam Luxuriasse Et ditum sodomie comississe […] horridam demonum Invocationem sepe et sepius fecisse […] fieri procurasse et eis sacrificasse et obtulisse et cum […] ipsis pactum fecisse Aliaque enormia Innormia In fide […] nostra perpetrasse Et in pluribus et diversis […] nomine et Commissarios […] procuratores nostros visitari Dedimus […] Egidium de Rays premissa perpetrasse Et alia flagitiosa In diocesi nostra comississe Super quibus publice et notorie apud bonos et graves […] et existit diffamatus

acted as clerk of the court, and four notaries—Jean Delaunay, Jean Petit, Guillaume Lesné, and Nicholas Géraud. Finally, there was Pierre de l'Hôpital, the president of Brittany, a man of singular probity who would preside over the secular trial. Of their presence, Huysmans writes:

> Outshone by the shimmer of the orphreys and the stones, the costumes of the other judges appeared darker and discordant. The black vestments of secular justice, the white and black robe of Jean Blouyn, the silk symars, the red woollen mantles, the scarlet chaperons lined with fur, seemed faded and common.
>
> The Bishops seated themselves in the front row, surrounding Jean de Malestroit, who, from a raised seat, dominated the court.
>
> Under the escort of the men-at-arms, Gilles entered.

The actual scene took place in the lower hall of La Tour Neuve. Here, for the first time since Gilles's arrest, he had an opportunity to see just what other effect, besides his nighttime pleasures, his murders had had. And it is just here, in an ambience far removed from Gilles's passionate bedrooms, that we get, from the pages of historical comments and the dry legalisms of the trial transcripts, the echo of that low-key groan of the parents and the relatives of the children who had come to be "a file of witnesses, poor folk weeping and sobbing, recounting with detail how their children had been stolen." [18]

It was October 13. The reading of the charges took a long time. There were forty-nine articles, many of which, in the style of legal garrulity, specified, qualified, and defined points of law as well as matters of substance. Pulsating among the legalisms, there was a "catalog of crime, a luxury of offenses that exhausted the prosecutor to qualify in proper terms and which, before a mixed assembly, could only be pronounced decently in Latin and not in vulgar language." [19] Thus, Thomas Wilson, writing in an age in which Latin was still used to hide, not horrid details, but sexual ones. The fact is that the children suffered and died, and their tormentor exulted over them in a common language—French.

The charges against Gilles and the Articles of Accusation follow:

> *Article I* establishes the Cathedral of Nantes as a center for archiepiscopal power.
> *Article II* further elaborates the powers of the bishopric and its rights to make ecclesiastical judgments.

Article III establishes the bishop's right to sit in judgment.

Article IV expresses the rights of the bishop to make censures, excommunications, punishments for excesses and crimes, and so on.

Article V specifies that Guillaume Merici, Inquisitor for Heresy in the realm of France, has been deputized to serve in this case.

Article VI specifies Merici's age, his quality: Professor of Holy Scripture.

Article VII specifies that the holy bishop of Nantes and the Inquisitor for Heresy have the right to inquire together into matters of apostacy, idolatry, divinations, superstitions—but principally, heresy.

Article VIII specifies that Guillaume Merici of the Order of Preaching Friars has the power to substitute in his place someone else.

Article IX makes clear that Gilles de Rais is a member of a "justiciable" parish.

Article X, that Gilles de Rais, from the time of his birth and adolescence, was subject to the spiritual authority of the bishop of Nantes and that of the Inquisitor.

Article XI reiterates Gilles's residence in the appropriate parish.

Article XII asserts that Guillaume Merici has deputized Jean Blouyn of the Order of Preaching Friars in his place.

Article XIII specifies Jean Blouyn's age—forty.

Article XIV specifies that everything preceding this article is well known by all to be true.

It is with Article XV that we come to the heart of the matter. Here we read that

[i]n consequence of public rumors and secret inquiry carried out by the Lord Bishop of Nantes in his towns and in his diocese as well as by his appointed commissioners in regard to the crimes developed further on, and in response to reiterated denunciations tearfully and dolefully uttered by various people of one and the other sex . . . [regarding] the loss and the death of their children, sons and daughters . . . as well in the town as in the [villages] of the diocese of Nantes [that these children] had been taken by Gilles de Rais, the accused, by Gilles de Sillé, by Roger de Briqueville, by Henri Griart, by Etienne Corrillault, otherwise known as Poitou, by André Buchet, by Jean Rossignol, by Robin Romulart, and by a certain Spadine, and by Hicquet de Bremont, cronies and dependents of the said accused Gilles de Rais, the accused, and by them these children had been inhumanly strangled, killed and afterward dismembered and burned, and in other ways tormented shamefully.

The prosecutor

> declares and intends to prove, if necessary, that for fourteen years,
> more or less during [all] those years, all those months, all those days, all
> those nights, all those hours of those fourteen years . . . that the said
> Gilles de Rais, imbued with a wicked spirit, and forgetful of his salva-
> tion, has taken boys and girls, that these children were killed,
> dismembered, burned and treated without humanity as without
> shame.[20]

Names, places, dates, details of torture, forms of invocation. Names, places, dates: Machecoul, Saint-Etienne-de-Mer-Morte, Saint-Cyr-en-Rais, Saint-Marie-de-Nantes. Heretic, relapsed, sorcerer, sodomist, invoker of evil spirits, magician, murderer of children, apostate, idolater.

The prosecutor's language has all the sonority that fits a trial in which not only punishment but also the salvation of the criminal are issues. For twentieth-century readers, there is a certain imbalance in the focus of the outrage on violations of faith and not on the torment and death of the children. But, in the view of the judges (and of Gilles), this world had hardly any significance in comparison with the world to come. The prosecutor could intone, "It is not fitting that Christians, who nurture the desire to be united one day with the angelic choir [that such Christians], should make their pasture of debauchery," [21] and feel perfectly certain that his auditors and the criminal in the dock shared his view that Gilles's crimes were enormous because of the ways in which he had incurred damnation.

Guillaume Chapeillon's voice droned on, but Gilles, better than Chapeillon, knew what his crimes were. Here, there was the rustle of paper, the sound of pens scraping hurriedly across pages, but there was nothing to suggest the sound of children whimpering; nothing to see that would suggest the pale finished look on the face of a child as it faded toward death; or that would suggest the spiritual affronts, the demonic strivings and erotic ingenuities that had engrossed the defendant. An artist given the task at that moment of making a drawing that would display the mind and soul of Gilles de Rais would pray for blindness. Albert Jean, in an inspired moment of his *Le Secret de Barbe-Bleue,* found the phrase that hints at what had happened to Gilles. "The human and the divine, joining together, ended by confounding each other." [22]

Gilles sat in the courtroom dressed, according to some accounts, in the white garb of the Carmelites; according to others, in red garments. I prefer to see him, as Vizitelly describes him, dressed in white, "wearing a doublet of pearl grey silk embroidered with golden stars edged with ermine and secured at the waist by a scarlet sash from which hung a dagger with a sheath of scarlet velvet. His *chapel,* or round cap, was bordered with ermine—which only the great feudatories of Brittany were privileged to wear—and from his neck hung certain orders of dignity or chivalry with a heavy gold chain to which a reliquary was attached." [23] Whether the relic it contained was the bit of the true cross Gilles wore while he was invoking Satan, we are not told. Nor are we told what was Gilles's mien as the charges were being read. Charles Lemire says that as Gilles sat, "the muscles of his face contracted. . . . Something sinister appeared in his face. He ground his teeth at intervals, like a ferocious animal deprived of its prey . . . his fixed eyes dilated in their sockets . . . his beard anointed with perfumed oil gave off bluish sparkles, like the wings of a raven. All who watched, shuddering with horror, cried, 'See him . . . Bluebeard.' " [24]

While the pen-and-ink men dickered over words, Gilles looked up and noticed, probably for the first time since he had become his crimes, that there was the rest of the world. That the room in which he sat contained any number of other selves, all of them as ambitious for ecstasy and sleep as he had been. With the possible exception of his relationship with Prelati, who had come too late, and in any case to no healing purpose, into his life, Gilles had lived since his retirement from the wars as if there were no other will in the world but his own.

He looked around the room and saw men and women there who were the parents of "his" children. Peasants, for the most part. Illiterate folk who had waited patiently for the Latin reading of the charges to end so they could hear them, as they were now being reread, in French—not as a courtesy to the common folk, but rather to ensure that Gilles, who prided himself on his elegant Latin, might by no means be able to complain that he had not understood the charges. These peasants or bakers or cobblers . . . the *menu peuple* . . . were hearing openly named what, for so many years, had only been whispered. What Gilles saw in their faces as they listened to the droning affidavits must have startled him. His victims had come from large families, or small ones. They had been cuffed and dandled, sent on errands, kissed, scolded . . . by fathers and mothers, uncles and aunts. They had all had sisters or brothers. The amazing thing was how the children were all *remembered,* while he who had known them more intimately than anyone in the world could not recall who they were or how many of them he had killed. Now, it appeared that they had been children with names and histories. For him they had been the raw material from which to shape ecstasies.

If ever there was to be a proper moment for Gilles to have a revulsion of feeling, to fall on his knees before parents and judges, surely this was it. Instead, Gilles, hearing his acts named, turned himself into a towering figure of scorn. When he was asked if he would reply to any of the Articles of Accusation, he answered "with pride and hauteur that he did not wish to respond to the various positions and articles." [25] These people—the bishop and the vicar of the Inquisition—were not, and had never been, his judges. "Simoniacs," he cried. "Ribalds. I'd rather be hanged by the neck than reply to the likes of such clerics and such judges. It is not to be borne . . . to appear before such as you." [26] Then, angrier still, he turned to the Bishop Malestroit, sneering, as if he were still a man with worldly gifts at his command, "I'll do nothing for you as Bishop of Nantes." [27] Patiently, the bishop bore the affront, then joined his colleague of the Inquisition, Jean Blouyn, in asking again whether Gilles wished to answer to the charges. One can see Gilles hiding behind the look of a stubborn twelve-year-old telling the grown-ups to go lump it, shaking his head. No. He would not reply to the charges. No. Not he.

Once. Twice. A third time and a fourth, he was asked to reply. "No," said Gilles, "*I* know the Catholic faith as well as those who have put forward these charges against me. I am as good a Christian, and as good a Catholic as they. And if I had done the things charged against me I would have directly committed a crime against the Catholic faith." [28] With a small boy's shrewdness, he tried to insert a wedge between his ecclesiastical judges and Pierre de l'Hôpital, who was in charge of the secular trial, crying out in mock astonishment that l'Hôpital would permit ecclesiastics to meddle with such crimes as were contained in the indictment.

It was a fine frenzy he went into. If it was a role he was playing, his judges were not impressed with his performance. When it was over, they declared him "manifestly contumacious"—in writing.

Gilles, as he had earlier appealed from the court itself, now appealed from the decree of excommunication. The judges, "given the nature of the case . . . and [of] the enormous and horrible crimes charged against the said Gilles," [29] denied the appeal. Then the letter from Guillaume Merici of the Order of Preaching Friars appointing Jean Blouyn as judge in his place was read. Gilles was asked if he had any comment. "No," he said. With that, the trial was adjourned for forty-eight hours. A fuming Gilles de Rais was led back to his chambers in La Tour Neuve.

Something inexplicable happened to Gilles de Rais in the forty-eight hours that intervened before his next appearance in the courtroom. There was no change in his imprisonment. He was still in the spacious rooms he had occupied from the beginning. But something had turned over in his soul. For the Abbé Bossard, the change in Gilles marks the beginning of a Christian miracle; Michel Bataille sees the change as a manifestation of Gilles's spiritual defeat, while Georges Bataille sees Gilles as entering a period of delirious despair. These are all points of view that can be reasonably held, but I would like to add that the change in Gilles may also be related to a sudden attack of downright fear. Gilles, as a soldier, had experienced plenty of physical danger, but always he had met it with a sword in his good right hand. In the courtroom, he had played out the imposture of the innocent boy tormented by mean grown-ups, and it had deceived no one. There, too, he had had a good strong whiff of the detestation his life and acts had created in the populace. So long as he had been free and powerful, suck folk could detest him all they liked. They were *canailles* whose best excuse for living was that they had begotten beautiful children who could, by force or wile, be brought to Gilles so that he might fondle them to death. But Gilles, the prisoner, had seen how in that courtroom the very body heat of the fathers and mothers had massed together to create a white hot conscience that neither Gilles nor his judges could ignore. And it had suddenly occurred to Gilles that his judges meant to kill him. That he, Gilles de Rais, would, like the children, be rendered bound and helpless, and made to die. It was a terrible thing to know.

It was in the grip of that despair, I think, that it occurred to Gilles, the theatrical man, the failed artist, that there might be something magnificent left for him to do in this life. He would mount one final stage play that would speak to all of the selves of Gilles de Rais: to the warrior, and to the comrade-in-arms of Jeanne d'Arc; to the torturer and murderer of children; to the passionate Christian. On the spot, he invented—not cynically—the "Mystery of Gilles de Rais." He would become a Christian allegory, and by dying well, he would, in Georges Bataille's splendid phrase, "Make a torch of a disaster."

Miracle or new charade, or something else again, the Gilles de Rais who made his appearance before the court on October 15 was a very different man from the one who had snarled at his judges two days earlier. For a moment, the change was not perceptible. Asked if he was ready to reply to the Articles of Accusation, he replied that he had nothing to say against them. He was then asked if he recognized the legitimacy of the court, to which, to everyone's astonishment, he replied, "Yes, I recognize as my judges the Bishop of Nantes [and] the Vicar of the Inquisition, Jean Blouyn." More than that, he "spontaneously avowed having committed and evilly perpetrated crimes in their jurisdiction." Then he suddenly dissolved into tears. Through his sobs he begged pardon of the judges for his earlier behavior, for his "sinister" and "wounding" speech. The judges accorded him their pardon and, in the bathos of the exchange, got Gilles to take the oath he had so long withheld. Then Jean Prégent, bishop of Saint-Brieuc, read the charges once more to Gilles, both in Latin and in French. Gilles this time acknowledged *some* of the charges but denied that "he had ever invoked or caused to be invoked evil spirits, or had offered or caused to be offered anything whatever in the way of sacrifice to such spirits." [30] This denial stands like an island of deception to which he felt he must cling. The matter was so important to him that he offered to submit himself to the Ordeal by Fire to prove he was telling the truth. He did admit, however, that he had borrowed a certain book on sorcery from a soldier at Angers, and that he had read it. But that was all. He had returned the book. In his rush of speech, he admitted having spoken to the Angers soldier about alchemy; and he acknowledged having studied and practiced that art.

Despite his refusal to admit any dealings with Satan, the general amity he had established with his judges was not marred, and the trial proceeded with the entry into the courtroom of his chief accomplices. For Gilles, they were familiar faces. For the audience, it was a sinister lineup: Henri Griart, Etienne Corillaut, known as Poitou, Blanchet, Prelati, and the murky Perrine Martin, nicknamed La Meffraye. Two people were missing from that crowd, Gilles's cousins, Roger de Briqueville and Gilles de Sillé, who had managed somehow to be elsewhere when Gilles and the others were arrested. Gilles was asked if he cared to question these witnesses and was offered a full day for such an interrogation, but he replied that he reposed confidence in them.

All of the accomplices then swore that "neither favor, nor resentment, nor fear, nor hatred, nor friendship, nor hostility would have any part in their testimony, and that they would put aside all partisan spirit and all personal affection, and that they would have only truth and justice in view." [31]

Having been sworn, Gilles's helpers were taken out of the courtroom so that they might be interrogated by various clerks. No sooner were they gone than Gilles threw himself on his knees and in a torrent of sobs begged the judges to remove from him his sentence of excommunication. The judges, moved by the sincerity of this anguished outburst, hastened to grant his request, and he became once again a communicant.

The sixteenth to the eighteenth of October were devoted to taking further testimony from the accomplices and other witnesses. The confessions of Prelati, Blanchet, Griart and Coriaullt (Poitou) form an important part of the trial transcript. Prelati and Blanchet give us much of what we know about Gilles's dealings with Satan, while Henriet and Poitou are especially detailed about Gilles's crimes against the children. On the seventeenth, Gilles heard more witnesses giving their depositions. As before, he was asked if he wished to question any of them. Again, he replied that he did not wish to. On October 19, in the course of a similar session, he was urged to "give, say, propose, allege or produce for his salvation and justification any important reason regarding his crimes, offences or facts urged against him"; [32] but Gilles declined this opportunity as well, saying, "I know of nothing other than what [I] have said and replied elsewhere." [33]

On the twentieth of October, with the court in session in the upper chamber of La Tour Neuve, the patient *promoteur*, Chapeillon, read *all* the testimony transcribed to that date. Once again, the flat dry voice with its "abovesaids," its "hereunders," its "items" and its "accuseds" sounded the role of Gilles's life achievements: dying children, ecstatic disembowelings, night visits to rainy fields in search of the devil; a tempestuous attack on a priest. The voice was dry as dust; the matter was death and desolation.

The reading done, Gilles was asked again the formulaic question, "Do you wish to reply to any of the charges or to interrogate or contradict any of the witnesses?" By this time, each and every one of Gilles's abominations had been frequently named, so that Chapeillon's request to the prisoner was made in an atmosphere of horror and loathing. Gilles's silence, if he persisted in it, would now be a tacit but imprecise confession. And imprecision would not do. In a medieval ecclesiastical court, conviction of the prisoner was not the issue. A full, detailed and "voluntary" confession was required. Vizitelly writes, "the Promoter rose to point out the gravity of the prisoner's reply, which showed that the alleged crimes had really been committed by him. But it was necessary that the tribunal should be fully enlightened, said Chapeillon." [34] But the court could not convict a man who merely assented vaguely. It wanted a detailed impeachment of the witnesses or a full and complete confession from Gilles. Nevertheless, when Gilles was, once more, asked whether he wished to comment on or to complain of the testimony given against him, he replied, as he had before, with a laconic no. In order therefore to "elucidate and scrutinize more amply the truth, the Promoter asked [that] torture or the Question, should be applied to the said Gilles, the accused." [35] The court, duly considering the matter, gave its assent. Gilles de Rais, perhaps the master torturer of all time, was to be put to the torture.

Here we come to a head-on collision about the moral cost of

The water torture.

justice as the majesty of the Church prepares to torment the handsome body of Gilles de Rais in order to make him say, for the sake of truth and the welfare of his soul, what has already been said by his accomplices and has been tacitly acknowledged by Gilles. The good torturer meeting the bad one? The responsible torturer meeting the selfish one? If we believe in society, our answer is a reluctant yes. The Church was willing to orchestrate pain for the sake of truth as Gilles had orchestrated it for the sake of pleasure. Still, something sticks in the throat. One cannot really bring oneself to judge a dialogue of torturers. Pain, one would think, should be the issue. Whether for humanity pain, deliberately, intelligently, and slowly applied, is a permissible implement in the pursuit of pleasure—or of truth and order.

In the Christian middle ages, torture was an established aid to the legal system, though "in practice," writes D. B. Wyndham Lewis, "it was ordered by medieval judges only when every other means of getting at the truth was exhausted. No Inquisitor could order it without consulting the bishop of the diocese or his official representative beforehand." [36]

The Question to which Gilles might be subjected could be applied in two categories. There was first, the *Question préparatoire* and then, the *Question définitive*. The first was employed *sur de simple indécis,* that is, against ordinary vagueness, to help the prisoner to a clear head; the second, the *Question définitive,* was used when the prisoner was already deemed guilty, but more information was required of him (names of accomplices, places, dates). The *Question définitive* in its turn had two parts: *définitif ordinaire* and *définitif extraordinaire.* The difference between the two, as their names suggest, is the intensity and duration of pain imposed on the prisoner. In Gilles's case, it was surely the *Question définitive* that would be required. Whether it became *définitif ordinaire* or *extraordinaire* would depend on Gilles's constitution and his power of resistance.

The most usual form of the Question was "with water." This required putting a funnel in the prisoner's mouth and making him swallow endless buckets of water. Or the water could be forced into his eyes or his ears, or his anus. Human ingenuity being what it is, there were a great many other forms of the Question. In Brittany, where Gilles lived, a favorite way of "putting the Question" required the victim to be strapped into an iron chair that was then slowly drawn closer and closer to a red-hot furnace. "In Normandy," Paul Lacroix tells us, "one thumb was squeezed in a screw in the ordinary, and both thumbs in the extraordinary torture. At Autun, after high boots made of spongy leather had been placed on the culprit's feet, he was tied onto a table near a large fire, and a quantity of boiling water was poured on the boots, which penetrated the leather, ate away the flesh and even dissolved the bones of the victim." [37] The *veglia*, a torture used in Italy, bears a grim resemblance, including a compassionate interlude, to one of Gilles's private scenarios. The victim of the *veglia* was "stretched horizontally by means of ropes passing through rings riveted into the wall, and attached to the four limbs, the only support given to the culprit being the point of a stake cut in a diamond shape, which just touched the end of the backbone. A doctor and a surgeon were always present, feeling the pulse at the temples of the patient, so as to be able to judge of the moment when he could not any longer bear the pain. At that moment he was untied, hot fomentations were used to revive him, restoratives were administered, and as soon as he had recovered a little strength, he was again put to the torture, which went on thus for six hours." [38]

It is both easy and embarrassing to human self-esteem to go on with the list of ways in which the Question could be put.[39] Gilles, we may be sure, knew about them all. What we do not know is how ꞏꞏles took the promoter's request for permission to put Gilles to ꞏhꞏ Question, nor how he reacted when the court named the very next day, Friday, the twenty-first of October, as the time for the torture to be administered; but we may assume that another fissure had opened in his already cracking facade of imperturbability. He knew too much about torture to consider for a moment submitting to it himself. Pain had been his elixir; it had served him as a source of energy flowing from the bodies of his victims, and it had sustained him on his desperate pilgrimage to the forbidden. This time, however, he, Gilles de Rais, would be the victim, helplessly bound, endlessly molested, elaborately hurt.

On Friday, the twenty-first, Gilles was brought to the lower hall of La Tour Neuve and was ordered to prepare himself for the torture. But Gilles fell on his knees and begged his judges to defer the execution of the torture for one more day, promising that at the end of that time he would have deliberated on his crimes to such effect that he would be able to answer his judges' questions in a way that would make torture unnecessary. He suggested that the bishop of Saint-Brieuc and Pierre de l'Hôpital, representing, respectively, the ecclesiastical and the secular courts, should prepare themselves to hear his confession "somewhere away from the torture chambers." [40]

The judges compromised. They delayed the torture until that afternoon at two. At that time, the bishop and Pierre de l'Hôpital, accompanied by the necessary scribes, clerks, and witnesses, including Jean Labbé, who had arrested him, met with Gilles. Jean Petit was also there to transcribe the proceedings.

In this meeting "in chambers" with representatives of the two courts, Gilles seems to be fighting a rearguard action. Though the transcript of the proceedings, ignoring the hovering threat of torture, says that Gilles spoke freely and without constraint, his confession is generalized. Yes, he says, he committed crimes against numerous children. Yes, he committed homicide and sodomy. Yes, he invoked demons. The admissions are there, but they are muffled, as if Gilles, though he had settled with himself that he would hang, could not bring himself to stipulate, in his own voice, precisely what he had done to deserve hanging.

And yet, it is in this muted confession that there occurs between Gilles and Pierre de l'Hôpital, the president of the secular court, the following remarkable exchange: When de l'Hôpital asked Gilles to say who had induced him to commit his crimes, the baron replied, "I did and perpetrated them following [the dictates] of my imagination and my thought, without the advice of anyone, and according to my own judgment and entirely for my own pleasure and physical delight, and for no other intention or end." [41]

De l'Hôpital, his mind still swarming with the frequently repeated details he had learned from other witnesses about Gilles's workshop of iniquity, shook his head and demanded a second time what motives Gilles could give for his treatment of the children. Gilles, "as if indignant at being thus solicited and interrogated, said in French to the Lord President, 'Alas, Monsieur, you torment yourself, and me as well.' To which the Lord President said in French, 'I do not torment myself at all, but I am very astonished at what you have told me, and, simply enough, I cannot be satisfied with [your reply]. But, I want and desire to know the pure truth.' "

Gilles answered with the utmost simplicity, " 'Truly, there was no other reason, no other end, no other intention except what I have said. I have told you greater things than this—enough to execute ten thousand men.' " [42]

Gilles, in the very few minutes the exchange had taken, had achieved a moment of greatness—from which later he would several times retreat. But here, the real Gilles de Rais takes on the stature of Milton's, or Victor Hugo's, fictional Satan. He alone was entirely responsible for his acts. All of them.

Pierre de l'Hôpital was silenced. There was a pause in the proceedings, then, at de l'Hôpital's signal, François Prelati was brought in. The handsome, glib young Italian had earlier made a very complete confession in which, while he acknowledged helping his master with alchemical experiments and demonic invocations, he had very carefully dissociated himself from anything involving the rape and death of children. This time, he was interrogated very briefly, along with Gilles. The story of the offer to the demon Barron of the hands, heart, eyes, and blood of a slain child was told once more, but Prelati stressed that the child whose remains were used was one whom he had seen already dead at Tiffauges.

Gilles, despite Prelati's deft distancing of himself from his crimes, seemed as dazzled as ever by the Italian. As his young lover was being led from the room, Gilles, "in tears, and sighing, embraced Prelati, saying, 'Adieu, François, my friend. We will never see each other again in this world; I pray God will give you good patience and understanding, and be sure that so long as you have good patience and hope in God that we will meet again in the great gladness of Paradise.' " [43]

For those who think that Gilles's closing days represent the triumphant struggle of a Christian sinner to achieve salvation, Gilles's confession on Saturday, October 22, has the ring of grandeur in it. "History," writes the Abbé Bossard, "shows him to us as he had been, [guilty] of crime and debauchery. It ought to do him the justice of showing him as he appeared in the final days of his mortal life, before God and before men: before God, so repentant as to make one believe that he had obtained His pity and pardon; before men, submissive enough to misfortune and justice to merit their mingling of hatred with pity, vengeance with prayer." [44]

More secular readers of the documents, like myself, are likely to see in Gilles's confession a model of hysteria endeavoring to achieve patience as he reaches into his soul and into the void and into his memories of how such things are done to find a rhetorical style that will somehow present him as a pitiable creature to the world. The confession stumbles forward or sideward or backward as Gilles moves from heartfelt truth to pathetic banalities. There are moments of grandeur that decline suddenly into petit-bourgeois phrases. There are admirable reachings for profundity that turn out to be overreachings. It is not easy to ad-lib greatness. Someone is always coughing or looking the other way. Gilles is at his worst whenever he tries to draw a moral from his life. Then there is a sharp drop in the mood of his speech and he sounds like a modestly endowed after-dinner speaker who is doing splendidly in his introductory remarks, until he discovers he has run out of content three minutes into a speech scheduled to last for an hour. He is at his most honest—because the details are so intractable—when he is specifying the manner of his crimes.

The session opened with the judges giving Gilles for the fifth or sixth time a chance to defend himself against any of the testimony heard to that point. Again, he replied that he had nothing to say. Then, like a chess player who has made a wrong move but who still holds the piece he is playing, he drew back his reply. "All of a sudden, without any pressure on him, without provocation of any sort, his features were convulsed; pain appeared in every line, reflecting the bitterness of his soul. Tears gushed from his eyes." [45] And speech from his throat in a deluge, as he reaffirmed the truth of his earlier but generalized confession. He begged for that confession to be read again so that he might correct and complete it publicly; then, without pause he plunged right in, crying, "From the time of my youth I have committed many great crimes against God and the Ten Commandments, crimes still worse than those of which I stand accused. And I have offended our Savior as a consequence of my bad upbringing in childhood, when I was left uncontrolled to do whatever I pleased [and especially] to take pleasure in illicit acts." [46]

He begged his judges to permit him to elaborate his crimes and urged that his full confession of them be published, in "the vulgar tongue," so that most of the audience, which did not know Latin, would know the full extent of his shame.

"When I was a child," he said, "I had always a delicate nature, and did for my own pleasure and according to my own will whatever evil I pleased." Then followed a piece of tastelessness as he deduced the easy moral: "To all [of you who are] fathers and mothers, friends and relatives of young people and children, lovingly I beg and pray you to train them in good morals, [teach] them to follow good examples and good doctrines; and instruct them and punish them, lest they fall into the same trap in which I myself have fallen." [47]

With that he went on to confess voluntarily and publicly before all that "for my ardor and my sensual delectation I took and caused to be taken a great number of children—how many I cannot say precisely, children whom I killed and caused to be killed; with them, I committed the vice and the sin of sodomy . . . and . . . I emitted spermatic semen in the most culpable fashion on the belly of . . . the children, as well before as after their deaths, and also while they were dying. I, alone, or with the help of my accomplices, Gilles de Sillé, Roger de Bricqueville, Henriet [Griart], Etienne Corrillaut (Poitou), Rossignol and Petit Robin, have inflicted various kinds and manners of torture on these children. Sometimes I beheaded them with daggers, with poignards, with knives; sometimes I beat them violently on the head with a stick or with other contusive instruments . . . sometimes I suspended them in my room from a pole or by a hook and cords and strangled them; and when they were languishing, I committed with them the vice of sodomy. . . . When the children were dead, I embraced them, and I gazed at those which had the most beautiful heads and the loveliest members, and I caused their bodies to be cruelly opened and took delight in viewing their interior organs; and very often, as the children were dying, I sat on their bellies and was delighted to see them dying in that fashion and laughed about it with . . . Corrillaut and Henriet, after which I caused [the children] to be burned and converted their cadavres into dust." [48]

From the details of the deaths of the children, he leaped to the stories of his invocations, reciting the details of those absurd flirtations with hell with the relentlessness of a metronome: stories of signs traced on the ground in the form of circles or of crosses. Spells recited by the light of the moon or of flickering torches; invocations with Prelati; invocations with Prelati's predecessors; the story of

Prelati's book of demonic names; his own role as a would-be Satanist who was willing to promise Satan everything but his life and soul.

For an instant, he was interrupted by a question: "Why had he maintained Prelati in his household?" Gilles, on trial for his life, could think of no better reason to give than that Prelati was a talented man with agreeable manners who spoke Latin with elegance and refinement. It was a lover's reply, not a defendant's.

But Gilles did not pause to correct it. He plunged on, describing more murders. Then, changing direction, he told the story of the assault on Saint-Etienne-de-Mer-Morte. Then, veering, more details of the deaths of children: two pages whose names, this time, he remembered: Guillaume Daussy and Pierre Jacquet, called Princé. Then the murder at Vannes.

Then, further satanic invocations with Prelati's predecessors: Dumesnil; Jean de la Rivière; a person named Louis; another named Antoine de Palerme; and another someone whose name he could not recall. Then the story of Satan in the form of a leopard; and the Satan who did not show up because Gilles, who hoped for power and wealth, *would* repeat a prayer to Our Lady as he waited for his visit from the Lord of the Flies.

Then a melancholy memory: He had meant to give up his wicked life and go on a pilgrimage to Jerusalem, "and to do all I could to obtain the mercy of my Redeemer and the remission of my sins." [49] Then more piety as Gilles advised his audience to venerate our Holy Mother the Church, urging as proof of her power that if he, Gilles, had not been firm in his faith, "the devil, by reason of the enormity of my crimes and wickedness, would long ago have destroyed my body and taken my soul." [50] Then, more advice on how to raise children: Do not dress them too delicately; do not permit them to live in idleness "since many evils come from idleness and excesses at table." [51]

One senses that Gilles was running out of steam, but he had not yet run out of breath. Fearful lest he lose the attention of his listeners, he made one final reach for something important to say and created a hellish moment. Turning to the spectators, he cried, "With humility and in tears I implore the mercy and the pardon of my Creator and very holy Redeemer, as well as the mercy and the pardon of the relatives and friends of the children [I have]

so cruelly massacred. . . . You, whoever you are whom I have
sinned against and injured, whether you are present now, or elsewhere, [give me] I beg, the succor of your Christian prayers." [52]
D. B. Wyndham Lewis thinks that here in our reading of the trial
transcript, "It is permissible to hear a tumult of astonished and
conflicting cries, not unmixed with weeping; but chiefly exclama-
tions of pity and forgiveness. . . . At any time before Gilles' last cry
the populace of Nantes might well have been capable of tearing
him in pieces. They now perceived him to be a miserable fellow
sinner facing death and in instant need of their help. It is impossible to believe that the prayers he begged were withheld from him,
or that he paced his chamber that night without feeling himself
ringed round with charity and supplications like a friendly
flame." [53] Lewis is, I think, badly mistaken. Gilles's turning to beg
forgiveness of the parents and friends of his victims is an act of
tactlessness as grating to one's moral sensibilities as his *fade* preach-
ments on how to raise children. Having excoriated the hearts of the
parents with the details of his lubricities, he had no right five
minutes later to ask anything of them; not their pardon; not their
prayers.

There is no reason to doubt that Gilles's piece of bad theater
moved his audience. The sight of an evil, rich, and powerful man
in tears begging for the prayers of the people whom he had most
abused makes an affecting allegory of the Fall of Princes. When it
was all over, a deep embarrassment must have fallen upon the
audience. This was supposed to be a court of law, a place for
justice. But there was no punishment fit to deal with the crimes
that had been so lavishly confessed. Or, if one could be devised, it
would have to be as creatively bestial as Gilles had been. Finally,
the judges turned aside from their quandary with an official gesture of delay. The trial was set over to the twenty-fifth of October
when their verdict, and their sentence, would be announced.

I must have justice, or I will destroy myself. And not justice
in some remote infinite time and space, but here on earth,
and that I could see myself. . . . But then there are the chil-

dren, and what am I to do about them? . . . Listen! If all must suffer to pay for the eternal harmony, what have children to do with it, tell me please?

—Fyodor Dostoevsky

On the twenty-fifth of October, the streets of Nantes were crowded with townsfolk and with visitors from the surrounding countryside. The great Lord Gilles de Rais, noble, illustrious, powerful, was to be sentenced on that day, and though the verdicts were a foregone conclusion, those who had lost children as well as those who only sensed that a unique historical event was about to take place were keyed to a pitch of excitement.

For Gilles, it was a time for wondering. Of memories of childhood; or the shape of a window recently seen; the look on the face of a squirrel confronting a cat. Death was coming soon and, with its coming, all that had once appeared strange or feverish flattened out and cooled. Until now, he might have dreamed of blustering or buying his way out of trouble, but that was all over now. Though he still breathed and walked and talked, the fact is that he had become a man whose will no longer had meaning. He might say or command what he liked, but his future was now fully in the hands of others, down to the most trivial detail. Like his victims, Gilles had become an object.

At nine o'clock, the court was convened. First, it was the turn of the ecclesiastical court to hand down its verdict. Before that could happen, a preamble insisting on the scrupulosity of the court had to be read. After that, the bishop of Nantes rose and read the sentence:

The holy name of Christ invoked, We, Jean, Bishop of Nantes, and Brother Jean Blouyn, bachelor in Holy Scriptures, of the Order of Preaching Friars of Nantes, delegate of the Inquisitor for heresy for the city and diocese of Nantes . . . after having examined the depositions of the witnesses . . . after having well weighed and considered all the other reasons which have affected our decision . . . after having heard his [Gilles de Rais's] own confession made spontaneously in our presence . . we pronounce, we declare, we decide that you . . . are shamefully guilty of heresy, apostasy, of the evocation of demons; that for these crimes you have incurred the sentence of excommunication, and all

other punishments required by law; and, . . . that you should be
punished, as both law and the holy canons require as a heretic, an
apostate and an invocator of demons.[54]

This was the sentence that satisfied the watchful Inquisition.
There was a second ecclesiastical sentence, handed down by the
bishop independently. In this one, the bishop said,

> We decree, we pronounce, we declare that you, Gilles de Rais, . . . have
> shamefully committed the crime against nature with children of one
> and the other sex; that you have violated the immunities of the
> Church; that by these crimes you have incurred the sentence of excom-
> munication and all other punishments fixed by law and that, in
> consequence, you should be punished and corrected for your salvation,
> as law and holy canons require.[55]

These sentences read, Gilles had to consider himself, as of that
moment, once again outside the spiritual protection of the Church.
That exile, as we have seen before, held special terrors for Gilles.
When he was asked if he would detest his crimes as a condition for
being reincorporated into the Church, he replied meekly: "I have
never known what heresy was, and I did not know that I had fallen
into my errors . . . but since the Church today has taught me that
my crimes have led me into heresy, I beg to be readmitted to the
bosom of our holy mother, the Church." [56] This was said on his
knees, and was followed by another outburst of grief in which he
asked to be reassured that both sentences of excommunication
would be lifted. The request was immediately granted. Then he
asked to be assigned a priest who should hear his confession. This,
too, was granted to him. Brother Jean Juvenel was assigned the
task, and with that, the ecclesiastical trial was over. It was eleven
o'clock in the morning.

Before the judgment of the secular court, under the presidency
of Pierre l'Hôpital, could pronounce its verdict, the bishop spoke
the formulary sentence, "Go in peace. The Church can defend you
no longer; it delivers you [now] to the secular arm." Traditionally,
the prelate was supposed to add a plea for clemency, but in this
case, the compassionate phrases were omitted. The Abbé Bossard
thinks that given the enormity of Gilles's crimes the gentle words
would have struck the wrong note. The abbé also observes, para-
phrasing Voltaire in another context, that "if the death penalty

had not existed in society, it is for such crimes as these that it would have had to be invented." [57]

In any case, the secular court's judgment was handed down in the Château du Bouffay, before which a huge crowd surged. First, Gilles reiterated the key elements of his confession. He accepted the responsibility for his attack against Saint-Etienne-de-Mer-Morte, specifying each of the illegal details of the foray: that he had taken the place by force; that he had mistreated Jean le Ferron. He acknowledged, too, having "killed a great number of little children, males, that he had caused them to be burned and turned to powder in order to suppress traces of his crimes . . . and that he had committed the other crimes described in his confession." [58] Once again, the detailed list of his crimes was given him to read. He read it, assenting to each of the details.

By now, the Baron Gilles de Rais had given over to the prisoner Gilles. For more than a month, he had sustained the chill, the freezing. Now, he was ready for the letting go. After the paradoxes of prayer and blood, then the alternations between mock and real humility, and the explosions of arrogance and straightforward lying, one senses that the last rigidity is leaving Gilles; that perhaps he has learned to acquiesce to the insignificance of his presence in the Creation. Even before the verdict of the court was sounded, one senses a new repose in Gilles. He yields to the bookkeeping of justice and specifies his acts. There is no further posturing. From now on he takes on the decent task of dying well.

This is not to say that the actor in him suddenly perished. The prospect of death does much for one's sense of humility, but it is unlikely to erase the very last of our self-delusions. Still, there was a great silence gathered around him now, and in that silence, perhaps for the first time, he actually heard the weeping of the children for what it was: the melody of *their* pain rather than sounds to entice him. Their pain; their cries; their death. And he had caused them to die. And it was too late.

It had taken him a long, long time, but finally, it had come to him that he was one of us. That death was not only a weapon to shake at an enemy—or a suave contrivance to rouse his lust— but also an end to somebody's life. That it was the common experience, as irreversible as being born. That it was an event so final it was beyond the reach of rhetoric. That it was about to happen to him.

This is all to say that even in a secular sense, Gilles de Rais, as he stood before Pierre l'Hôpital to hear the verdict of the court, was ready for salvation.

The sentence read aloud was almost an anticlimax. It was the verdict of the secular court that Gilles "deserved to die." And that he should be "hanged and burned . . . and that the sentence would be carried out on the following day, at eleven o'clock." [59]

There was a pause. No one knows quite what to do with the silence that follows on a death penalty. Then Gilles spoke. He had some final requests to make. One was that he begged to die before either Poitou or Henriet, his accomplices, lest they, going to their death, might at the last moment believe that Gilles, given his power and connections, might yet escape punishment. His other request was that his body, unlike that of his accomplices, was to be taken down from the gallows shortly after the noose and the flames had killed him, so that his remains might be buried. This request, too, was granted Gilles in consideration of his high rank. The bodies of his accomplices, commoners, would be reduced to ashes by the flames.

There was a brief exchange of courtesies between the condemned man and his judges that so heartened Gilles that he was emboldened to make one more request of them. And here, I think, we have one more flaring up of the Gilles de Rais who had spent a fortune on *Le Mistère du Siège d'Orléans*. Gilles, the theatrical man, could not resist asking that there be a solemn procession the next day from his prison to the gallows. Such a procession would more than likely have taken place in any case since both the duke and the bishop would want to make a display of their justice. Gilles's request was instantly granted and he was led away. He had one final dark night of the body and soul to endure.

EXPIATION

This innocence, unlike the Biblical one, comes after the complete awareness of sin, beyond the hope of redemption.

—Lorenza Trucchi

Gilles waited for his death without much earthly consolation. His shadowy wife, Catherine, kept to her lonely grounds at Pouzauges where, for years, she had stayed out of Gilles's way—except when she joined Gilles's brother, René, in petitioning the king to interdict Gilles's spending. Catherine was not present at his trial, and she did not appear for any reconciliatory meeting with him on the night before he died. As for René, whose entire energies had been poured into heading off the ruin of Gilles's fortune, he too found reasons to be elsewhere. Marie, Gilles's ten-year-old daughter, was also somewhere else. One wonders what she had been told of her father, or his crimes. Did she know, for instance, that he had once signed over to his cousin Roger de Briqueville a document giving that parasite the legal power to arrange for Marie's wedding? Did Gilles think of her and what she faced when, one day, she learned why he had died? She was ten years old, the same age as dozens of his victims . . . boys and girls.

It is all conjecture. A sackful of "maybes" and "supposes." We know only that he was alone on the night before he died. Neither his wife, nor his brother, nor his daughter came to ease his final agony. He had lived for years as if they had no place in his life; now they kept to the outer circle to which he had relegated them.

He would be hanged and burned. Tomorrow.

There was nothing to do but follow the advice his judges had given him: "Prepare to die well." It was what he meant to do, but for a man with *his* crimes on his conscience, that might prove more difficult than for the usual pious criminal. Gilles had been taught that God was infinitely compassionate; but had God ever had to deal with the likes of Gilles de Rais who had lived as if he meant to test the limits of His mercy? "I have told you greater things. Enough to execute ten thousand men." Or, what if, in the hours ahead, Gilles should experience a resurgence of his former pride? Or—another terror—suppose Gilles discovered that all those tears and confessions, and public appeals for forgiveness were so much tinsel dust flung into the world's eyes? Worse still, what if, unable to be truly sorry, he died, enveloped in his sins and moved, there-fore, from the flames of the executioner's pyre directly to the blaz-ing pits of hell?

Somehow, Gilles got through the night. In the morning, he made his appearance entirely composed. He had asked for a pro-cession, and Nantes was thronged with citizens moving to the sound of church bells toward the place of execution on the Ile de Biesse. "No doubt Gilles felt himself at peace, perhaps for the first time. He had brought his adventure to its close. There was nothing more for him to do," writes Michel Bataille.

Perhaps. But there was still the walk to the gallows and the pyre, and that had to be managed with dignity if he would make a torch of a disaster. At the instance of his guards, he and his accomplices, Griart and Poitou, took their places at the rear of the procession and moved at a snail's pace toward the Ile de Biesse. Gabory says that "the cortege crossed the bridges. . . . The banks of [the Loire] were black with people; a great number of distinguished indi-viduals could be observed, even the duke of Britany according to certain old accounts."

Arrived at the place of execution, Gilles, who had been exhort-ing his underlings, continued to preach to them and to the multi-tude. His voice now confident, he cried that "there is no sin, no matter how great, that God cannot pardon. . . ." He pleaded with Griart and Poitou to resist diabolical temptation now, in the final moments of their lives. "Death," he urged, "is but a small depar-ture, without which one may not attain to the glory of God. . . . And well it is to desire to be quit of this world in which there is nothing but misery. . . . [Moreover] we, who have committed evil

The execution of Gilles de Rais.

together will see each other again in glory in Paradise, once our souls have left our bodies."

Gilles, it is clear, glowed with increasing piety the closer he approached his death. What is touching here is not his language, which is merely a rush of "sound Catholic doctrine," as Lewis calls it. What is touching is the willed innocence with which Gilles summons up the familiar teachings to simplify the final moments of his life. Because he was moving toward the gallows and the pyre where he would be required to expiate with his stopped breath the torn flesh of the children; because his evil had been sophisticated and eloquent—he needed the pieties, the easy, ancient pieties of contrition and salvation, to help him invent the sweet mood of ending, that yearned-for sleepiness of the spirit that would enable him to step off the wheel of consciousness.

He talked for a long time, as if his speech were a murmuring lullaby. When he was done, Griart and Poitou thanked their master for his pious counsels and in their turn pleaded with him to be of good courage in the hour of his death.

The sun was now well up in the sky. It was almost time for the culmination of the mystery play the multitude was waiting for. Gilles commended his soul to Saint James and to Saint Michael. As he turned to face the crowd, it hushed: "I am your brother in Christ," he said to the upturned faces. "By Our Lord's Passion, I implore you, pray for me. Forgive me."

The hangman stepped forward now and arranged Gilles for the final act. As Gilles had requested, he would be the first to die. His hands were bound; the noose was tied around his neck and he mounted the hanging stool. Gilles stood for a moment, high above the multitude, breathing the moist October air, feeling the mild sunlight on his face. Then the executioner signaled to an assistant who held a lighted torch beside the brush stacked around the platform. The torchbearer and the hangman moved together. As the hangman kicked Gilles's stool out from under him, the assistant fired the brush. A sigh of satisfaction passed like a breeze through the crowd, as Gilles writhed and dangled and scorched. When he stopped twitching, the flames were extinguished and his body was cut down. Then it was Griart's turn and Poitou's. Their bodies, left to the mercy of the flames, were reduced to ashes. Gilles's charred remains were claimed by four "ladies of high rank" who may have been related to him. These ladies prepared Gilles de Rais for burial in the Carmelite church, as he had requested.

On the Ile de Biesse, the multitude, with nothing more dramatic to see but a thick column of smoke rising to the heavens, slowly dispersed.

It was Wednesday, October 26, 1440. The Baron Marshal Gilles de Rais had been fully awake that morning. At eleven o'clock, when he died, he was thirty-six years old.

EPILOGUE

How to attune oneself to Gilles de Rais without risking the scorn of Isaiah who admonishes, "Woe unto them that call evil good, and good evil; that put darkness for light, and light for darkness; that put bitter for sweet, and sweet for bitter! / Woe unto them that are wise in their own eyes, and prudent in their own sight!"

Peace to Isaiah. Gilles was wicked. The wickedest man in the world. It does not matter that his prey was Immanence. It was wicked to bait his trap for God with the anguished flesh of children. Gilles deserved to hang; he deserved to burn.

Then, how to attune oneself to Gilles de Rais who was not a tiger or a dragon. Who was not a madman. By making an act of recognition—which is not the same as compassion or forgiveness. He was one of us . . . another one of us who stepped through a door leading to the abyss and found himself on a windswept stairway contending, under the glittering stars, with time and vanity. I do not salute him, as D. B. Wyndham Lewis does "with that salute due to a soldier, a victor, perhaps already a citizen of Paradise." Instead, I acknowledge him. I see him for what he is: a crystallization out of the human essence. A miserable instance of who else we are.

APPENDIX

THE BLUE BEARD

However it is, we are at the antipodes of reason," writes George Bataille, commenting on the way in which the story of Gilles de Rais has, in the folk imagination, been linked with the mythological Blue-beard. Certainly, Charles Perrault who, in the seventeenth century, gave the ancient tale its present form did not have Gilles in mind; nor does the content of the Blue-beard tale have any resemblance to the details of Gilles's life. It may be, as Bataille suggests, that terror is what links the two stories: the terrifying realities of Gilles's crimes require mythologizing. What is curious and poignant and worth mulling over is that in the process by which Gilles's name and Blue-beard's have been confounded, the child murderer has been transformed and softened into a man who murders his wives. Humankind, as T. S. Eliot reminds us, cannot bear too much reality.

There was once upon a time a man who had several fine houses both in town and country, a good deal of silver and gold plate, embroidered furniture, and coaches gilt all over with gold. But this same man had the misfortune to have a *Blue Beard*, which made him so frightfully ugly that all the women and girls ran away from him.

One of his neighbors, a lady of quality, had two daughters who were perfect beauties. He desired by her one of them in marriage, leaving to her the choice of which of them she would bestow upon him. They would neither of them have him, and sent him backward and forward from one another, being resolved never to marry a man that had a *Blue Beard*. That which moreover gave them the greater disgust and aversion was that he had already been married to several wives, and nobody ever knew what were become of them.

The *Blue Beard*, to engage their affection, took them with my lady their mother, and three or four other ladies of their acquaintance, and some young people of the neighborhood, to one of his country seats, where they stayed full eight days. There was nothing now to be seen but parties of pleasure, hunting of all kinds, fishing, dancing, feasts, and collations. Nobody went to bed, they past [*sic*] the night in rallying and playing upon one another: In short, everything so well succeeded, that the youngest daughter began to think that the master of the house had not a *Beard* so very *Blue,* and that he was a very civil gentleman.

As soon as they returned home, the marriage was concluded. About a month afterward, the *Blue Beard* told his wife that he was obliged to take a journey into a distant country for six weeks at least, about an affair of very great consequence, desiring her to divert herself in his absence, send for her friends and acquaintances, carry them into the country, if she pleased, and make good cheer wherever she was: "Here," said he, "are the keys of the two great rooms that hold my best and richest furniture; these are of my silver and gold plate, which is not to be made use of every day; these open my strongboxes, which hold my gold and silver money; these, my caskets of jewels; and this is the master key that opens all my apartments. But for this little one here, it is the key of the closet at the end of the great gallery on the ground floor. Open them all, go into all and every one except that little closet, which I forbid you, and forbid you in such a manner that if you happen to open it, there is nothing but what you may expect from my just anger and resentment." She promised to observe everything he ordered her, who, after having embraced her, got into his coach and proceeded on his journey.

Her neighbors and good friends did not stay to be sent for by the new married lady, so great was their impatience to see all the rich furniture of her house, not daring to come while the husband was there, because of his *Blue Beard,* which frightened them. They ran through all the rooms, closets, wardrobes, which were all so rich and fine that they seemed to surpass one another. After that, they went up into the two great rooms where were the best and richest furniture; they could not sufficiently admire the number and beauty of the tapestry, beds, couches, cabinets, stands, tables, and looking glasses, in which you might see yourself from head to foot; some of them were framed with glass, others with silver and silver gilt, the finest and most magnificent as ever were seen. They never ceased to extol and envy the happiness of their friend, who in the meantime no ways diverted herself in looking upon all these rich things, because of the impatience she had to go and open the closet of the ground floor. She was so much pressed by her curiosity that without considering that it was very uncivil to leave her company, she went down a back pair of stairs, and with such an excessive haste that she had like to have broken her neck two or three times.

Being come to the closet door, she stopped for some time, thinking upon her husband's orders, and considering what unhappiness might attend her were she disobedient; but the temptation was so strong she could not overcome it. She took then the little key and opened it in a very great trembling. But she could see nothing distinctly, because the windows were shut; after some moments, she began to observe that the floor was all covered over with clotted blood, on which lay the bodies of several dead women ranged against the walls. (These were all the wives that the *Blue Beard* had married and murdered one after another.) She thought that she should have died for fear, and the key that she pulled out of the lock fell out of her hand. After having somewhat recovered her surprise, she took up the key, locked the door, and went upstairs into her chamber to recover herself, but she could not, so much was she frightened. Having observed that the key of the closet was stained with blood, she tried two or three times to wipe it off, but the blood would not come out; in vain did she wash it and even rub it with soap and sand, the blood still remained, for the key was a Fairy, and she could never quite make it clean; when the blood was gone off from one side, it came again on the other.

The *Blue Beard* returned from his journey the same evening and said he had received letters upon the road informing him that the affair he went about was finished to his advantage. His wife did all she could to convince him she was extremely glad of his speedy return. The next morning he asked for the keys, which she returned, but with such a trembling hand that he easily guessed what had happened. "What is the matter," said he, "that the key of the closet is not amongst the rest?" "I must certainly," said she, "have left it above upon the table." "Do not fail," said the *Blue Beard*, "of giving it to me presently." After several goings backward and forward, she was forced to bring him the key. The *Blue Beard*, having very attentively considered it, said to his wife, "How comes this blood upon the key?" "I don't know," said the poor woman paler than death. "You don't know," replied the *Blue Beard*, "I know very well, you were resolved to go into the closet, were you not? Very well, Madam, you shall go in, and take your place amongst the ladies you saw there."

Upon this, she threw herself at her husband's feet and begged his pardon with all the signs of a true repentance, and that she would never more be disobedient. She would have melted a rock, so beautiful and sorrowful was she; but the *Blue Beard* had a heart harder than the hardest rock! "You must die, Madam" said he, "and that presently." "Since I must die," said she, looking upon him with her eyes all bathed in tears, "give me some little time to say my prayers." "I give you," said the *Blue Beard*, "a quarter of an hour, but not one moment more."

When she was alone, she called out to her sister, and said to her, "Sister Anne," for that was her name, "go up, I desire thee, upon the top of the tower, and see if my brothers are not coming. They promised me that they would come today, and if thou seest them, give them a sign to make haste." Her sister Anne went up upon the top of the tower, and the poor afflicted lady cried out from time to time, "Anne, sister Anne, dost thou see nothing coming?" And sister Anne said, "I see nothing but the sun that makes a dust, and the grass that grows green." In the meanwhile the *Blue Beard*, holding a great cutlass in his hand, cried out as loud as he could to his wife, "Come down presently, or I'll come up to you." "One moment longer, if you please," said his wife, and immediately she cried out very softly, "Anne, sister Anne, dost thou see nothing coming?" "I see, replied sister Anne, "a great dust that comes on this side here." "Are they my brothers?" "Alas! no, my dear sister. I see a flock of sheep." "Will you not come down?" cried the *Blue*

Beard. "One moment longer," said his wife, and then she cried out, "Anne, sister Anne, dost thou see nothing coming?" "I see," said she, "two horsemen coming, but they are yet a great way off. God be praised." said she immediately after, "they are my brothers. I have made them a sign as well as I can to make haste." The *Blue Beard* cried out now so loud that he made the whole house tremble.

The poor lady came down and threw herself at his feet all in tears with her hair about her shoulders. "This signifies nothing," says the *Blue Beard.* "You must die." Then taking hold of her hair with one hand, and holding up the cutlass with the other, he was going to cut off her head. The poor lady, turning about to him and looking at him with dying eyes, desired him to afford her one little moment to recollect herself. "No, no," said he, "recommend thyself to God." For at this instant, there was such a loud knocking at the gate, that the *Blue Beard* stopped short of a sudden. They opened the gate, and immediately entered two horsemen who, drawing their swords, ran directly to the *Blue Beard.* He knew them to be his wife's brothers, one a dragoon, the other a musketeer, so that he ran away immediately to save himself, but the two brothers pursued him so close that they overtook him before he could get up the steps of the porch, when they ran their swords through his body and left him dead.

The poor lady was almost as dead as her husband, and had not strength enough to rise and embrace her brothers. The *Blue Beard* had no heirs, and so his wife became mistress of all his estate. She made use of one part of it to marry her sister Anne to a young gentleman who had loved her a long while, another part to buy captains' commissions for her brothers, and the rest to marry herself to a very honest gentleman who made her forget the ill time she had passed with the *Blue Beard.*

THE GOOD VIRGIN,
MILK-CREATOR

There is an ironic footnote to Gilles's death. Some years afterward, his daughter, Marie, had a stone memorial constructed on the site of his execution. This structure contained a niche that, over the years, came to be regarded by the local population as a holy altar to which the name *"Bonne Vierge de Crée-Lait"* ("The Good Virgin, Milk-Creator") was given. To this altar, believed to be under the protection of Saint Anne, generations of pregnant women came to pray for plentiful milk for their infants. The memorial, of which no trace now exists, was destroyed by rioting Jacobins during the French Revolution.

HE WAS INNOCENT!

Not surprisingly, in a century that loves conspiracy theories, Gilles de Rais has found advocates to assert his innocence. Salomon Reinach, in 1902, moved by the spirit of Dreyfus, published an article arguing that Gilles had been the victim of a judicial lynch mob: "Of all the alleged proofs which went to compose this procedure [the trial] not one would be admissible in a modern civil trial. . . . They are the confessions extorted from Gilles under the menace of torture, and they correspond, even to the most unlikely details, with those obtained from witnesses on the rack" *(Le Signal,* October 21).

A greatly amplified version of Reinach's views was published by Fernand Fleuret in 1922. Fleuret, writing under the pseudonym of Dr. Ludovico Hernandez, demanded to know whether one would "let it be said that the companion of a saint and the guardian of the Holy Ampul of the Anointment made human sacrifices to demons, and that he wallowed in the most abominable lusts?" Beyond this rhetorical outrage directed chiefly against the Abbé Bossard, Fleuret argued, following Reinach, that Gilles's trial was concocted by Jean de Malestroit, the bishop of Nantes and his cousin, Jean V, the duke of Brittany. Fleuret asserted that the testimony of the witnesses was suborned; that Gilles's confession was extracted from him by torture; and that, finally, Gilles had been a victim of society's hostility against homosexuals. Fleuret wrote, "Say of someone that he is a liar, a drunkard, a debauchee, a perjuror, a traitor to his country; that he is harsh to his children, and you stain his memory only partially, but say that he is a pederast, invent some stories, and there he is—an outcast from humanity" (page iii, *Le Procès Inquisitorial de Gilles de Rais, Maréchal de France*).

The charge that homosexuals have been harassed by society is sound enough, as is the assertion that the bishop of Nantes and the duke of Brittany stood to gain by Gilles's condemnation and death. But these truths are not sufficient to overturn the great weight of the evidence of Gilles's guilt provided by the trial transcripts, Gilles's confession, and those of his accomplices. And to say that Gilles did not have a trial that would have sustained the scrutiny of modern jurisprudence is pretty much beside the point. No fifteenth-century trial could meet that test.

The main weakness of the Reinach-Fleuret thesis is that, for it to hold up, one has to imagine a conspiracy in which there were nearly one hundred and forty participants, all of whom had been coached to give testimony which, woven together, make such an elaborate and compelling tapestry of greed, lust, pain, betrayal, and pride that only a genius possessed of the literary skill of a whole pantheon of writers could have woven it.

Finally, there is common sense. If the bishop and the duke wanted to rid themselves of Gilles by a judicial procedure in a court that they controlled, what need was there to produce so many witnesses or to adduce such appalling crimes. One foul crime and a couple of witnesses would have sufficed.

NOTES

INTRODUCTION, PAGES x–xi

1 Michel Guimar, *Annales Nantaises,* pp. 221–22.
2 D. B. Wyndham Lewis, *The Soul of Marshal Gilles de Raiz,* p. 1.
3 Albert Jean, *Les Secret de Barbe-Bleue,* p. 155.
4 Thomas Mann, "Dostoyevski—Within Limits," in *The Thomas Mann Reader,* ed., Walter Angell, p. 435.
5 *Ibid.,* p. 435.
6 Maurice Saillet, "In Memoriam: Antonin Artaud," in *The Theater and Its Double,* p. 152.

PROLOGUE, PAGES 1–2

1 T. F. Powys, "The Hunted Beast," in *Wolf's Complete Book of Terror,* pp. 132–39.
2 Edgar Allan Poe, "The Black Cat," in *The Complete Works of Edgar Allan Poe,* vol. 5, p. 146.
3 Fyodor Dostoevsky, *Stavrogin's Confession,* p. 43.
4 Fyodor Dostoevsky, *The Brothers Karamazov,* p. 289.

CHAPTER ONE, PAGES 3–8

1 Philippe Contamine, *La Vie Quotidienne Pendant la Guerre de Cent Ans: France et Angleterre, XIVe Siècle,* p. 160.
2 Michel Bataille, *Gilles de Rais,* pp. 49–50.
3 Edward Lucie-Smith, *Joan of Arc,* p. 8.
4 "The Vision of Saint Paul" in William Matthews' *Later Medieval English Prose,* pp. 111–12.
5 John Le Patourel, "The Origins of the War," in *The Hundred Years War,* p. 29.
6 D. B. Wyndham Lewis, *The Soul of Marshal Gilles de Raiz,* p. 29.
7 Edouard Perroy, *The Hundred Years War,* p. 226.

225

8 Lewis, *op. cit.*, p. 21.
9 Perroy, *op. cit.*, p. 229.
10 *Ibid.*, p. 227.
11 Janet Shirley, ed., *A Parisian Journal 1405–1449*, pp. 170–75 *passim*.
12 Régine Pernoud, *Joan of Arc*, trans. Edward Hyams, p. 20.

CHAPTER TWO, PAGES 9–31

1 Michel Bataille, *Gilles de Rais*, p. 47. There are those who suggest that the change of heart was contrived by de Craon himself, who saw his opportunity to add estates to those of his already wealthy family.
2 Ernest Alfred Vizitelly, *Bluebeard*, pp. 116–20.
3 Philippe Contamine, *La Vie Quotidienne Pendant la Guerre de Cent Ans: France et Angleterre, XIVe Siècle*, p. 164.
4 *Ibid.*, p. 165.
5 *Ibid.*, p. 166. Contamine's description of child-rearing is followed closely here.
6 L'Abbé Eugène Bossard, *Gilles de Rais, Maréchal de France Dit Barbe-Bleue*, p. 9.
7 *Ibid.*, p. 9.
8 Vizitelly, *op. cit.*, p. 120.
9 Bossard, *op. cit.*, p. 11.
10 Michel Bataille, *op. cit.*, pp. 56–57.
11 Vizitelly, *op. cit.*, p. 122.
12 Emile Gabory, *Alias Bluebeard: The Life and Death of Gilles de Rais*, trans. Alvah C. Bessie, p. 11.
13 Vizitelly, *op. cit.*, p. 124.
14 Roland Villeneuve, *Gilles de Rays: Une Grande Figure Diabolique*, p. 24.
15 Jean Benedetti, *Gilles de Rais*, p. 35.
16 Georges Bataille, *Le Procès de Gilles de Rais*, p. 28.
17 Bossard, *op. cit.*, pp. 14–15.
18 Georges Bataille, *op. cit.*, p. 242. The citizens of Nantes, anyhow, took Gilles's words to heart. For some years after his execution, they whipped their sons on the anniversary of his death.
19 Kenneth Fowler, *The Age of Plantagenet and Valois*, p. 79.
20 Janet Shirley, ed., *A Parisian Journal 1405–1449*, pp. 95–96.
21 Georges Bataille, *op. cit.*, p. 244.
22 Fowler, *op. cit.*, p. 107.
23 Syr Jean Froissart, *The Chronicle of Froissart*, trans. Sir John Bourchier, Lord Berners, vol. I, p. 171.
24 Geoffrey Chaucer, *The Works of Geoffrey Chaucer*, p. 42.
25 Jean de Bueil in Le Jouvencel, cited in *The Age of Plantagenet and Valois*, Kenneth Fowler, p. 181.
26 Sidney Painter, *French Chivalry*, p. 51.
27 Chaucer, *op. cit.*, p. 41.
28 Edouard Perroy, *The Hundred Years War*, p. 119.

29 William Matthews, *Later Medieval English Prose,* p. 172.
30 *Ibid.,* pp. 169–70.
31 J. K. Huysmans, *Là-Bas (Down There),* trans. Keene Wallace, p. 162. Huysmans gives these fantasies to Gilles much later in his life, after he has joined his crimes.
32 Albert Jean, *Le Secret de Barbe-Bleue,* p. 29.
33 Jean Benedetti, *Gilles de Rais,* p. 37; Georges Bataille, *op. cit.,* p. 82.
34 Bossard and Vizitelly assert that the young candidates died. Vizitelly adds further that there are legendary accounts of other engagements and other deaths, and that these misfortunes, "In Brittany and the adjacent province of La Vendée, these numerous alleged betrothals, always followed by death of the fiancees, gave rise, in later days, to the tradition that Gilles had been married repeatedly, and that all his brides, save the last, had mysteriously disappeared. In that one legend alone lay the germ of a 'Bluebeard' story" Vizitelly, *op. cit.,* p. 127).
35 Perroy, *op. cit.,* p. 114.
36 Gabory, *op. cit.,* p. 87.
37 Dom Morice, *Histoire de Bretagne,* vol. I, p. 476.
38 Vizitelly, *op. cit.,* p. 133.
39 *Ibid.,* pp. 133–34.
40 Dom Morice in Bossard, *op. cit.,* p. 18.
41 Bossard, *op. cit.,* p. 20.
42 Vizitelly, *op. cit.,* p. 135.
43 *Ibid.,* p. 136.
44 Bossard, *op. cit.,* p. 23.
45 *Ibid.,* p. 16; Vizitelly, *op. cit.,* p. 137.
46 Tennille Dix, *The Black Baron: the Strange Life of Gilles de Rais,* p. 44.
47 D. B. Wyndham Lewis, *The Soul of Marshal Gilles de Raiz,* p. 58.
48 *Ibid.,* p. 58.
49 Benedetti, *op. cit.,* p. 47.
50 Michel Bataille, *op. cit.,* p. 74.
51 *Ibid.,* p. 74.
52 *Ibid.*
53 *Ibid.* Surely Bataille, or his unspecified source, is being fanciful here. The abduction, the prison cell, the starvation make a kind of de Craon sense. But the leather sack and the tentative dips into the water are baroque elements—not really Jean de Craon's style.
54 *Ibid.*

CHAPTER THREE, pages 32–38

1 Edouard Perroy, *The Hundred Years War,* p. 244.
2 *Ibid.,* p. 243.
3 L'Abbé Eugène Bossard, *Gilles de Rais, Maréchal de France Dit Barbe-Bleue,* p. 25.

4 *Ibid.* To show their good faith, the principals at the meeting arranged a marriage between Isabelle of Brittany and Louis III of Aragon, Yolande's son (Georges Bataille, *Le Procès de Gilles de Rais,* p. 86).

5 M. G. A. Vale, *Charles VII,* pp. 28–29.

6 *Ibid.,* p. 11.

7 Jean Benedetti, *Gilles de Rais,* p. 56.

8 Michel Bataille, *Gilles de Rais,* pp. 89–90.

9 Bossard, *op. cit.,* p. 30.

10 Vale, *op. cit.,* p. 42.

11 Georges Bataille, *op. cit.,* p. 37.

12 Michel Bataille, *op. cit.,* pp. 80–81.

13 *Ibid.,* p. 85.

CHAPTER FOUR, PAGES 39–76

1 W. P. Barrett, trans., *The Trial of Jeanne d'Arc,* p. 43.

2 Régine Pernoud, *Joan of Arc,* trans. Edward Hyams, p. 17.

3 Barrett, *op. cit.,* p. 43.

4 *Ibid.,* pp. 43–44.

5 D. B. Wyndham Lewis, *The Soul of Marshal Gilles de Raiz,* p. 32.

6 Pernoud, *op. cit.,* p. 31.

7 Vita Sackville-West, *Saint Joan of Arc,* p. 55.

8 W. P. Barrett, *op. cit.,* p. 44.

9 *Ibid.*

10 Pernoud, *op. cit.,* p. 31.

11 Barrett, *op. cit.,* p. 159.

12 Pernoud, *op. cit.,* p. 33.

13 Sackville-West, *op. cit.,* p. 98.

14 Frances Winwar (pseud.), *The Saint and the Devil: Joan of Arc and Gilles de Rais,* p. 56.

15 Because the English forces commanded by Sir John Fastolfe were on a provisioning expedition to Orléans and carried with them a plentiful supply of Lententide herrings. The Battle of the Herrings was another of those apparently unnecessary defeats sustained by the French. Sir John Fastolfe, commanding 1,700 men of whom "only 600 were true-born Englishmen," arrived at the village of Rouvray where his small force was set upon by three or four thousand soldiers commanded by the duke of Bourbon. The battle was fought three hours after midnight of the first Sunday in Lent (February 12, 1429). Despite their numerical superiority, the French were unable to disrupt the convoy and the herring reached the troops before Orléans (Enguerrand de Monstrelet in *Contemporary Chronicles of the Hundred Years War,* p. 296).

16 Pernoud, *op. cit.,* p. 39.

17 *Ibid.,* p. 40.

18 Barrett, *op. cit.,* p. 160.

19 *Ibid.,* pp. 162–63.

20 *Ibid.,* pp. 161–62. "There were many, even great lords," writes M. Petitot, "[who] undertook to find out if they might have her carnal company, and to that end came before her pleasingly attired, but as soon as they saw her, all [their] bad wishes ceased: and when one asked of her why she was in men's garments, she replied that she had been so ordered, and that principally it was to guard her chastity more easily: moreover, it would be considered too strange [if she were] to be seen riding in woman's clothes among so many men-at-arms." Jeanne was elaborately careful to guard her physical privacy. Petitot adds, "No man had ever seen her bathe or purge [herself], and she always did it secretly, and if it happened that she camped outdoors with the men-at-arms, she never removed her armor" (M. Petitot, *Collection complète des Mémoires Rélatifs à l'Histoire de France,* pp. 194–95).

21 Andrew Lang, *The Maid of France,* p. 77.

22 *Ibid.,* p. 77.

23 *Ibid.,* p. 79.

24 Tennille Dix, *The Black Baron: The Strange Life of Gilles de Rais,* p. 107.

25 Raffaele Ciampini, *Barba-Blu,* p. 64.

26 *Ibid.,* pp. 65–67.

27 Michelet, as if to specify that she was not fully a woman, says of her that "she grew up to be robust and handsome but the curse of women never affected her" (Jules Michelet, *Joan of Arc,* trans. Albert Guerard, p. 9).

28 Charles Lemire, *Un Maréchal et un Connétable de France,* p. 12.

29 Pernoud, *op. cit.,* p. 49.

30 Michel Bataille, *Gilles de Rais,* p. 99.

31 Pernoud, *op. cit.,* pp. 58–59; Petitot, *op. cit.,* p. 267: "The examination took place in [the Queen of Sicily's] presence and before the ladies Gaucour and Trèves: it was acknowledged that [Jeanne] was a true and entire virgin, in whom there appeared no corruption or violence."

32 Fr. Funck-Brentano, *The Middle Ages,* trans. Elizabeth O'Neill, p. 515.

33 J. Cousinot, *Chronique de la Pucelle ou Chronique de Cousinot,* p. 281; W. S. Scott, *Jeanne d'Arc,* pp. 43–44.

34 L'Abbé Eugène Bossard, *Gilles de Rais, Maréchal de France Dit Barbe-Bleue,* p. 37.

35 Petitot, *op. cit.,* p. 158.

36 M. G. A. Vale, *Charles VII,* pp. 39–40.

37 E. Coseneau, *Le Connétable de Richemont,* pp. 143–44.

38 M. Vallet de Viriville, ed., *Histoire de Charles VII,* pp. 169–70.

39 Ernest Alfred Vizitelly, *Bluebeard,* p. 156.

40 *Ibid.*, p. 156. The Abbé Bossard and D. B. Wyndham Lewis are scandalized by de Viriville's suggestion. Lewis is particularly vitriolic. "Like many people, [de Viriville] assumed bad men to be all of a piece, all black, dancing at all times to the Devil's beck." And Lewis concludes, "The case for Gilles de Raiz is clear. He had neither art nor part, as Scots lawyers say, in St. Joan's disaster" (Lewis, *op. cit.,* pp. 83–84).

41 Bossard, *op. cit.,* p. 35.

42 In fact, the death penalty was rarely invoked against homosexuals for the very good reason that the punishment was so wildly disproportionate to the "crime" that few people were heartless enough to press charges. Gilles's grandfather, Jean de Craon, for example, appears to have kept his knowledge of Gilles's homosexuality to himself.

43 There is some ambiguity about the dating of Gilles's first crimes. At Gilles's trial, Poitou, one of his accomplices, testified that the murders began in 1426 (as the indictment charged). Gilles himself said that they did not happen until the year in which Jean de Craon, his grandfather, died (November 1432). Georges Bataille gives good reasons to take Gilles at his word (Georges Bataille, *Le Procès de Gilles de Rais,* pp. 97–98).

44 Sackville-West, *op. cit.,* p. 145.

45 Pernoud, *op. cit.,* p. 61; Petitot, *op. cit.,* p. 15.

46 Cousinot, *op. cit.,* pp. 281–82.

47 Pernoud, *op. cit.,* pp. 70–71; Petitot, *op. cit.,* pp. 161–62.

48 Pernoud, *op. cit.,* p. 82.

49 Jean Benedetti, *Gilles de Rais,* p. 78.

50 Sackville-West, *op. cit.,* p. 163.

51 Cousinot, *op. cit.,* p. 290.

52 *Ibid.,* p. 288.

53 Benedetti, *op. cit.,* p. 80.

54 Cousinot, *op. cit.,* p. 291.

55 Pernoud, *op. cit.,* p. 86.

56 *Ibid.,* p. 88.

57 *Ibid.,* p. 90.

58 Benedetti, *op. cit.,* p. 83.

59 Pernoud, *op. cit.,* p. 92; Sackville-West, *op. cit.,* pp. 192–93.

60 Pernoud, *op. cit.,* p. 91.

61 *Ibid.,* pp. 91–92.

62 Sackville-West, *op. cit.,* p. 201.

63 *Ibid.,* p. 202.

64 Vizitelly, *op. cit.,* p. 158.

65 Jeanne and d'Alençon had received orders from the king to have nothing to do with de Richemont, whom they met at Beaugency; but La Hire and others urged her not to spurn de Richemont's offer of help. There was a moment when Jeanne suggested fighting the constable, but she was persuaded to change her mind. De Richemont is

reported to have said to her: "Jeanne, they have told me that you want to fight me. I don't know if you are from God or not. If you are from God, I am not afraid of you, because God knows my intentions are good; if you are from the devil, I fear you even less" (Coseneau, *op. cit.*, pp. 168–69).

66 Petitot, *op. cit.*, pp. 187–88.

67 Sackville-West, *op. cit.*, p. 212.

68 Michelet, *op. cit.*, p. 38.

69 *Ibid.*, p. 39.

70 Coseneau, *op. cit.*, p. 171.

71 Sackville-West, *op. cit.*, p. 215.

72 Vizitelly, *op. cit.*, pp. 160–61.

73 Petitot, *op. cit.*, p. 203.

74 Michelet, *op. cit.*, p. 52.

75 Scott, *op. cit.*, p. 61. W. S. Scott notes that the tax forgiveness lasted until the French Revolution, after which it was rescinded and military honors to Jeanne's house were substituted. Scott writes: ". . . the last time that military honours were paid to the house the regiment in question was a German one, shortly before the defeat [in WWII] of Germany" (Scott, *op. cit.*, p. 220, n. 17).

76 Sackville-West, *op. cit.*, p. 225.

77 Michelet, *op. cit.*, p. 52.

78 Petitot, *op. cit.*, p. 212.

79 Bossard, *op. cit.*, p. 32.

80 Janet Shirley, ed., *A Parisian Journal 1405–1449*, pp. 240–41.

81 Enguerrand de Monstrelet, in *Contemporary Chronicles of the Hundred Years War*, p. 311.

82 Vizitelly, *op. cit.*, p. 166.

83 Bossard, *op. cit.*, pp. 32–33.

84 Sackville-West, *op. cit.*, p. 252.

85 Lang, *op. cit.*, p. 212.

86 *Ibid.*, p. 213.

87 Whether Jeanne's capture was the result of a conspiracy against her in which Guillaume de Flavy played a part is still debated. Most contemporary biographers think de Flavy was only doing his duty when he ordered the portcullis dropped. Summarizing the grounds for suspecting de Flavy, W. S. Scott writes: "it must not be forgotten that the Governor [de Flavy] was appointed to his post by La Trémoïlle . . . ; de Flavy was also a relative of Regnault de Chartres, Archbishop of Rheims, one of Jeanne's most jealous enemies, who happened—a suspicious circumstance—to be at Compiègne just ten days before Jeanne's capture" (Scott, *op. cit.*, pp. 80–81). If de Flavy was guilty, he got what was coming to him later in life when his unfaithful wife stabbed him to death in their marriage bed.

88 Lang, *op. cit.*, p. 214.

89 Arthur Tilley, *Medieval France*, p. 129.

90　Michel Bataille, *op. cit.*, p. 134.
91　Edouard Perroy, *The Hundred Years War*, p. 289.
92　In Thomas Shipman's Restoration drama, *Henry the Third of France*, cited by Lewis, *op. cit.*, p. 83.
93　Sackville-West, *op. cit.*, p. 277.
94　Edward Kennard Rand, *Founders of the Middle Ages*, pp. 192–93.
95　Barrett, *op. cit.*, p. 177.
96　Pernoud, *op. cit.*, p. 210.
97　Lang, *op. cit.*, p. 256.
98　Scott, *op. cit.*, p. 102.
99　Barrett, *op. cit.*, pp. 147–48.
100　Pernoud, *op. cit.*, p. 174.
101　Michelet, *op. cit.*, p. 79.
102　*Ibid.*, p. 77.
103　Pernoud, *op. cit.*, p. 209.
104　*Ibid.*, p. 210.
105　*Ibid.*, p. 212.
106　Lang, *op. cit.*, p. 258.
107　There is evidence that Jeanne never truly signed the abjuration at all. Régine Pernoud quotes Haimond de Macy as saying that "the secretary of the King of England who was there, called Laurent Calot, drew from his sleeve a little written *cédule* which he held out to Joan that she might sign it; and she answered that she could neither read nor write. Despite which this Laurent Calot . . . handed Joan the paper and a pen that she might sign, and by way of derision Joan drew a circle. Then Laurent Calot seized Joan's hand with the pen in it and made Joan make a mark which I no longer remember" (cited in Pernoud, *op. cit.*, p. 213).
108　Michelet, *op. cit.*, p. 107.
109　Scott, *op. cit.*, p. 119.
110　Lang, *op. cit.*, p. 274.
111　Pernoud, *op. cit.*, p. 228.
112　Barrett, *op. cit.*, p. 362.
113　Scott, *op. cit.*, p. 122. Jules Michelet asserts that "the pyre had been made so high, so that the executioner could only reach its base; he would not be able to dispatch the victim, as he usually did, and so . . . spare her the flames. In this case, they wanted to make sure that justice would not be cheated . . . they wanted her to be literally burnt alive" (Michelet, *op. cit.*, p. 116).
114　Scott, *op. cit.*, p. 125.
115　Mark Twain, *Personal Recollections of Joan of Arc*, note on p. 457.
116　Shirley, *op. cit.*, p. 263.
117　Pernoud, *op. cit.*, p. 259.
118　*Ibid.*, p. 265.
119　*Ibid.*, p. 269.
120　Vale, *op. cit.*, p. 68.

CHAPTER FIVE, PAGES 77–81

1 Mourain de Sourdeval, *Les Sires de Retz,* p. 177.
2 D. B. Wyndham Lewis, *The Soul of Marshal Gilles de Raiz,* p. 203.
3 Edward Lucie-Smith, *The Dark Pageant, A Novel about Gilles de Rais,* p. 182. In his novel, Lucie-Smith makes René the adulterous father of little Marie. He portrays Gilles as complacent about the adultery.
4 Ernest Alfred Vizitelly, *Bluebeard,* p. 340.
5 Jean Benedetti, *Gilles de Rais,* p. 126.
6 *Ibid.*
7 L'Abbé Eugène Bossard, *Gilles de Rais, Maréchal de France Dit Barbe-Bleue,* p. CLV.

CHAPTER SIX, PAGES 83–98

1 D. B. Wyndham Lewis, *The Soul of Marshal Gilles de Raiz,* p. 93.
2 L'Abbé Eugène Bossard, *Gilles de Rais, Maréchal de France Dit Barbe-Bleue,* pp. 57–58.
3 Norman O. Brown, "Sexuality and Childhood," extract from *Life Against Death,* in Leonard Wolf, ed., *The Uses of the Present,* p. 289.
4 Georges Bataille, *Le Procès de Gilles de Rais,* p. 252.
5 Albert Jean, *Le Secret de Barbe-Bleue,* p. 40.
6 Philippe Contamine, *La Vie Quotidienne Pendant la Guerre de Cent Ans: France et Angleterre, XIVe Siècle,* p. 227.
7 Paul Lacroix, *France in the Middle Ages,* pp. 131–32. Meanwhile, life for the poor was wretched: "Alas! when a poor man shall have paid his impost, his villein tax, his salt tax, his hearth money, his fourth, the King's spurs, the Queen's belt, the customs, the road tax, the tolls—not much remains to him. Then will come another levy newly created. . . . The poor man will have no bread to eat except by chance some little rye or barley; his poor wife will be in childbirth, and will have four or six little children round the hearth—or by the oven, if it chance to be warm—asking for bread and crying with the desperation of hunger. . . . How could it be worse for a poor fellow? It could hardly be worse. . . . And there are thousands and thousands, and more than ten thousand in the land in a worst state than I have described" (Gerson, in Fr. Funck-Brentano, *The Middle Ages,* p. 498).
8 Lewis, *op. cit.,* p. 36.
9 Geoffrey Chaucer, *The Works of Geoffrey Chaucer,* p. 150.
10 Lacroix, *op. cit.,* pp. 152–53.
11 *Ibid.,* p. 153.
12 Lewis, *op. cit.,* p. 36.
13 Jean, *op. cit.,* pp. 40–41; M. Bataille, *Gilles de Rais,* p. 162.
14 Michel Bataille, *op. cit.,* p. 146.

15 M. Vallet de Viriville, ed., *Chronique de la Pucelle ou Chronique de Cousinot,* pp. 412–13.
16 Julio Cortázar, "Axolotl," in *End of the Game,* trans. Paul Blackburn, p. 9.
17 Michel Foucault, *Madness and Civilization: A History of Insanity in the Age of Reason,* p. x.
18 Georges Bataille, *op. cit.,* p. 42.
19 *Ibid.,* p. 93.
20 Jean Benedetti, *Gilles de Rais,* p. 104.
21 Lewis, *op. cit.,* p. 89.
22 Robert Jay Lifton, "Psychological Effects of the Atomic Bomb in Hiroshima: The Theme of Death," in Leonard Wolf, ed., *The Uses of the Present,* p. 41.
23 J. K. Huysmans, *Là-Bas (Down There),* trans. Keene Wallace, p. 52.
24 Frances Winwar [pseud.], *The Saint and the Devil: Joan of Arc and Gilles de Rais,* pp. 236–37.
25 Michel Bataille, *op. cit.,* pp. 136–37.
26 *Ibid.,* pp. 135–36.
27 *Ibid.,* p. 138–39.
28 *Ibid.,* p. 142.
29 Ernest Alfred Vizitelly, *Bluebeard,* p. 171.
30 Bossard, *op. cit.,* p. 60.
31 *Ibid.,* p. 62.
32 Vizitelly, *op. cit.,* p. 183.
33 Bossard, *op. cit.,* p. 65.
34 *Ibid.*
35 *Ibid.*
36 Leonard Wolf, *A Dream of Dracula,* p. 56.
37 Benedetti, *op. cit.,* p. 125.
38 J. Huizinga, *The Waning of the Middle Ages: A Study of the Forms of Life, Thought and Art in France and the Netherlands in the XIVth and XVth Centuries,* p. 248.
39 Chaucer, *op. cit.,* p. 18.
40 Arthur Tilley, *The Dawn of the French Renaissance,* p. 58.
41 Barbara W. Tuchman, *A Distant Mirror,* p. 426.
42 M. A. Racinet, *Le Costume Historique,* vol. 5.
43 Bossard, *op. cit.,* p. 60.
44 *Ibid.,* p. CLV.
45 *Ibid.,* p. CLVI.
46 *Ibid.,* p. CLVII.

CHAPTER SEVEN, PAGES 99–114

1 Georges Bataille, *Le Procès de Gilles de Rais,* p. 270.
2 St. Jerome's Epistle XXII in Edward Kennard Rand, *Founders of the Middle Ages,* p. 12.

3 Rand, *op. cit.,* pp. 70–71.

4 L'Abbé Eugène Bossard, *Gilles de Rais, Maréchal de France Dit Barbe-Bleue,* p. 71.

5 *Ibid.,* p. 70.

6 Georges Bataille, *op. cit.,* p. 108.

7 Bossard, *op. cit.,* pp. 61–62.

8 Ernest Alfred Vizitelly, *Bluebeard,* p. 201.

9 Bossard, *op. cit.,* p. 61.

10 Georges Bataille, *op. cit.,* p. 279.

11 The duke of Brittany, to whom the *Mémoire des Héritiers* was addressed, was not horrified by the establishment of the Chapel of the Holy Innocents. In his reply to the *Mémoire,* he says "that it was not prodigality, because as regards God, His honor and His service, one cannot spend excessively because everything comes from God, and if everyone who ever kept chapels for a time, or who founded them and richly endowed and embellished them into perpetuity, were reputed to be notorious prodigals, there would be many such in this realm among those who are held [now] to be good people" (Bossard, *op. cit.,* p. CLVII).

12 The Bible, Exod. 1:15–16.

13 *Ibid.,* 1:22.

14 St. Matt. 2. From a mystery play put on in Paris in 1431 whose staging extended "from a little beyond [the Rue] St. Sauveur to the end of the Rue Darnetal," we learn that Herod had "seven score and four thousand men-children (144,000)" beheaded or killed (Janet Shirley, *A Parisian Journal 1405–1449,* p. 269).

15 David Bevington, *Medieval Drama,* pp. 67–72.

16 St. Matt. 2:18.

17 The word *mystery* used to describe medieval plays like *The Mystery of the Siege of Orléans* tends to idealize the genre a little. There is nothing essentially mysterious about such plays. W.T.H. Jackson writes of the word *mystery* that it is "an odd but traditionally sanctified term of origin still unexplained" (W.T.H. Jackson, *The Literature of the Middle Ages,* p. 289). Michel Bataille says the word is derived from Latin *"ministerium* meaning a representation" (Michel Bataille, *Gilles de Rais,* p. 161). This etymology is rejected by Jackson who says it is based on a confusion between *mysterium* and *ministerium.*

18 The morality plays were allegorical satires in which personified abstractions were the dramatic characters. Thus, Faith, Hope, Charity, Reason pranced about the stage in encounters with Vainglory, Nobility, Poverty, Labor, and Folly. The Farce, says Bossard, "was born of the popular malice . . . [and was] a sort of joyful *fabliau* set in dialogue instead of being recounted" (Bossard, *op. cit.,* p. 87). The *moresque,* says Michel Bataille *(op. cit.,* p. 168), is what we now call the flamenco; while the *sotie* was a genre "intermediate between the Morality and the Farce, taking its intrigue from the Farce and its allegorical characters from the Moralities" (Bossard, *op. cit.,* pp. 87–88).

19 Bossard, *op. cit.*, p. 85.
20 Vizitelly, *op. cit.*, p. 190.
21 Georges Bataille, *op. cit.*, p. 115.
22 Leo van Puyvelde, *Flemish Painting*, p. 45.
23 Bossard, *op. cit.*, pp. 95–98.
24 Emile Gabory, *Alias Bluebeard: The Life and Death of Gilles de Rais*, trans. Alvah C. Bessie, p. 55.
25 Bossard, *op. cit.*, p. 96.
26 It is not clear whether any children were actually killed at Orléans.
27 Georges Bataille, *op. cit.*, p. 214.
28 Richard Cavendish, *The Black Arts*, p. 233.
29 Fr. Funck-Brentano, *The Middle Ages*, p. 517.
30 *Ibid.*
31 Gabory, *op. cit.*, p. 59.
32 Bossard, *op. cit.*, p. 105.
33 Vizitelly, *op. cit.*, p. 197.
34 *Ibid.*, p. 198.
35 Bossard, *op. cit.*, p. 108.

CHAPTER EIGHT, PAGES 115–129

1 "They promise those things for which they have no evidence."
2 J. K. Huysmans, *Là-Bas (Down There)*, trans. Keene Wallace, p. 76.
3 Arthur E. Waite, *Alchemists through the Ages*, p. 96.
4 *Ibid.*, p. 97.
5 *Ibid.*, p. 98.
6 *Ibid.*, p. 99.
7 *Ibid.*
8 *Ibid.*, p. 100.
9 *Ibid.*, p. 101.
10 *Ibid.*, p. 103.
11 *Ibid.*, p. 107.
12 *Ibid.*, p. 108.
13 *Ibid.*, pp. 110–11.
14 Du Guesclin died on July 13, 1380, besieging a pack of *routiers* at Châteauneuf-de-Randon. While it is unlikely that Gilles learned his vices at the Sabbath of Saint Denis, du Guesclin, a great constable of France, was Gilles's paternal great-great uncle.
15 Jules Michelet, *Satanism and Witchcraft*, pp. 121–22.
16 Waite, *op. cit.*, p. 12.
17 L'Abbé Eugène Bossard, *Gilles de Rais, Maréchal de France Dit Barbe-Bleue*, p. 73.
18 *Ibid.*
19 *Ibid.*, p. 77.
20 *Ibid.*, p. 73.

21 *Ibid.*, p. 78.
22 Georges Bataille, *Le Procès de Gilles de Rais,* pp. 224–25.
23 Emile Gabory, *Alias Bluebeard: The Life and Death of Gilles de Rais,* trans. Alvah C. Bessie, p. 113.
24 From here on in this chapter, unless page numbers are specified, the dialogues quoted are reconstructions derived from the trial transcript, *passim.*
25 Georges Bataille, *op. cit.,* p. 251.
26 *Ibid.*, p. 271.
27 *Ibid.*, p. 262.
28 *Ibid.*, p. 264.
29 *Ibid.*, p. 263.
30 *Ibid.*, p. 264.
31 *Ibid.*, p. 263.
32 *Ibid.*, p. 270.

CHAPTER NINE, PAGES 130–146

1 Michel Bataille, *Gilles de Rais,* p. 151.
2 Raffaele Ciampini, *Barba-Blu,* pp. 115–16. Ciampini derives the notion of the book written in red characters from the deposition of the priest André Buchet, who claimed to have seen in the "archives of the said accused Gilles de Rais five or six sheets of paper with wide margins on which there was red writing; which writing, he, the witness, presumed and suspected to have been [written] in human blood, basing himself on what he had formerly heard: that the said Gilles killed children to use their blood to write books with (Georges Bataille, *Le Procès de Gilles de Rais,* p. 270).
3 Georges Bataille, *op. cit.,* p. 278.
4 *Ibid.*, p. 284.
5 Fyodor Dostocvsky, *The Brothers Karamazov,* p. 283.
6 *Ibid.*, p. 287.
7 Jean Benedetti, *Gilles de Rais,* p. 112.
8 J. Huizinga, *The Waning of the Middle Ages: A Study of the Forms of Life, Thought and Art in France and the Netherlands in the XIVth and XVth Centuries,* pp. 162–63.
9 *Ibid.*, p. 163.
10 Georges Bataille, *Le Procès de Gilles de Rais,* p. 275.
11 Thomas Wilson, *Bluebeard: A Contribution to Historical Folklore,* pp. 65–68.
12 Georges Bataille, *op. cit.,* p. 269.
13 *Ibid.*, pp. 300–301.
14 L'Abbé Eugène Bossard, *Gilles de Rais, Maréchal de France Dit Barbe-Bleue,* p. 183.
15 Georges Bataille, *op. cit.,* p. 303.

16 *Ibid.,* p. 302.
17 *Ibid.,* p. 308.
18 *Ibid.,* pp. 312–13.
19 Wilson, *op. cit.,* p. 69.
20 Georges Bataille, *op. cit.,* p. 308.
21 *Ibid.,* p. 304.
22 Bossard, *op. cit.,* p. 183.
23 Georges Bataille, *op. cit.,* p. 316.
24 Roland Villeneuve, *Gilles de Rays: Une Grande Figure Diabolique,* p. 146.
25 Norman Mailer, *Genius and Lust,* p. 16.
26 Michel Bataille, *op. cit.,* p. 186.
27 Georges Bataille, *op. cit.,* p. 283.
28 *Ibid.,* p. 243.
29 *Ibid.,* p. 283.
30 *Ibid.*
31 *Ibid.,* p. 243.
32 *Ibid.*
33 *Ibid.,* p. 285.
34 *Ibid.,* p. 243.

CHAPTER TEN, PAGES 147–154

1 Emile Gabory, *Alias Bluebeard: The Life and Death of Gilles de Rais,* p. 130.
2 Georges Bataille, *Le Procés de Gilles de Rais,* p. 300.
3 Roland Villeneuve, *Gilles de Rays: Une Grande Figure Diabolique,* p. 83.
4 The trial transcript gives this laconic account of how Poitou was inducted into his master's secrets: "He [Poitou] says and deposes that when the said Gilles de Rais had recovered from the said Lord de la Suze the castle of Champtocé, and when he went there to give it over and deliver it into the possession of the Lord Duke of Brittany, to whom he had already transferred the lordship of that same place, then, first, he made him, the witness, swear not to reveal the secrets he would show him. . . . Gilles then commanded Poitou to go with Gilles de Sillé, Henriet Griart, Hicquet de Brémont, and Robin Romulart to a tower in the castle at Champtocé where there were the bodies and the bones of thirty-six or forty-six children" (Georges Bataille, *op. cit.,* p. 274).
5 Michel Bataille, *Gilles de Rais,* p. 175.
6 Georges Bataille, *op. cit.,* p. 277.
7 *Ibid.,* p. 274.
8 *Ibid.,* p. 285.
9 Michel Bataille, *op. cit.,* pp. 180–81.
10 L'Abbé Eugène Bossard, *Gilles de Rais, Maréchal de France Dit Barbe-Bleue,* p. 203.

11 *Ibid.,* p. 204.
12 The word *meffraie* imitates the sea hawk's cry.
13 Jules Michelet, *Histoire de France,* tome V, in Bossard, *op. cit.,* p. 206.
14 Bossard, *op. cit.,* p. 208.
15 *Ibid.*

CHAPTER ELEVEN, PAGES 155–167

1 Maurice Saillet, "In Memoriam: Antonin Artaud," in *The Theater and its Double,* Antonin Artaud, p. 147.
2 Roland Villeneuve, *Gilles de Rays: Une Grande Figure Diabolique,* p. 54.
3 *Ibid.*
4 *Ibid.,* pp. 56–57.
5 Albert Jean, *Le Secret de Barbe-Bleue.*
6 Ernest Alfred Vizitelly, *Bluebeard,* p. 345.
7 Raffaele Ciampini, *Barba-Blu,* p. 18.
8 *Ibid.,* p. 20.
9 *Ibid.,* p. 77.
10 *Ibid.*
11 *Ibid.,* p. 80.
12 *Ibid.,* p. 81.
13 Edward Lucie-Smith, *The Dark Pageant, A Novel about Gilles de Rais,* p. 22.
14 *Ibid.*
15 *Ibid.,* pp. 30–31.
16 *Ibid.,* p. 29.
17 Bernard L. Diamond, M.D., "The Psychiatric Prediction of Dangerousness," *University of Pennsylvania Law Review,* p. 442.
18 *Ibid.,* p. 444.
19 *Ibid.*
20 *Ibid.*
21 Georges Bataille, *Le Procès de Gilles de Rais,* pp. 238–39.
22 *Ibid.,* p. 116.
23 Charles Lemire, *Un Maréchal et un Connétable de France,* p. 18.
24 Suetonius Tranquillus, Gaius, *Lives of the Caesars,* trans. Robert Graves, p. 222.
25 *Ibid.,* p. 224.
26 *Ibid.*
27 *Ibid.,* p. 228.
28 *Ibid.,* p. 238.
29 *Ibid.,* p. 163.
30 *Ibid.,* p. 167.
31 *Ibid.,* p. 173.
32 Régine Pernoud, *Joan of Arc,* trans. Edward Hyams, p. 242.
33 *Ibid.,* pp. 242–43.

34 *Ibid.,* pp. 243–44.
35 *Ibid.,* p. 245.
36 Janet Shirley, ed. and trans., *A Parisian Journal 1405–1449,* p. 337.
37 *Ibid.,* p. 338.

CHAPTER TWELVE, PAGES 168–179

1 Michel Bataille, *Gilles de Rais,* p. 234.
2 Albert Jean, *Le Secret de Barbe-Bleue,* p. 182.
3 L'Abbé Eugène Bossard, *Gilles de Rais, Maréchal de France Dit Barbe-Bleue,* p. 237.
4 Such rumors are cited in Blanchet's confession (Georges Bataille, *Le Procès de Gilles de Rais,* p. 271).
5 Bossard, *op. cit.,* p. 177.
6 *Ibid.*
7 *Ibid.*
8 Georges Bataille, *op. cit.,* p. 267.
9 Bossard, *op. cit.,* p. 233.
10 Ernest Alfred Vizitelly, *Bluebeard,* p. 317.
11 *Ibid.,* p. 318.
12 Bossard, *op. cit.,* p. 232.
13 Michel Bataille, *op. cit.,* p. 237.
14 Georges Bataille, *op. cit.,* p. 267. Vizitelly believes that there was already a reconciliation between Gilles and the duke effected by de Richemont. That, indeed, Gilles was on his way to collect money owed to him by the duke for a previous real estate transaction (Vizitelly, *op. cit.,* p. 321).
15 Michel Bataille, *op. cit.,* p. 242.
16 J. K. Huysmans, *Là-Bas (Down There),* trans. Keene Wallace, p. 208.
17 Georges Bataille, *op. cit.,* p. 281.
18 *Ibid.*
19 Michel Bataille, *op. cit.,* p. 242.
20 *Ibid.,* pp. 242–43.
21 *Ibid.,* p. 246.
22 Bossard, *op. cit.,* pp. 250–51.
23 *Ibid.,* p. 251.
24 *Ibid.*

CHAPTER THIRTEEN, PAGES 180–211

1 L'Abbé Eugène Bossard, *Gilles de Rais, Maréchal de France Dit Barbe-Bleue,* p. 252.
2 *Ibid.,* p. 253.
3 *Ibid.,* pp. 253–54.
4 Raffaele Ciampini, *Barba-Blu,* p. 177.

 5 *Ibid.,* p. 178.

 6 Georges Bataille, *Le Procès de Gilles de Rais,* p. 285.

 7 Albert Jean, *Le Secret de Barbe-Bleue,* p. 14.

 8 Bossard, *op. cit.,* p. 256.

 9 *Ibid.,* p. 268.

10 *Ibid.,* p. 238.

11 See pages 120–121 for Jean de Malestroit's financial dealings with Gilles.

12 Jean, *op. cit.,* p. 185.

13 Georges Bataille, *op. cit.,* p. 191.

14 *Ibid.,* p. 200.

15 *Ibid.*

16 *Ibid.,* p. 202.

17 J. K. Huysmans, *Là-Bas (Down There),* trans. Keene Wallace, pp. 230–31.

18 Jules Michelet in Bossard, *op. cit.,* p. 270.

19 Thomas Wilson, *Bluebeard: A Contribution to Historical Folklore,* p. 119.

20 Bossard, *op. cit.,* p. 281.

21 Georges Bataille, *op. cit.,* p. 211.

22 Jean, *op. cit.,* p. 165.

23 Ernest Alfred Vizitelly, *Bluebeard,* p. 345.

24 Charles Lemire, *Un Maréchal et un Connétable de France,* p. 40.

25 Georges Bataille, *op. cit.,* p. 203.

26 *Ibid.* In the third person in the trial transcript.

27 *Ibid.* In the third person in the trial transcript.

28 *Ibid.,* p. 204. In the third person in the trial transcript.

29 *Ibid.,* p. 205.

30 *Ibid.,* p. 225; Bossard, *op. cit.,* pp. 297–98.

31 Bossard, *op. cit.,* p. 299; Georges Bataille, *op. cit.,* p. 227.

32 Georges Bataille, *op. cit.,* p. 232.

33 *Ibid.,* p. 230. In the third person in the trial transcript.

34 Ernest Alfred Vizitelly, *Bluebeard,* p. 356.

35 Georges Bataille, *op. cit.,* p. 234.

36 D. B. Wyndham Lewis, *The Soul of Marshal Gilles de Rais,* p. 180. It will be remembered, of course, that in Gilles's case both the Inquisitor and the bishop were already in place as *Gilles's judges.*

37 Paul Lacroix, *France in the Middle Ages,* p. 408.

38 *Ibid.,* p. 410.

39 To compound the embarrassment, a reader should turn the pages of *Amnesty International: Report on Torture* (1975).

40 Lewis, *op. cit.,* p. 181.

41 Georges Bataille, *op. cit.,* p. 239. In the third person in the trial transcript.

42 *Ibid.* In the third person in the trial transcript.

43 *Ibid.,* p. 240. In the third person in the trial transcript.

44 Bossard, *op. cit.,* p. 309.

45 *Ibid.*
46 Georges Bataille, *op. cit.*, p. 242. In the third person in the trial transcript.
47 *Ibid.*, p. 243. In the third person in the trial transcript.
48 *Ibid.*, p. 244. In the third person in the trial transcript.
49 *Ibid.*, p. 252. In the third person in the trial transcript.
50 *Ibid.* In the third person in the trial transcript.
51 *Ibid.*
52 *Ibid.*, p. 253—in the third person in the trial transcript; Lewis, *op. cit.*, p. 186.
53 Lewis, *op. cit.*, p. 186.
54 Georges Bataille, *op. cit.*, p. 259.
55 *Ibid.*
56 *Ibid.*, p. 256. In the third person in the trial transcript.
57 Bossard, *op. cit.*, p. 319.
58 *Ibid.*, p. 324.
59 *Ibid.*, pp. 329–30.

A NOTE ON SOURCES

Bluebeard: The Life and Crimes of Gilles de Rais is not a work of original scholarship. I have discovered no new facts either about Gilles or about Jeanne d'Arc with whom Gilles was involved. What I have attempted is a reconstruction of Gilles's life that is founded on such facts as have come down to us. To these, I have added what I must believe are instructed insights and speculations of my own.

The primary sources for most of what we know about Gilles are to be found in the transcripts [1] of Gilles's ecclesiastical and secular trials and in the pages of the *Mémoire des Héritiers,* which Dom H. Morice includes in his *Mémoires Pour Servir de Preuves, etc.* Manuscript copies of the trial transcripts are to be found in the Bibliothèque Municipale at Nantes, and in Paris at the Bibliothèque de l'Arsenal and the Bibliothèque Nationale. These Latin transcripts are included in the appendix of the Abbé Bossard's *Gilles de Rais, Maréchal de France Dit Barbe-Bleue,* published in 1886. In our own day, French versions of the transcripts have been made by Fernand Fleuret and, most recently, by Georges Bataille. No English translation exists.

The Abbé Bossard's *Gilles de Rais* was the first thorough study of Gilles's life, and it is still, after the passage of nearly a hundred years, one of the best; but the abbé's work is marred by his need to make of Gilles's story a demonstration of the healing powers of Catholic Christianity. Bossard, too, like many of the writers before and after him, treats Gilles's homosexuality as one of his crimes. In 1897 Thomas Wilson, an American, published *Bluebeard: A Contribution to Historical Folklore.* Wilson's small book is, for its day, a surprisingly lucid and balanced work, though it moves around the subject of Gilles's crimes in a gingerly fashion. Three years later, in England, Ernest Alfred Vizitelly published his *Bluebeard, An Account of Comorre the Cursed and Gilles de Raiz.* Vizitelly's book, as its title suggests, is only half about Gilles, and that half, though it is detailed and scholarly, relies heavily on long paraphrases from the Abbé Bossard.

Since Vizitelly's time, there have been a great many versions of Gilles's life published in England, France, Germany, and Italy. Most of what has been written has proved useful to me in one way or another. Early in my work, Frances Winwar's *The Saint and the Devil,* in which the story of Gilles is contrasted with that of Jeanne d'Arc, proved stimulating. D. B. Wynd-

---

[1] The transcripts, like those we have of Jeanne d'Arc's trial, are by no means verbatim accounts of the proceedings. They are, rather, summaries of what took place, and they are signed by whichever team of notaries made them at any given time.

ham Lewis's *The Soul of Marshal Gilles de Raiz* has also affected my thinking. Lewis, even more fervently than the Abbé Bossard, is determined to transform Gilles into a heroic pilgrim toward Christian salvation, but his bias, which after all, Gilles shared, is important. Emile Gabory's *Alias Bluebeard: The Life and Death of Gilles de Rais,* and Jean Benedetti's later *Gilles de Rais* are crisp and factual, while Albert Jean's *Le Secret de Barbe-Bleue,* Michel Bataille's *Gilles de Rais,* and Tennille Dix's *The Black Baron* are in varying degrees interesting but speculative accounts. Roland Villeneuve's *Gilles de Rays,* while it can be helpful, suffers from its author's rabid antihomosexuality. Raffaele Ciampini's *Barba-Blu* and Edward Lucie-Smith's *The Dark Pageant* are novelizations of Gilles's life. Of the two, Ciampini's blood-and-thunder version has the greater verve and insight.

If there is any one work after Bossard's that is indispensable to Gilles de Rais studies, it is surely Georges Bataille's edition of the trial transcripts, *Le Procès de Gilles de Rais.* Bataille provides his readers with a provocative, if cranky introduction to Gilles's life as well as with an annotated chronology that is worth its weight in gold.

BIBLIOGRAPHY

Appia, Adolphe. *The Works of Living Art: A Theory of the Theater.* Coral Gables: University of Miami Press, 1960.

Archives de Bretagne, publiées par la Société des Bibliophiles Bretons. Vols. I–II. Documents inédits. Nantes, 1884.

Archives de Nantes: Procès de Gilles de Rais. E 289.

Artaud, Antonin. *The Theater and Its Double.* Translated by Mary Caroline Richards. New York: Grove Press, Inc., 1958.

Barchillon, Jacques. *The Authentic Mother Goose.* Denver: Alan Swallow, 1960 (1729 facsimile).

Barrett, W. P. (trans.) *The Trial of Jeanne d'Arc.* U.S.: Gotham House, Inc., 1932.

Basin, Thomas. *Histoire de Charles VII.* 2 vols. Paris: Editions C. Samaran, 1933.

Bataille, Georges. *Death and Sensuality.* New York: Walker and Co., 1962.

———. *Le Procès de Gilles de Rais.* Paris: Jean-Jacques Pauvert, 1965.

Bataille, Michel. *Gilles de Rais.* Paris: Editions Planète, 1966.

Belloc, Hilaire. *Joan of Arc.* New York: The Declan X. McMullen Company, Inc., 1929.

Benedetti, Jean. *Gilles de Rais.* New York: Stein and Day, 1971.

Bernelle, Frédéric Henri. *La Psychose de Gilles de Rais.* Paris: Jouvet et Cie., 1910.

Bernheimer, Richard. *Wild Men in the Middle Ages.* Cambridge, Mass.: Harvard University Press, 1952.

Beyle, Marie Henri [Stendhal] *Oeuvres Complétes (Mémoires d'un Touriste).* Paris: Librairie Honoré Champion, 1932.

Blanchet, Maurice. *Lautréamont et Sade.* Paris: Les Editions de Minuit, 1949.

Bossard, l'Abbé Eugène. *Gilles de Rais, Maréchal de France Dit Barbe-Bleue.* Paris: H. Champion, 1886 (2d ed.).

Bourdeaut, l'Abbé M. A. *Champtocé, Gilles de Rais et les Ducs de Bretagne.* Brest: Mémoires de la Société de l'Histoire et de l'Archéologie de Brest, 1924.

Brissard, André. *Les Agents de Lucifer.* Paris: Périn (Librairie Académique), 1975.

Bullen, A. H., ed. *The Works of Christopher Marlowe.* New York: AMS Press, 1970.

Campbell, Leroy A. *Mithraic Iconography and Ideology.* Leiden: E. J. Brill, 1968.

Capellanus, Andreas. *The Art of Courtly Love.* Edited by John Jay Parry. New York: W. W. Norton and Co., 1960.

Carter, Dagny. *The Symbol of the Beast.* New York: Ronald Press Company, 1957.

Carus, Paul. *The History of the Devil and the Idea of Evil.* New York: Bell Publishing Company, 1969.

Cavendish, Richard. *The Black Arts.* New York: Capricorn Books, 1967.

————. *A History of Magic.* London: Weidenfeld & Nicolson, 1977.

Champion, Pierre. *Splendeurs et Misères de Paris.* Paris: Calmann-Lévy, 1934.

Le Château de Gilles de Retz et Son Histoire. Olonne-Beauvoir: Lussaud Frères, 1957.

Chaucer, Geoffrey. *The Works of Geoffrey Chaucer.* Edited by F. W. Robinson. Boston: Houghton Mifflin Co., 1957.

Ciampini, Raffaele. *Barba-Blu.* Firenze: Fussi, 1948.

Clemens, Samuel Langhorne [Mark Twain]. *Personal Recollections of Joan of Arc.* New York: Harper & Brothers Publishers, 1896.

Cole, David. *The Theatrical Event: A Mythos, A Vocabulary, A Perspective.* Middletown: Wesleyan University, 1975.

Colquhoun, Ithell. *Sword of Wisdom.* New York: G. P. Putnam's Sons, 1975.

Contamine, Philippe. *Guerre, Etat et Société à la Fin du Moyen Age: Etudes sur les Armées des Rois de France, 1337–1494.* Paris: Mouton et Cie., 1972.

————. *La Vie Quotidienne Pendant la Guerre de Cent Ans: France et Angleterre, XIVe Siècle.* [Paris]: Hachette, c. 1976.

Contemporary Chronicles of the Hundred Years War from the works of Jean le Bel, Jean Froissart, and Enguerrand de Monstrelet. Translated and edited by Peter E. Thompson. London: The Folio Society, 1966.

Coseneau, E. *Le Connétable de Richemont.* Paris: Librairie Hachette et Cie., 1886.

Cousinot, J. *Chronique de la Pucelle ou Chronique de Cousinot.* Edited by Vallet de Viriville. Paris: Adophe de la Hays, 1859.

Davenport, Millia. *The Book of Costume.* New York: Crown Publishers, 1948.

Dervenne, Claude. *Hommes et Cités de Bretagne.* Paris: Editions du Sud, 1965.

Diamond, Bernard L., M.D. "Identification and the Sociopathic Personality," in *Archives of Criminal Psychodynamics,* Summer 1961, vol. IV, no. 3.

————. "The Psychiatric Prediction of Dangerousness." *University of Pennsylvania Law Review* 123:439–52.

Dictionnaire de la noblesse. Vol. XVI. Paris: Schlesinger Frères, 1870.

Dix, Tennille. *The Black Baron: The Strange Life of Gilles de Rais.* Indianapolis: Bobbs-Merrill, 1930.

Dostoevsky, Fyodor. *The Brothers Karamazov.* translated by Constance Garnett. New York: Modern Library, Random House, 1950.

———. *Stavrogin's Confession.* Translated by S. S. Koteliansky and Virginia Woolf. London: Haskell House Publishers, 1972.

Ducasse, Isidore. *Les Chants de Maldoror.* New York: New Directions, 1965.

Duckett, Eleanor Shipley. *The Gateway to the Middle Ages: France and Britain.* Ann Arbor: University of Michigan Press, 1938.

Elst, Baron Joseph van der. *The Last Flowering of the Middle Ages.* Port Washington, New York: Kennikat Press, Inc., 1969.

Endore, Guy. *The Werewolf of Paris.* New York: Farrar and Rinehart, 1933.

———. *Satan's Saint: A Novel about the Marquis de Sade.* New York: Crown Publishers, 1965.

Evans, Joan, ed., *The Flowering of the Middle Ages.* London: Thames & Hudson, 1966.

Fairbairn, W.R.D. *An Object Relations Theory of the Personality.* New York: Basic Books, 1962.

Fleuret, Fernand [Dr. Ludovico Hernandez]. *De Gilles de Rais à Guillaume Apollinaire.* Poitiers: Marc Tézier, 1933 (3d ed.).

———. *Le Procès Inquisitorial de Gilles de Rais avec un Essai de Réhabilitation.* Paris: Bibliothèque des Curieux, 1921.

Foucault, Michel. *Discipline and Punish.* Translated by Alan Sheridan. New York: Pantheon Books, 1977 (1975).

———. *Madness and Civilization: A History of Insanity in the Age of Reason.* New York: Random House, 1965.

Fowler, Kenneth. *The Age of Plantagenet and Valois.* New York: G.P. Putnam's Sons, 1967.

———. *The Hundred Years War.* New York: Macmillan, 1971.

Froissart, Syr Jean. *The Chronicle of Froissart.* Translated by Sir John Bourchier, Lord Berners, with introduction by William Paton Ker, vols. V and VI. New York: AMS Press, Inc., 1967 (1902).

Funck-Brentano, Fr. *The Middle Ages.* Translated by Elizabeth O'Neill, M.A. London: William Heinemann, Ltd., 1922.

Gabory, Emile. *Alias Bluebeard: The Life and Death of Gilles de Rais.* Translated by Alvah C. Bessie. New York: Brewer & Warren, 1930.

Giron, Aimé. *Les Amours étranges.* Paris: Michel-Lévy Frères, 1864.

———, et Tozza, Albert. *La Bête de luxure.* Paris: Ambert, 1903 (4th ed.).

Goethe, Johann Wolfgang von. *Faust: A Tragedy.* Translated by Bayard Taylor. Boston: Houghton Mifflin, 1912.

Guépin, M. A. *Histoire de Nantes.* Nantes: Librairie Prosper Sébire, 1839.

Guessard, F., et Certain, E. de. *Le Mistère du Siège d'Orléans.* (Publié pour la première fois d'après le manuscrit unique conservé à la bibliothèque du Vatican.) Paris: Imprimerie Imperiale, 1862.

Guimar, Michel. *Annales Nantaises.* Nantes: à l'imprimerie de l'auteur; X Année de la République.

Guizot, François. *A Popular History of France.* Translated by Robert Black. Illustrated by A. de Neuville. Vols. I & II; III & IV. Boston: Colonial Press Co., 1870.

Hartmann, Franz. *Magic, White and Black.* New Hyde Park, New York, University Books, 1970.

Hernandez, Dr. Ludovico, pseud. Fernand Fleuret. *Le Procès Inquisitorial de Gilles de Rais avec un Essai de Réhabilitation.* Paris: Bibliothèque des Curieux, 1921.

Hoffman, Martin. *The Gay World: Male Homosexuality and the Social Creation of Evil.* New York: Basic Books, Inc., 1968.

Hogg, Garry. *Cannibalism and Human Sacrifice.* New York: Citadel Press, 1966.

Hone, Joseph. *W. B. Yeats.* New York: The Macmillan Company, 1943.

Hugo, Victor. *La Légende des Siècles.* Paris: Librairie Gallimard, 1950.

Huizinga, J. *The Waning of the Middle Ages: A Study of the Forms of Life, Thought and Art in France and the Netherlands in the XIVth and XVth Centuries.* London: Edward Arnold (Publishers) Ltd., 1955.

Huysmans, J. K. *Là-Bas, (Down There).* Translated by Keene Wallace. New York: Dover Publications, Inc., 1972.

Huxley, Aldous. *The Devils of Loudun.* New York: Harper & Row, Publishers, Inc., 1952.

Institoris, Henricus [Jakob Sprenger, Heinrich Kraemer]. *Malleus Maleficarum.* Translated with an Introduction, Bibliography, and Notes by the Rev. Montague Summers. New York: Benjamin Blom, Inc., 1928.

Jackson, W. T. H. *The Literature of the Middle Ages.* New York: Columbia University Press, 1960.

Jean, Albert. *Le Secret de Barbe-Bleue.* Paris: SFELT, 1950.

Johnson, Pamela Hansford. *On Iniquity.* New York: Charles Scribner's Sons, 1967.

Jonas, Hans. *The Gnostic Religion.* Beacon Hill, Boston: Beacon Press, 1958.

Jones, Ernest. *On the Nightmare.* New York: Liveright Publishing Co., 1951.

Kaiser, Georg. *Gilles und Jeanne.* Potsdam: Gustav Kiepenheuer Verlag, 1923.

King, Francis. *The Magical World of Aleister Crowley.* New York: Coward, McCann & Geoghegan, Inc., 1977.

Kinsley, David R. *The Sword and the Flute: Kali and Krasna.* Berkeley: University of California Press, 1978.

Kittredge, George Lyman. *Witchcraft in Old and New England.* Cambridge: Harvard University Press, 1929.

Krafft-Ebing, Richard von, M.D. *Psychopathia Sexualis.* New York: Pioneer Publications, 1950.

Kramer, Noah Samuel, ed. *Mythologies of the Ancient World.* New York: Doubleday Anchor, 1961.

Lacroix, Paul. *France in the Middle Ages.* New York: Frederick Ungar Publishing Co., 1963 (republished).

———. *Military and Religious Life in the Middle Ages and the Renaissance.* New York: Frederick Ungar Publishing Co. (1874), republished 1964.

Lamartine, Alphonse de. *Méditations Poétiques, Suivies de Poésies Diverses* (Préface, Notices et Notes de Marius-François Guyard). Paris: Livre de Poche, 1963.

Lang, Andrew. *Magic and Religion.* London: Longmans, Green & Co., 1901.

———. *The Maid of France.* London: Longmans, Green and Co., 1924.

Lautréamont, Comte de. *Les Chants de Maldoror.* New York: New Directions, 1965.

Lea, Henry Charles. *History of the Inquisition of the Middle Ages.* 3 vols. London: 1888.

Lecky, W.E.H. *History of European Morals.* New York: D. Appleton and Co., 1917.

Lederer, Wolfgang. *The Fear of Women.* New York: Grune and Stratton, 1968.

Lely, Gilbert. *The Marquis de Sade, a Biography.* New York: Grove Press, Inc., 1961.

Lemire, Charles. *L'Episode de Barbe-Bleue au Théâtre.* Paris: Trebse et Stock, 1898.

———. *Un Maréchal et un Connétable de France.* Paris: E. Leroux, 1886.

Lemoisne, Paul André. *Gothic Painting in France, Fourteenth and Fifteenth Centuries.* Translated by Ronald Boothroyd. New York: Hacker Art Books, 1973.

Lescadieu, A., and Laurant, A. *Histoire de Nantes.* Paris: A. Pougin, 1836.

Lewis, D. B. Wyndham. *The Soul of Marshal Gilles de Raiz.* London: Eyre & Spottiswoode, 1952.

Lobineau, Dom Gui Aléxis. *Histoire de Bretagne.* Tome I. Paris: La Veuve François Muguet, 1707.

Lucie-Smith, Edward. *The Dark Pageant, A Novel about Gilles de Rais.* London: Blond & Briggs, 1977.

———. *Joan of Arc.* London: Allen Lane, 1976.

Luria, Maxwell S., and Hoffman, Richard L. *Middle English Lyrics.* New York: W. W. Norton & Company, Inc., 1974.

Mailer, Norman. *Genius and Lust: A Journey through the Major Writings of Henry Miller.* New York: Grove Press, 1979.

Mann, Thomas. *Dr. Faustus.* New York: Alfred A. Knopf, 1948.

———. *Last Essays.* New York: Alfred A. Knopf, 1959.

Matthews, William. *Later Medieval English Prose.* New York: Appleton-Century-Crofts (Meredith Publishing Co.), 1963.

Meuret, F. C. *Annales de Nantes.* Nantes: C. Mersort, 1840.

Michaud et Poujoulat. *Mémoires pour Servir à l'Histoire de France,* 3e tome. Paris: Edouard Proux, 1837.

Michelet, Jules. *Histoire de France.* Vols. V and VI. Paris: Flammarion.

———. *Joan of Arc.* Translated with Introduction by Albert Guérard. Ann

Arbor: University of Michigan Press, 1957.

———. *La Sorcière.* Tome I. Paris: Librairie Marcel Didier, 1952.

———. *Satanism and Witchcraft.* Translated by A. R. Allinson. New York: The Citadel Press, 1930.

Monstrelet, Enguerrand de. *Chronique.* 6 vols. Paris: Editions L. Douet d'Arcq, 1857–62.

Morice, Dom H. *Histoire de Bretagne.* Tome I. Paris: Imprimerie de la Guette, 1750.

———. *Mémoires pour Servir de Preuves, etc.* Nantes: Charles Osmont, 1746.

Munro, Dana Carleton. *The Middle Ages.* New York: Century Co., 1922.

Murray, Margaret Alice. *The God of the Witches.* London: Faber and Faber Ltd., 1931.

Nietzsche, Friedrich. *The Birth of Tragedy and the Genealogy of Morals.* Garden City: Doubleday, 1956.

O'Flaherty, Wendy D. *The Origins of Evil in Hindu Mythology.* Berkeley: University of California Press, 1978.

Painter, Sidney. *French Chivalry.* Ithaca, New York: Great Seal Books (Cornell University Press), 1957 (1940).

Pauphilet, Albert, ed. *Poètes et Romanciers du Moyen Age.* Paris: Librairie Gallimard, 1952.

Papini, Giovanni. *Il Diavolo.* Firenze, Italy: Vallecchi Editorie, 1969.

Parry, John Jay, ed. *The Art of Courtly Love,* by Andreas Cappellanus. New York: W. W. Norton & Company, Inc., 1960 (1941).

Pernoud, Régine. *Joan of Arc.* Translated by Edward Hyams. New York: Stein and Day, 1966.

Perrault, Charles. *Tales of Mother Goose.* Introduction, Critical Text by Jacques Barchillon. New York: Pierpont Morgan Library, 1966.

———. *Histoires, ou Contes du Temps Passé.* Paris: Editions Barbin, 1697.

Perroy, Edouard. *The Hundred Years War.* Introduction by David C. Douglas. Bloomington: Indiana University Press, 1962.

Petitot, M. *Collection Complète des Mémoires Rélatifs à l'Histoire de France.* Tome VIII. Paris: Foucault, 1825.

Plutarch. *Moralia.* Volume V. Translated by Frank Cole Babbitt. London: William Heinemann, Ltd., 1957.

———. *De Iside et Osiride.* Edited with Introduction, translation, and commentary by J. Gwyn Griffiths. [Wales]: University of Wales Press, 1970.

Poe, Edgar Allan. *The Complete Works of Edgar Allan Poe.* Vol. 5. New York: AMS Press, Inc., 1965.

Praz, Mario. *The Romantic Agony.* New York: Meridian, 1956.

Prével, Louis. *Histoire de Tiffauges.* Nantes: Imprimerie Vincent Forest et Emile Grimaud, 1874.

Puyvelde, Leo van. *Flemish Painting from the Van Eycks to Metseys.* New York: McGraw-Hill Book Co., 1968.

Quicherat, J. *Histoire du Costume en France.* Illustrations by Chévignard, Pauquet et P. Sellier. Paris: Librairie Hachette, 1875.

———. *Procès de Condemnation et de Réhabilitation de Jeanne d'Arc.* 5 vols. Paris: Renouard, 1841–1849.

Racinet, M. A. *Le Costume Historique.* 500 illustrations. Paris: Librairie Firmin, 1888.

Rand, Edward Kennard. *Founders of the Middle Ages.* New York: Dover Publications, Inc., 1928.

Read, John. *The Alchemist.* London: Thomas Nelson and Sons, Ltd., 1947.

Reinach, Salomon. *Revue de l'Université de Bruxelles,* October 1904, pp. 161–87.

Rhodes, Henry Taylor-Fowkes. *The Satanic Mass: A Sociological and Criminological Study.* London: Rider and Co., 1954.

Ring, Grete. *A Century of French Painting 1400–1500.* New York: Phaidon Publishers, Inc., 1949.

Rose, Elliot. *A Razor for a Goat.* Toronto, Canada: University of Toronto Press, 1962.

Roughead, William. *Classic Crimes.* London: Cassel, 1951.

Roy, Claude. *Les Arts Fantastiques.* Paris: Encyclopédie Essentielle, 1960.

Russell, Jeffrey Burton. *The Devil.* Ithaca, New York: Cornell University Press, 1977.

Sackville-West, Vita. *Saint Joan of Arc.* New York: Doubleday Doran, 1936.

Schafer, Stephen. *The Victim and His Criminal: A Study in Functional Responsibility.* New York: Random House, 1968.

Schneider, Marcel. *La Littérature Fantastique en France.* Paris: Fayard, 1964.

Scholem, Gershom G. *Major Trends in Jewish Mysticism.* New York: Schocken Books, 1941.

Scott, W. S. *Jeanne d'Arc.* London: George G. Harrap, 1974.

Seabrook, William. *Witchcraft.* London: Sphere Books. Ltd., 1942.

Seaver, Richard, and Wainhouse, Austryn, eds. *The Marquis de Sade, The Complete Justine, Philosophy in the Bedroom and Other Writings.* New York: Grove Press, Inc., 1966.

Shah, Sayed Idries. *Oriental Magic.* England: Octagon Press, 1968 (1956).

Shirley, Janet, ed. and trans. *A Parisian Journal 1405–1449.* London: Oxford University Press, 1968.

Sinan, A. *Le Vieux Nantes.* Paris: Floch, 1935.

Sourdeval, Mourain de. *Les Sires de Retz.* Tours: Imprimerie de Marne, 1845.

Stoller, Robert J. *Perversion: The Erotic Form of Hatred.* New York: Pantheon Books (Random House), 1975.

Suetonius Tranquillus, Gaius. *Lives of the Caesars.* Translated by Robert Graves. England: Penguin Books Ltd., 1957.

Symonds, John. *The Great Beast, The Life and Magick of Aleister Crowley.* London: Macdonald & Co. (Publishers) Ltd., 1971.

Thompson, Peter E., ed. *Contemporary Chronicles of the Hundred Years War.* London: The Folio Society, 1966.

Thompson, Richard Lowe. *History of the Devil.* London: K. Paul, Trench, Trubner and Co., Ltd., 1929.

Thorndike, Lynn. *A History of Magic and Experimental Science.* Vols. III and

IV: fourteenth and fifteenth centuries. New York: Columbia University Press, 1934.

Tilley, Arthur. *The Dawn of the French Renaissance.* Cambridge: Cambridge University Press,

———. *Medieval France.* Cambridge: Cambridge University Press, 1922.

Trachtenberg, Joshua. *The Devil and the Jews.* New Haven: Yale University Press, 1943.

Travers, l'Abbé. *Histoire Civile, Politique et Religieuse de la Ville de Nantes.* Vol. I. Nantes: Vincent Forest, 1836.

Tuchman, Barbara W. *A Distant Mirror.* New York: Alfred A. Knopf, 1978.

Turner, J. M. W. *Liber Fluviorum or River Scenery of France.* London: Henry G. Bohn, 1853.

Vale, M.G.A. *Charles VII.* Berkeley: University of California Press, 1974.

Vallet de Viriville, M., ed. *Chronique de la Pucelle ou Chronique de Cousinot.* Paris: Adolphe de la Hays, 1859.

Vermaseren, M. J. *Mithras: The Secret God.* New York: Barnes and Noble, Inc., 1959.

Villeneuve, Roland. *Le Diable: Erotologie de Satan.* Paris: Jean-Jacques Pauvert, 1963.

———. *Gilles de Rays: Une Grande Figure Diabolique.* Verviers (Belgique): Editions Gérard & Cie., 1973 (1955).

Vizitelly, Ernest Alfred. *Bluebeard.* London: Chatto & Windus, Ltd., 1902.

Wagenknecht, Edward, ed. *Joan of Arc: An Anthology of History and Literature.* New York: Creative Age Press, 1948.

Waite, Arthur E. *Alchemists through the Ages.* Blauvelt, New York: Rudolf Stein Publications, 1970.

Whibley, Charles. *A Book of Scoundrels.* New York: Benjamin Blom, Inc., 1971.

Willoughby, Harold R. *Pagan Regeneration.* Chicago: University of Chicago Press, 1929.

Wilson, Colin. *The Occult.* New York: Vintage Books, 1971.

Wilson, Thomas. *Bluebeard: A Contribution to Historical Folklore.* New York: G. P. Putnam's Sons, 1897.

Winwar, Frances [pseud.]. *The Saint and the Devil: Joan of Arc and Gilles de Rais.* New York: Harper, 1948.

Wismes, Armel de. *Nantes et le Pays Nantais.* Nantes: Editions France-Empire, n.d.

Wolf, Leonard. *A Dream of Dracula.* Boston: Little, Brown and Company, 1972.

———. ed. *The Uses of the Present.* New York: McGraw-Hill Book Company, 1970.

Yates, Frances A. *Giordano Bruno and the Hermetic Tradition.* Chicago: University of Chicago Press, 1964.

INDEX